INESSA

INESSA
Lenin's Mistress

Michael Pearson

Duckworth

First published in 2001 by
Gerald Duckworth & Co. Ltd
61 Frith Street, London W1D 3JL
Tel: 020 7434 4242
Fax: 020 7434 4420
Email: enquiries@duckworth-publishers.co.uk
www.ducknet.co.uk

A catalogue record for this book is available
from the British Library

ISBN 0 7156 3048 2

Typeset by
Derek Doyle & Associates, Liverpool
Printed in Great Britain by
Bookcraft (Bath) Ltd, Midsomer Norton, Avon

CONTENTS

For Robert, my son

A PERSONAL NOTE

I first discovered Inessa Armand many years ago when I was researching *The Sealed Train – Journey to Revolution, Lenin, 1917*.

No one knew much about her then because there was very little in the way of available sources. And it is astonishing, given that she became arguably the most powerful woman in post-revolutionary Moscow, that even today hardly anyone, outside the small academic world historians of Russia, has ever heard of her.

I found Inessa totally fascinating, partly because she had five children and often seemed to have a couple with her – which is odd for a revolutionary – and partly because she clearly had an extraordinary marriage, to a wealthy husband, who accepted her lifestyle and her decision to live openly with his brother. And finally, of course, because she was the rumoured mistress of Lenin, with suggestions of a *ménage à trois* with his wife.

She was an attractive, vivacious woman who was said to have been fluent in four languages and a brilliant pianist, to have been jailed three times and to have escaped from exile in Archangel.

Much of the information then available under Communist rule was wrong. For example, she was said to have been raised in the Armand household near Moscow, where her aunt was a tutor, which was pure fiction.

What was clear, however, from the many letters from Lenin then available in *The Works Of Lenin*, was that she had, as a party comrade, been very important to him, acting as a troubleshooter, a confidante, organiser, translator, even speaking at conferences in his place. They were mostly friendly letters, often laced with jokes, but nothing to suggest the reality of their relationship – and subject, of course, to censorship or held back from publication altogether.

She died in 1920 aged only forty-six, in dramatic conditions in the

Caucasus akin to scenes from Boris Pasternak's *Dr Zhivago*. Ironically, it was Lenin's concern for her that was partly responsible for her death.

She remained vividly in my mind. I felt her life would lend itself to operatic treatment, toyed with writing a novel about her, but once the Central Party Archives (now known as the RTsVKhIDNI) were opened, giving access to her files, she seemed an ideal subject for a biography.

A few months of a story – the journey back to Russia with Lenin in the Sealed Train in April, 1917 and the events leading to the Bolshevik strike for power in November – were told in detail in *The Sealed Train* and I have leaned heavily on it and its sources for this short period of her life.

There is no doubt now that she was Lenin's mistress. Over the years, however, especially in the frustration of exile, the relationship went through various phases. At first, she worshipped Lenin, but in time came to challenge him. At one stage she was barely talking to him; at another she went quite happily back to Russia for him, knowing she would be jailed.

At times she played with him, refusing to answer his letters, or writing only to his wife Nadya, or declined to translate the passages in his articles with which she disagreed.

But, only days before she died, she was to admit that, together with her children, Lenin – and the cause they shared – had been her life.

Lenin, of course, was different from most lovers. He planned to change the world and, to the end, she had total faith in this vision.

THE LETTERS

I quote from many letters written by Lenin or Inessa. All originals are held in the RTsVKhIDNI Archives (Russian Centre for the Conservation and Study of Documents of Contemporary History), previously the Central Party Archives in Moscow.

However, most of Lenin's letters are to be found in his Collected Works. The 5th Edition of this has been published only in Russian. The 4th Edition was translated into English and Volume 43 of this contains letters written between 1893 and 1917, published for the first time in the Russian 5th Edition – some sixty of them to Inessa.

So my notes refer mainly, until 1917, to the English edition. Some of the letters quoted do appear in the Russian 5th Edition, especially those written after 1917, and in various Russian journals as well as the 40-volume *Leninskii Sbornik* and the 12-volume *Vladimir Ilyich Lenin Biograficheskaia Khronika*.

Inessa's letters to her husband, Alexander, his brother and her lover, Vladimir, her children and her friends are in date order within their addressee sections, in Fond 127 of the Central Archive above, though some have been published in edited form in I.F.Armand, *Stat'i*, *Rechi*, *Pis'ma* and in 'Pis'ma Inessy Armand', in *Novyi Mir*, 6 (1970) 196-218, and also in journals. Inessa and Lenin often omitted to date their letters, archivists sometimes relying on the contents to indicate, very roughly, especially with Inessa's, when they were written.

Since her relations with Lenin have been a delicate area for the Soviet leadership, the collected works have been subject to censorship and omission, as indicated above. Now, however, all previously censored letters are available in the archives. There are also three published sources – Richard Pipes, *The Unknown Lenin*, the Ros

Archiv, and E.G.Latyshev, *Rassekreechennyi* – purely about the previously censored material.

PHOTOGRAPHS

Most of the photographs were obtained from the Central Party Archive in Moscow, now known as the RTsVKhIDNI, the David King Collection, or from descendants of Inessa herself.

In order of appearance:

(1–5) courtesy of RTsVKhIDNI; (6) courtesy of Blona Yakovlevna Romas, Varvara Armand's daughter; (7) courtesy of the David King Collection; (8) Blona Yakovlevna Romas; (9) David King Collection; (10) RTsVKhIDNI; (11) courtesy of Renee Pavlovna Armand, Inessa's great-niece; (12) courtesy of Vsevolod Markovich Fedoseyev-Yegorov, Vera's grandson; (13) courtesy of Sergei Yakovlev; (14–22) RTsVKhIDNI; (23–36) David King Collection.

ACKNOWLEDGEMENTS

Firstly, I must thank Professor Robert Service who, learning of my interest in Inessa, suggested I should write a book about her for the general reader and guided me on Moscow sources. Secondly, I am grateful to Patrick Walsh, a new agent, for his enthusiasm and active promotion of the project from our first meeting.

I am also especially indebted to two previous biographers of Inessa: Dr R.C.Elwood, Professor of History at Carleton University and author of the scholarly *Inessa Armand – Revolutionary And Feminist*, who has corresponded with me at length by email and telephone and given me most useful help on sources; also to Georges Bardawil, author of the fine *Ines Armand*, published in French, which explored newly available sources. He most generously loaned me his extensive notes and documents for my use and discussed Inessa's character with me at length.

I have been extremely fortunate to receive co-operation, and indeed hospitality, from many members of the Armand family, in particular from: Blona Yakovlevna Romas, Inessa's granddaughter (Varvara's daughter) and Vsevolod Markovich Fedoseyev-Yegorov (grandson of Inessa's sister-in-law Vera); and also from: Vladimir Andreyevich Armand (Inessa's grandson, Andre's son); Rene Pavlovna Armand (granddaughter of Inessa's sister Renee); Klavdia Ivanovna Armand (wife of Vladimir, son of Inessa's husband Alexander by his second marriage).

Also from Yevgeny Alexandrovich Armand and Sergei Alexandrovich (grandsons of Inessa by her son Alexander) and Natalya Sergeyevna Yevseyeva-Armand (Sergei's daughter) who kindly came with us to Pushkino with her friend and distant cousin, Maria Vladimirovna Armand. I am also indebted to Maria's uncle, Alexei Davidovich Armand, who made available to me the unpublished autobiography of his father; and finally to Galina, wife of Alexander Evgenevich (Inessa's great grandson).

I would like to thank Larissa Nikolayevna Malashenko who led us so efficiently through Inessa's Fond in the Central Archives and I appreciate, too, the aid of her colleague Yelena Yefimovna Kirillova.

I must record my deep gratitude to Lena Yakovleva, an Inessa admirer herself, who made all arrangements for me in Moscow, organised introductions, as well as interpreting, making translations and exchanging what must have been a hundred emails on my return to my desk; and also to my son Robert, an Oxford University history graduate, to whom this book is dedicated. He travelled with me to Russia, provided stalwart and organised support with the research and, because of his prodigious memory and perception, has shared with me many conversations since our return.

I am also grateful to my editors, Sarah Such and Lee Boudreaux for their patient assistance and creative enthusiasm from an early stage; and to Dr Harold Shukman, late of St Anthony's College, Oxford, who has written much about Lenin himself and has kindly read the manuscript and answered many questions. I have appreciated too the help with translation in my home country given by Olga Haigh and Frederic Constant; the transcription of my notes by Jean Rayment; and the staff of the British Library, whose Russian holdings are wonderfully extensive; the London Library as always, the University of London's School of Slavonic and East European Studies and the London School of Economics & Political Science. All have made my task much easier.

Finally, I have to thank Susan, my wife, and our family for their tireless support and the endless discussions that accompany the writing of a book of this nature.

ONE

Pushkino 1893

It was before the early snows in October 1893, and already dark by mid-afternoon, that Inessa Stephane married Alexander Armand in the church of St Nikolai in the little town of Pushkino – and embraced a future that would take her eventually into the highest levels of power in Russia.

Until that day, as an educated, unmarried girl the only occupation open to her in Russia would have been that of tutor and even this was in question since technically Inessa was illegitimate.

Now, as she walked behind the Ikon Boy in his scarlet shirt into that beautiful church, ablaze with candles, and shared with Alexander the rituals, such as the kissing of the rings and the circling of the praying desk beneath the crowns of silver, she became a young wife with status and wealth. Her husband was the eldest son in a large family that owned local textile plants as well as estates in the region and property in Moscow.

A slight, pretty girl with auburn hair and green eyes, she was imma- ture even for her nineteen years, but she had an attractive vitality, if touched at times by bleak depressions. Certainly, the letters she had written to Alexander before the marriage suggest emotional muddle.

There was no doubt, however, of her artistic potential. She was well read, fluent in four languages and a talented pianist, able to play classics from memory for two hours at a stretch. But none of the people in the church that day would have guessed that she also had the qualities it would take to hold her own in the intellectual rough- and-tumble of Lenin's years in exile; nor that she could ever stay stubbornly cool on the platform against such formidable heavy- weights as Trotsky or Plekhanov or Axelrod, while Lenin himself would usually lose his temper.

1

Inessa Armand was to become Lenin's lover in a relationship that was volatile but which bound them by deep emotional ties, even when she was barely speaking to him. She was his troubleshooting lieutenant, his 'front' when he wished to stay in the background, and a friend who could discuss tactics with him, console him at times of setback and share his victories. At meetings and conferences, some of which she organised, she helped to execute the tortuous strategies that would ultimately yield him greater authority than even the Tsar could command.

He had already been married for some years, but Nadya – Nadezdha Konstantinovna whose cover name was Krupskaya – looked after the back office, the running of his faction of the party, the coded correspondence with its members.[1] Inessa, though, would be out there in the field, directing the hand-to-hand combat in the large exile community, riddled with frustrations and conflicts, that was preparing for the day they all dreamed of, even if they disagreed about the form it would take.

All that, of course, lay years ahead. At nineteen, Inessa was politically innocent, even uninterested, but her wedding was the first link in the chain of events that was to take her within the fringes of history. For without this marriage and possibly this husband, she might never have met Lenin nor, for that matter, gained the kind of power in the Russia of 1918 that enabled her to write to the commissar of a military district, as she did for a childhood friend, requesting the 'Respected Comrade' to 'receive my acquaintance'. She would be confident that her wish would be enough to achieve the object, since anyone in authority knew how close she was to the ruler of all the Russias.

The church of St Nikolai, with its twin bell towers and blue and gold cupola, was on a hill that overlooked Pushkino. In the 1890s the forest town, with its lake, two rivers, a thriving summer theatre, and only an hour by train from Moscow, was a favoured place for holiday dachas, especially with the families of the city's French community, in which the Armands were prominent. It was also a company town. Two tall brick chimneys, which still exist today, reached high above the Armand textile plant. Armand workers' cottages, built in timber, with carved wooden friezes, lined the roads.

And the Armand family home was extraordinary. Based originally on four separate houses, it had become a strange, sprawling complex of carved and decorated timber, linked by galleries at ground-floor level and flanked by verandas, simple to extend if more children made this necessary. It also had elaborate gardens, featuring gazebos and an avenue, bordered on each side by poplars.

At the centre of the house was a large covered area, containing an eighteen-foot dining table, and this was used for parties, children's games, 'Name day' celebrations, and impressive theatrical productions with elaborate programmes, designed by Alexander's sister Maria. It was here that Alexander's father Eugene – or Evgeny Evgenevich – lived with his two brothers, Emil and Adolf, each family occupying a separate house within the complex.

Like many French Muscovite families, the Armands had settled in Russia early in the nineteenth century, Alexander's ancestor Paul having died in Napoleon's retreat from the city. Legend has it that his son, Ivan, was captured by peasants at the same time and, on being released, started a wine import business, only to be threatened with failure by the sinking of a delivery ship. But it was *his* son, the first Eugene, Alexander's grandfather, who placed the Armand fortunes on a more stable footing through a factory in Pushkino, making army uniforms, and the purchase of property with the profits.

Foreign families were required by law to take Russian nationality, but only as 'Honorary Citizens', not as fully-fledged Russians. Second class, in other words, and ignored by the local socially-conscious nobility as a result. Even so, Alexander's father had made some concession to his country of residence by converting from the Roman Catholic faith to that of the Russian Orthodox, and Alexander, like most of his brothers and sisters, had followed him.

Inessa's mother, Natalie Wild, also came from a French family that had settled in Moscow, albeit from Franche-Comté, at the time a Protestant area of France. Her father was a language teacher and the Wild family, acquainted with most of the French families in the city, naturally came to know the Armands.

3

Inessa, though, had been born in Paris, for Natalie had run away from her Moscow home to live with a French opera singer, Theodore Stephane. Originally called Elise – Elisabeth or Elisaveta in Russian – Ines, as she was known by then, was the eldest of three girls, being born four months before her parents were married. Later, in Russia, this was to cause problems that Natalie tried to solve by having her wedding to Theodore officially noted – or, rather, forged – on Inessa's birth certificate, stating it legitimised her. By then Inessa was seventeen and, if she was to be a tutor, which was the only obvious profession for her, she required an unblemished background. In fact, although she had a few students for a while, it proved to be hardly necessary.

Inessa was five when her father's contract with the Grand-Théâtre in Lyons was ended. He was a man of buoyant spirits and great optimism, which came to infuriate Natalie, who feared this had little base in reality, though quite why is not clear. The notices of his performances in such operas as *The Thief of Baghdad*, *Rigoletto* and even *Faust* were often good, and were enough, when he died, to earn him an obituary in *Le Figaro*.[2]

The break with the Lyons opera house seemed to confirm Natalie's suspicions, however. The family returned to Paris, where Theodore rejoined the Théâtre de la Gaietie, but the marriage remained troubled and the couple parted, with Natalie, pregnant, facing the prospect of raising three children under five on her own.

To ease the burden, Natalie's mother and her sister, who had visited Paris in 1879, probably to help while she bore Anna, her third child, took Inessa back with them to Moscow. Natalie's sister, Sophie, was herself a tutor to various Moscow families, possibly at times to the Armands, and she and her mother educated Inessa at home.[3]

Unlike much of her adult life, Inessa's childhood in Russia remains obscure. According to early accounts, including that of Lenin's wife, Nadya, on the death of her father Inessa had been taken into the Armand home by her aunt who was a full-time tutor at Pushkino, and brought up with the family's children. This story, though attractive, is now seen clearly to be wrong, and probably fabricated by Soviet propagandists as a tutor (an employee) and a poor fatherless little girl fitted the picture they liked to draw of the proletarian revolution, though virtually all its prominent figures were bourgeois. Inessa's father, as testified by his death certificate, in fact lived for six years after she had left Paris.

Her daughter Inna has confirmed that Inessa was brought up by her aunt and grandmother, and her letters to Alexander before their marriage confirm much of this picture. The Wilds probably lived in an apartment near Kouznietsky-Most, the French business area of old Moscow. The education the two women gave her – especially in music, languages and literature – was obviously very sound and ideal for a good marriage but, as she was to be sensitively aware for much of her life, it was not intellectual.

In 1891, when Inessa was seventeen, her grandmother died and Natalie brought her other two daughters to Russia to live in the Moscow apartment. A few months later, Alexander Armand, who had been away from Pushkino for some years, training to take his place in the family business, returned home.

He already knew Inessa quite well. In the summertime she had often been to Pushkino, where the Wilds had friends, and she had mixed with the Armand children in the huge, rambling house. But Inessa had matured since Alexander had last seen her, blossoming into a young woman he found totally compelling – and he quickly fell in love with her.

Inessa encouraged him, writing in May under the pretext of wanting the address of a mutual friend. In the same letter she spoke of what she had been doing and thinking about since she last saw him, though it had been only the previous night!

With her sister Renee, she visited the lake near Pushkino after a chance meeting with Alexander that in fact seems to have been contrived. He took them out in a boat. She was relieved that, as she indicated, no one saw them. Alexander made her promise to keep the meeting secret, since a younger sister was hardly an adequate chaperone, but the moment she got home she could not resist telling her mother.

A few days later Inessa sent him an invitation to a small party for her birthday. 'Please come. We'll be expecting you. There will be a lot of young ladies for only four or five young men.'

During the next year, Inessa and Alexander came to know one another and although she was callow and lacked experience, her letters are interesting, if voluble and self-condemning. 'I am horribly thoughtless. I'm boring you abominably by always asking services from you. I never stop complaining. I have become capricious and nervous.'[4]

She would seem to have been expecting a denial, which she probably received. However, she constantly attacked men, such as those invited by her friends, whom she finds 'condescending. They think they are masters of creation. They have an absolute disdain for women that finds expression in their respect for feminine weakness. For these men,' she mocked, 'believe themselves generous, terribly generous, under the cover of amiability, false respect, and a patience with women they would grant to a child. Women believe anything and men lie endlessly.' For a woman who was to become a leading feminist of her day this statement is, perhaps, generalising and simplistic, but the anger was to remain.

She accepted acidly that men believe that 'a woman has a little intelligence, just a little bit, and also a soul, like they do themselves,' but feared 'on reading this, I know you will take offence, that you will cease to be my friend, but I think it is better that I should tell you the whole truth so that you know the depth of my thoughts. And men in general have good qualities,' she asserted, softening the blow. 'I hold you, for instance, in great esteem and I would be very sorry if we ceased to be friends. However men make me angry, they exasperate me. But enough on that subject. Above all, I don't want you to be upset.'

And Alexander wasn't; he was five years older than her and this chattering perhaps appealed to him. She may have been disappointed by young men in general, but she made it clear that he stood out among the crowd as a shining exception.

Later letters were more concerned with their relationship. 'It is true that I do not have a complete trust in you because you do not know me. You know only my good sides, not the bad ones. And because the opinion of others is very precious to me, it would be unpleasant for me to think that [even the bad aspects] were not good in your eyes. What's more I have the impression that, if I disappointed you, you would end our friendship. I would be sorry. See how frank I am with you.'

She wrote later: 'There are people whom I trust more than myself because I know that, even if I became the worst of women, the nastiest and most odious of people, they would remain my friends, but it seems to me that if I became bad you would cease to be my friend. I know what I am telling you will probably be disagreeable. I don't want to cause any bad feelings between us but I prefer to be sincere with you.'

What she was seeking, it seems, was an assurance that he would rather die than cease to be her friend. 'Anyway,' she ends, 'I find I trust you more now than before, don't you find? Well I do anyway.'

She is reaching for an honesty between them, even if her aim is calculating, but she guesses he's keeping too much of himself hidden from her. 'Yesterday you had a very strange expression, as though you didn't have a happy heart, yet you went on smiling and being friendly. And if you want to know I find it infinitely disagreeable that you can't tell me [what is worrying you], that you are going to put on a mask and smile when you don't want to smile.

'But maybe I am fooling myself and you're [always] going to be smiling when you're sad or angry – and note these future tenses and see how, without noticing it, they are committing us to a future. Marriage, as they say, would seem to be "in the air".'

Which was outrageously forward for the period since it would appear that Alexander had not yet proposed. However, it shows early signs of the determination she is later to demonstrate.

At other times, she was worried by the reproaches she imagines in his letters and, by contrast to her previous attacks on his sex, suggests that 'You are a man and I am a woman and that means that you are more intelligent than I am. I'm always scared of saying stupid things and this curbs my confidence. Fear of ridicule prevents me from saying all that I have in my mind. I know that you would not deliberately make fun of me but involuntarily you might do so.' Is there an element of friendly sarcasm? Or does she really mean that he, as a person, is more intelligent than herself, even though she puts it in a sexual context? There is a hint of the manipulative techniques she will develop later with Lenin and *for* Lenin, who was a master of the art.

Her mother, Natalie, was causing Inessa some concern and three weeks before her marriage the young girl wrote Alexander what seems an odd letter: 'It is a long time since I have written to you, Alexander Evgenevich. I have all my time taken up with lessons with Anna [her youngest sister] and my other affairs. How are you all in Pushkino? It is such a long time since I have been there and in Moscow the weather is bad and everywhere there is noise and chaos. But in Pushkino everything is so good.

'What's more I have been a little sad for a while and I would like to tell you why but I would bore you. All right, perhaps I will tell you. I won't be so sad if I tell you.

'My mother torments me so much. She has such a passionate and violent nature and her limitless capacity to love so deeply causes her constant suffering that hurts me terribly because I think it is incurable. What will become of her when I leave her?

'In me she has put all her love. When I think about that I have such sadness I feel no tears could express it. I would give anything to appease her but she is so full of contradictions. She makes demands on me that are totally impossible. She would like me to love no one else. And even if I submitted, she would not be satisfied. She'd find another reason to torment herself.'

This shows clearly from where Inessa inherited her own agonised conflicts, but she was, in due course, to reveal a hard core of intelligence beneath the emotional froth and a formidable will which her mother perhaps lacked.

Also, the cool tone of the letter, from a woman we know to be passionate, is marked. She is three weeks from a wedding that she does not even mention and, while it may have been custom to call her fiancé by the formal Alexander Evgenevich, she says nothing about missing him or looking forward to being his wife. However, the last lines of the letter have been lost and these might have been more intimate.

The real nature of the problem with her mother is not clear. Inessa had, of course, seen little if anything of Natalie since she had been taken from her as a five-year-old – possibly blaming the parting on herself, for some unknown fault as children often do. Now, in her late teens, she had lived with her for little more than a year.

Natalie was clearly obsessive. To run away from home to live with a lover who did not even have the obstruction of a marriage, as she did with Theodore, was at that time very unusual. And she was to do it again, leaving Moscow just before – not after – Anna's wedding, to set up house with a new lover, Charles-Louis-Joseph Faure, of the theatre-owning family that had employed her husband. Set against the cultural background of the nineteenth century, it was the behaviour of a wilful, unstable and probably unhappy woman.

But was Inessa making too much of it? Presumably Natalie loved her other daughters too. So what happened to the relationship after Inessa's marriage? Inessa, who wrote at such length to her husband, lover and children, often discussing very minor details of her life, rarely mentioned her mother.

Inessa's relationship with her sisters whom, for all practical purposes, she met for the first time at seventeen, is also interesting. Anna, the third child, had been only twelve when she came to Moscow, but Inessa claims to have got on well with Renee, then sixteen, until there was a bitter quarrel between them in 1899, the cause of which is obscure.

In this angry dispute, Inessa speaks of Renee's accusation of 'her own sister ... poisoning her against their own mother,' and trying to force her to take Anna's side. This could possibly have arisen from Natalie's decision to leave Moscow so precipitately for Paris and her new lover.

Inessa claims total innocence of Renee's charges and appeals simply to her 'sisterly love. But it seems I am such a villain ... that I can't see how you can ever trust me. We have known each other for eight years, and quite closely it seems to me ... Au Revoir, my Renee,

I bid you farewell with a very heavy heart,' she writes, adding a PS: 'I'll be sad not to see any more of Kolia, my little god-child.'[5]

She is being dramatic and obviously does not mean what she is saying. Relations were, in time, to be re-established. When later they both lived in Moscow, their homes were in the same street in the Arbat district. Renee, who had married Nikolai, Alexander's brother, clearly helped with the children when Inessa was first arrested and almost certainly provided cover for her to meet them in later years when she was in Moscow illegally.

Meanwhile, in 1893 Inessa and Alexander began what was to develop into a rare and fascinating relationship. In its early stages, the marriage was traditional enough. Within three months Inessa was pregnant. A handsome home in the European style was available to them at Eldigino, some fifteen miles away on one of the Armand estates, but they seem to have been slow to take advantage of it, living in the family complex at Pushkino, until the birth of the baby – a son, also to be named Alexander.

Years later, Inessa would tell her daughter Inna that she had always felt an outsider among the Armands,[6] but she appeared to join in the family entertainments with some enthusiasm. Two months after her wedding, as part of the New Year celebrations, she had a role in a play, *A Tale of Summer*, that was to have resonance in later years. The programme, beautifully decorated by Maria, features the cast list in both Russian and French: Alexander's sister and brother, Eugenie and Nikolai; Inessa's two sisters, Renee and Anna Stephane; and three who came from other French families, Georges Gautier and Emma and Georges Wilken. Both the Gautiers and the Wilkens were to seek Inessa's help in the chaos that was so disastrous for such middle-class families in 1918. Inessa was listed there too, of course, under her new name: Madame Ines Armand.[7]

Certainly, Inessa loved the theatre and one reason she was happy to stay in the Armand home instead of at the somewhat remote Eldigino, was Pushkino's position on the railway line, with easy access to Moscow. She was, after all, a city girl. Even so, during the early months of the marriage, she seems to have developed something of a new persona. Alexander often took her to Moscow, to plays, concerts, the opera, ballets. The Armands also maintained a home in the city where the young couple would spend the night.

Inessa entered into the city's social life, bought stylish hats and dresses and, more importantly, became part of an artistic avant-garde set. With Alexander she was invited to the Mamontovs, one of the old industrialist families of Moscow, who owned a theatre where Chaliapin sometimes sang and Chekhov attended rehearsals of his own plays. The Mamontovs entertained lavishly at their big home on Sadovaya Koltso and their country mansion at Abramtsevo, the guests including actors and writers.

Another important hostess was Minna Gorbunova-Kablukova, who held open house every Sunday for people with new ideas: philosophers, poets, thinkers, artists. Minna claimed to be a correspondent of Engels, who was still alive two years after Inessa's marriage. It was in Minna's home that Inessa met such writers as Valeri Brionsov, seen as the 'new Pushkin'; she was reading Pushkin at the time in Verlaine's translation.[8]

It was here, too, that there was much talk of 'Zhenskii vopros', the 'woman question', and if Inessa's remarkable transition from the giddy young girl that Alexander had married to the skilled, clear-thinking revolutionary she became is to be wondered at, then the feminist Minna certainly played a great part in it.

So, too, did Alexander's married sister, Anna, eight years older than Inessa, who often joined her in her social round, in lieu of Alexander. Inessa was to see a lot of Anna in Europe later, during her exile. And in 1917 Anna would return from Switzerland to St Petersburg with Inessa in the famous 'Sealed Train' that took Lenin and his party across a Germany that was still slaughtering Russian troops on the Eastern Front.

Alexander lived the way men often live. He liked shooting in the forest and enjoyed male company at Le Club des Marchands, sometimes preferring this to the fashionable friends of his young wife.

After the baby Alexander's birth they moved at last to Eldigino, which was beautifully set on a hill in the forest. A wall plaque at Eldigino records that Inessa Armand lived there from 1894 to 1904,

11

but much of this time was, in fact, spent at Pushkino, the centre of the Armand family's activities.

Inessa planned to keep a diary, in a red velvet cover with edges of gold leaf, in which she would record occasional thoughts. She persuaded Alexander to supply the first entry. 'What shall I write to you?' he wrote. 'Do I write that I love you, that you are my life, the light which illuminates for me every thing in every place – but all this you well know. I am nothing without you.'[9]

Alexander was a member of the Moscow Region Zemstvo, an official but autonomous body that had authority in such areas as education and, in particular, public health. Inessa would join him in visits to the poorest families in the cottages around Pushkino and the Moscow slums. She was shocked by what she saw. She knew that such conditions existed in the villages and the city, but she had never before witnessed them close up. In fact, she would have seen them in any Western country at the turn of the century: the homeless; the dreadful, overcrowded housing, starvation, poverty, disease, appalling sanitation, as well as the effects of despair, such as drunkenness and prostitution, which was illegal outside Moscow's brothels though still practised elsewhere in secret.

Perhaps it was these experiences that inspired her to adopt a child, Vladimir, who had been born to poor parents in Moscow's Khitrov Street Market. This was a kind of charity, customary for rich families, though Vladimir would be raised almost like her own children.[10]

Inessa saw an answer to at least some of the social devastation she had witnessed as lying in education on a broader scale. 'Oh what misery in the cottages,' she wrote in her diary. 'What riches in the books.'[11] She initiated plans that she had discussed with her sister-in-law, Anna, and two of the Pushkino tutors: a young left-wing Social Democrat named Eugene Kammer and an older teacher, also with Marxist views, named Nikolai Ivinsky, who was tutor to her husband's youngest brother, also called Vladimir. With their help, and Alexander's, she started a school for the sons of the Armand workers and local peasants.

On one occasion, she matched Alexander's passionate entry in her diary with a scribbled note that must have pleased him. 'Dear and beloved Sacha. Excuse my absence but you are late and I must leave for the school. I love you madly with all my heart. You are my beloved, my darling.'[12]

At about this time, in St Petersburg, some four hundred miles to the north, an angry young lawyer named Vladimir Ilyich Ulyanov had just become a member of a small revolutionary group with plans to start a political journal called *Robotnik* (The Worker).[13] For some months during 1895 he had travelled round Europe, meeting the leading Social Democrats such as Georgi Plekhanov, Paul Axelrod and Paul Lafargue, who had married Laura, one of Karl Marx's daughters. He returned to Russia, with some useful European links and a suitcase with a false bottom, packed with illegal literature.

While he had been away, another activist, Yuli Martov, had linked his friends with a group of his own. Ulyanov, or Lenin which was to be his cover name, had so far worked with his comrades to frame their policies by group discussion, reading the key banned books and writing articles that were hard to place. Martov, though, was urging direct action, awakening unrest in the factories and helping striking workers.

It was a vision that appealed to Lenin, who nursed a great hatred against the establishment and the bourgeois middle class that was never to leave him. Born of minor nobility, his father had been an Inspector of Schools in the Volga River town of Simbirsk. His elder brother Sasha had been on the fringe of a student plot against the Tsar that failed. Despite the pleas of his mother, Sasha had claimed that he was one of the leaders when he was not and this had led to his being hanged in 1887. As a result, Lenin and his family had been ostracised in Simbirsk and forced to leave the town in disgrace. Now Lenin ached for revenge, as the St Petersburg police probably guessed. In December 1895, he was arrested for planning to provoke strikes. His friend Martov was taken a few days afterwards.

In Pushkino a few months later, three years after her marriage, Inessa bore Alexander another son, Fedor, but the political future in Russia was looking darker. Revolution had become fashionable, openly discussed by people who would not, in most cases, dream of being part of a secret cell – the same sort of people who had ostracised the Ulyanovs in Simbirsk. Revisionist writers like Turgenev and Chernyshevsky, with new ideas about marriage and society, were popular.

There was possibly a strain of resentment within the Armands. As well as being classified as second ranking 'Honorary Citizens,' they were also in 'trade', which excluded them from the higher social circles. Evgeny Evgenevich, Alexander's father, was a man of liberal views, but hardly radical, unlike most of his children, nearly all of whom became politically active.

Anna, Alexander's elder sister, was to be banished as Alexander was himself for a period, after a short spell in prison, though he was not a revolutionary by nature. His sisters Sofia and Varvara married activist Social Democrats (the party that was, after various splits, to become the Communist Party). Maria and Sergei were to join the rival Socialist Revolutionary Party, with its Terror Brigade. Vladimir, who was later to become so important to Inessa, was only eleven but would in due course become a dedicated revolutionary.[14]

And then there was Kammer.

Eugene Kammer was a young medical student who had been taken on as a tutor. Everyone liked him, and his sister was later to marry Alexander's brother, Sergei.

In 1896 Kammer told two of his pupils – Alexander's young brother Boris and his cousin Lev Armand – that he was a member of a student group that promoted propaganda among the workers, supported political strikes and was a source of forbidden books. The two boys were caught by Kammer's enthusiasm and were eager to become involved.

It took only a few months for the police to learn from an informer that there was a printing press in the Armand home together with a secret network spreading illicit literature. It was with some embarrassment that they approached Evgeny Evgenevich, who was so important in the area, and said they were under orders to search his home. He laughed. 'Search if you want to, but you won't find anything.'

But they did. Tapping on the floorboards, they noted that some had a hollow sound. On lifting them they found a hidden part of the cellar, with equipment ranging from a printing press to four linotype machines, and a store of illegal leaflets.

Kammer, together with Boris and Lev, was arrested: they were the first of the Armands to be taken. Kammer, though, accepted full responsibility, insisting that the boys were innocent. The Armands backed him, paying for his lawyers and putting up the bail for his release from jail. With their help, he escaped to Germany. Years later, Inessa was to support Kammer's application to join the Bolshevik Party, when it was deemed a great honour to be a member.

Lev's father, Emil, was told to send his son abroad for a few months in lieu of formal exile and eighteen-year-old Boris had a restriction put on his movements at home.[15]

The Kammer case brought a cold realism into the Armands' world but, if anything, this increased the temperature of their revolutionary ambitions. And it was not limited to the family. The local doctor and his nurse in Pushkino were activists. So, too, was the man who ran the local library. All played their role in the party networks that were soon to be re-formed.

It is tempting to wonder what all these rich young people thought they were working to achieve – and not only them, for many of the leaders of the revolutionary parties came from bourgeois and intellectual backgrounds. Most of the Armands were Marxists, yet a declared aim of the Communist Manifesto, published by Marx and Engels in 1848, had been state control of 'the means of production, distribution and exchange,' which was pretty well everything on which the Armands' fortunes were based.

It was, of course, expected that in time change would come to the antiquated Tsarist society. It was only forty years since serfdom had ended and Russia, with its autocracy and semi-divine image of the Tsar as a 'Holy Father', still lagged way behind most Western nations.

The Armands were good, progressive employers, but it is doubtful if they realised that they would lose their factories, their homes, their way of life, or had considered the possibility of a dictatorship, even more rigid and ruthless than the Tsar's, that would rule by terror. Probably they were expecting some kind of democratic system, when rule would come from below, by election, and be truly by the people.

For some seventy years, since the Decembrist uprising of young aristocrats in 1825, Russia's history had been marked by men and women who had fought the autocracy, being seen by many as heroes, and by others as tolerable villains. The list is long – including such men as Petrashevsky, with a circle that included the writer, Dostoevsky, who was actually facing the firing squad when a messenger galloped up with an amnesty; Karakozov who was tortured so badly he could hardly walk the short distance to the scaffold; Nechaev whose 'Catechism of a Revolutionary' clothed revolution in religious tones; who, when writing materials were denied him, wrote in his own blood. And there would be others to come, during Inessa's early life.

In 1898 Inessa had borne her third child – Inna. She was accustomed by now to motherhood but it was the first of her pregnancies to expose her to bitter humiliation: she was refused admission to a church on the grounds that, being with child, she was 'unclean'. According to her friend Polina Vinogradskaya she had been devout in her teens but the shock of this made her question the tenets of her faith.[16] It may well have done so, and she would certainly become an atheist in time, but the political circles with which she was soon to become involved –being already on their fringes – would probably have made her question it anyway.

She had always questioned much, even in the confusion of her teens, and now she had grown older, the problems of marriage were starting to be apparent. At fifteen, she had been appalled by Tolstoy, in *War and Peace*, describing Natasha as becoming, with her marriage, a 'complete woman', a *samka* – the implication being that a woman needed a man, children and the world of a wife in order to be whole. 'It hit me like a whip,' she wrote, years later to Inna.[17] She swore she wouldn't become a *samka* but now, five years into marriage, she seems to have feared she was getting close to it.

16

Although a friend of Kammer, she had not been involved with the secret printing press, possibly because she had been spending more time at Eldigino. Also, she was not yet fully committed to activism. 'Marxism for me was not a youthful enthusiasm,' she was to write to Alexander's brother Vladimir in 1903, 'but a long evolution from right to left.'[18]

She had, though, seen much of Minna Gorbunova-Kablukova, being a fairly regular guest at her Sunday salons.[19] Three years earlier, in 1895, Minna had asked official permission to start the Moscow Society for Improving the Lot of Women, but the Ministry of the Interior had refused. What was going on at Pushkino was also happening elsewhere, and the government was growing increasingly nervous. Philanthropic groups were acceptable but anything that was even remotely political, for which these societies could provide good cover, was opposed. And this included active feminism, which was implicit in the Moscow Society's proposed title.

In 1899, however, the Minister relented and permission was granted. The society was ambitious, encompassing demands for women's political and legal rights, promoting their education and technical training, as well as trying to divert country girls, who flocked into the city, from prostitution.

Inessa became secretary of the society and, using her languages, tried to broaden its remit by writing to Adrienne Veigele, secretary of the Women's International Progressive Union in London. The two women exchanged frequent letters that developed, though they never met, into a close friendship. Inessa told Adrienne that, like many fashionable women in Moscow, she had become a vegetarian and later, rather to Veigele's surprised disappointment, had abandoned it. She described the progress of her new baby, Inna.

Veigele suggested that the Moscow Society should become the Moscow branch of her Progressive Union – and even claimed in print that this arrangement was already in place. But although Inessa – international, even then, in her thinking – was in favour, Minna was not. The police, too, were none too happy for reasons of control. Minna had a point. The London union had broad, lofty

17

feminist aims whereas the ladies of the Moscow Society were out there working directly at the grass-roots level.

The next year Inessa was appointed President of the society but, with the Kammer case behind her, she was being watched by the Okhrana, the Tsarist political police. She applied successively, in the name of the society, for permission to open a Sunday school for women; to publish a regular news leaflet that might grow into a fully-fledged newspaper for women; to open a library with books of feminine interest. All were approved by the police and overruled by the Okhrana, the latter believing that they could all be exploited for 'anti-loyal' propaganda.

The Okhrana were to play an ever-growing role in Inessa's life. They were the descendants of Ivan the Terrible's *oprichniki*, who wore black uniforms and rode black horses, each with a dog's head attached to its saddle. Their orders had been to exterminate treason, which remained the aim of the Okhrana though their remit was now somewhat wider. They were often ruthless and, although some of their surveillance can now be seen to have been hopelessly misdirected, their success at getting spies into the high levels of the main revolutionary parties was formidable.

Inessa decided to break with Minna and set up her own Society for the Protection and Emancipation of Women and a Sunday school where prostitutes were welcome. Neither the police nor, surprisingly, the Okhrana took exception, mistakenly seeing this as a society for fallen women, with no political element to it.

In 1890, Moscow had 105 brothels and 1178 registered prostitutes. A member of the society approached Tolstoy for advice on what action they could take to persuade girls to renounce the life, but he was gloomy. 'It was thus before Moses. It was thus after Moses. Thus it was … thus it will always be.' [20]

Which was ultimately Inessa's reluctant conclusion. It did nothing to help her morale. 'I'm a little unhappy,' she wrote in her diary. She took the children for a holiday in Yalta where she read the agrarian socialist Peter Lavrov's *The Problem of Understanding History* and was impressed by his radical answers to the peasant problem. 'It's been a long time,' she wrote to Alexander, 'since I read a book which more closely conforms with my own opinions.'[21]

Within months of her return she was away again, this time to the Swiss resort of Montreux, taking one of her sons for foreign medical treatment. 'Darling, it's wonderful here,' she wrote to Alexander, 'but I'll be glad to be back home again in Eldigino. The sunset was beautiful today. I walked along the bank of the lake for quite a long time. The water was tranquil. The sun was just below the horizon lighting up the mountains in different colours and you can't imagine what this sight did to me. It seems that the mountains are like one's soul which grows high above everything. They make me feel unformed and immature, small and lacking in harmony. I want to cry.'

She was also reading Jerome K. Jerome. 'He says that we are never content and happy with what we have. He says that even Cinderella, once she'd got her prince and all the riches, would still have wanted more.'[22]

As, of course, did Inessa herself. She was thinking of studying chemistry, of helping with the Workers' Association, presumably linked to the Armand factories. 'Then I intend to write something.'

Meanwhile, Alexander was taking on more. In 1901, he became a member of the Moscow City Duma and he was already working for the Moscow Forest Protection Committee. He had his place on the Zemsto, was supporting several charities and, of course, helping his father run the Armand companies.

Inessa, who was becoming busier with her societies' work and who was pregnant for the fourth time, began to spend more time in Moscow, in an apartment of a house the Armands owned – 6 Ipatievsky Lane in the Arbat, the district favoured by artists, writers and intellectuals.[23]

Any of the family could use this on visits to the city, but Vladimir, Alexander's brother and the Armands' youngest son, lived there most of the time, since he was reading biology at Moscow University.

With Vladimir, everything would change.

TWO
Moscow 1902

In 1902 Vladimir was seventeen. Inessa was twenty-eight and, since bearing her second daughter Varvara in October 1901, the mother of four children. She had known Vladimir since he was a child, before her wedding, when he was eight and, since then, of course, as her youngest brother-in-law.

If revolution was affecting the younger generation in such families as the Armands in Pushkino, it was not strange that the Moscow students were even more militant, and obviously so. Vladimir had aleady started to hold meetings of the students' Executive Committee in the family apartment. Sometimes Inessa was present at these, probably briefly while passing through, since she spoke later of becoming involved with 'underground revolutionary people' in 1902, suggesting she didn't take these earlier contacts too seriously. However the police learned of these meetings soon enough and, as early as February 1901, they had raided the apartment and arrested several students whom they believed to be planning street protest marches, which were illegal.

Vladimir, or Volodya as Inessa called him, was a quiet, serious, rather frail young man with a short beard, sincere brown eyes, and had what a friend described as 'an uncommon, apostolic simplicity about him.' This was hardly the material of a great lover, but he had certainly some quality that, in time, caught Inessa's attention. He was a radical activist but no leader. He wouldn't be out there at the front or storming the barricades, but he *would* be doing the political thinking. At this early stage he had not made up his mind if he was going to join the Social Democrats or the Socialist Revolutionaries.

The SRs and the SDs had similar aims. They both sought revolution and an end to the evils of society, which is why they could sometimes work together, but they had radically different views about methods and theory. The SRs, with their deep agrarian roots and a vivid revolutionary tradition behind them, believed that the road to socialism lay in the peasant communes. The SDs were Marxists who believed that capitalism had within it the seeds of its own destruction, though force, in the form of revolution, might be needed at the final stage, when those in power tried to cling onto it.

The SDs' main purpose was to educate the people, and the workers in particular, so they were ready to exploit that collapse when it came, which was why it was illegal to hold meetings promoting this idea or to publish books, journals or leaflets that discussed it. The SRs, however, were committed to terror and the 'People's Will' party, predecessors of the SR, had indeed shocked the nation with the successful murder of Tsar Alexander II in 1881. As a result, five people had been hanged in public in Semenovsky Square, in black clothes on a black scaffold. Two of them, Andrei Zhelyabov and Sofia Perovskaya, had been lovers – she the daughter of an aristocrat, he the son of a serf. He had been allowed to kiss her farewell before the executioner, dressed in scarlet, had put the noose around her neck, making her the first woman in Russia to be executed in public.

And this execution didn't halt the killings. In fact, the actions of the SR's Terror Brigade were to hinder the Marxist SDs, who saw violence as achieving nothing, and also coloured the attitude of the police, who were not always sure which party they were dealing with.

Even so, the authorities could be punitive to excess. Soon after the raids on the Armand flat in 1901, the students of Moscow University went on strike. In response, several hundred were herded into the riding school and charged by mounted Cossacks, who flogged them with their knouts, their vicious whips. Some of the girl students were raped.[1] This cruelty turned one easy-going non-political student, Yegor Sazonov, into an active SR terrorist, who was later to murder Vyacheslav Konstantinovich Plehve, a particularly brutal Interior Minister.

Inessa, like Volodya, was still a long way off joining either party but she was growing disenchanted with her societies, which were

22

only a slight improvement on the usual 'good works' of many rich young wives. By contrast, she found the meetings of excited and courageous students, intent on creating a better world by revolution, extremely attractive. Drawn by this emerging cause, even though it was not yet fully formed in her mind, or probably in the minds of those students, she grew closer to Volodya.[2]

The age difference between them was wide, which perhaps blinded them to the emotional dangers. She was a mother and well read in the mainstream literature but Volodya, in his late teens, was probably more acquainted with the works of Karl Marx and other revolutionary thinkers. The two elements merged in them, each finding the other highly stimulating, and attuned to a common purpose – maybe intellectually in the early months, when each may have seemed out of reach to the other, and then at last with recognisable emotion. The fact is that, during the course of 1902, they formed a deep attachment that, though unusual in certain aspects, was clearly demanding.

Inessa has often been compared to Vera Pavlovna, the much-admired heroine of *What Is To Be Done?*, Nikolai Chernyshevsky's novel, written while he was in prison in the Fortress of Peter and Paul. The book caught the imagination of a Russian generation before it was eventually banned, and so impressed Lenin that he gave the same title to a major work of his own.

Vera Pavlovna lived on equal terms with her husband, and had her own room in the marital home where she could entertain her friends and lovers. And when she decided to leave him – and, in time, his successor – the parting was without jealousy or rancour, both being seen as degrading emotions. Personal freedom was thought to override all against the background of the repression of marriage. Certainly, Inessa and Alexander were about to behave in a way that Vera Pavlovna would have approved of.

Quite when Inessa told Alexander of her emotional involvement with his brother is not clear. But she had been discontented for a while – and her behaviour at home and indeed the marriage itself had reflected this. She began to quarrel with Alexander, according to an old family servant named Ivan, often screaming at him and stamping her feet with a petulance that seems childish and is, again, in striking contrast to the strong character that would later emerge in her.[3] While she was to be petulant at times with Lenin, who certainly wouldn't spoil her, this was more calculated, a weapon of maturity that she deployed with some skill.

Meanwhile, Alexander and Inessa were playing out a drama that is common enough. With all Alexander's new work he was often away from home and Eldigino, in its forest, was remote. Also, Inessa's life was in stark contrast to her somewhat simple past. On her marriage into wealth, with a husband keen to please her, she could have anything she wanted. She could buy any clothes she chose. She had servants. She was able to travel abroad on a whim. It was enough to go to any young woman's head.

Whether or not Volodya was a factor, Inessa took to suddenly running away from the house, often not returning until hours later. More than once, though, she did this after dark in her nightdress. A desperate Alexander, terrified she might take her life, would summon teams of local workers to help search for her with lanterns, systematically scouring the immediate area – the park, the forest, even the wells. Then at sunrise, Inessa would emerge unharmed from an outhouse or a barn, having been listening all night to the commotion of the search.

And, while many husbands would, and perhaps should, have reacted with fury, Alexander would fall to his knees in front of their servants and beg her to forgive him for whatever he was supposed to have done. 'She just wanted to punish the master,' said Ivan. 'What a character she was!'[4] And Alexander should not be dismissed too easily as being weak for, like his capricious young wife, he, too, was later to reveal a character of some steel and even acumen.

The crisis of Inessa's new passion for Volodya came to a head and Ivan, who speaks of them as 'wonderful people', described the scene in Eldigino. 'The three of them were sitting on a couch for hours, with Inessa between them, and all of them were crying. "I can't divide myself," she kept insisting, "I feel so sorry."' Ivan, who sounds as though he was a little in love with her himself, remarks, 'She wasn't just crying for herself. And all the servants in the house were crying too.' [5]

Like Dmitri Lopuklov, Vera Pavlovna's husband in Chernyshevsky's novel, Alexander accepted the fact that his wife had fallen in love with Volodya. But instead of leaving like Lopuklov, he continued to maintain Inessa, supporting her various causes, paying her bail when she was jailed, as she often would be, and, despite her requests for no favours, using what influence he could to gain her release. He aided her escapes when she had to cross borders illegally. He brought up the children when she was away in exile or prison and made sure that the Pushkino home was always available to her as a haven. He became a stalwart friend as she recognised with gratitude repeatedly.

There was little doubt Inessa felt love for Alexander, though it differed in character from her feelings for Volodya. When he was away she would keep him chattily up to date with the progress of the children and, when she herself was away from them, she would often express anxiety about them – ranging from their teachers to their health – and ask him to take specific action.

In January, 1903, the lovers left Russia for the Mediterranean and a holiday on the Neapolitan coast which had all the colour of a honeymoon. They visited the Isle of Capri, went south to Sorrento, travelling on to Amalfi and Ravello, set on huge, high cliffs. As a coastline of sheer beauty, it rivals any in the world and it seemed in keeping that Inessa became pregnant with Volodya's child.

They returned to Moscow, living together in the Armand apartment as an unmarried couple with the children. In July, when her pregnancy was becoming evident, Inessa left for Martheray-Lausanne in Switzerland – taking all the children with her, but not her lover. 'When are you coming to join us?' little Fedor asked his father, Alexander, in a PS to one of Inessa's letters from the Alps.

They were to be in the mountains for almost a year and, although part of the reason may have been the imminent birth of a new child – a last discreet nod to the bourgeois life and perhaps concern for Alexander's position – there is a sense that Inessa needed a period of peace to sort out the direction of her life. This possibly explains why she was willing to be parted for so long from a lover who had overwhelmed her enough to make her leave her husband. Before leaving

Moscow, she had also broken off all connection with the Moscow Society and her other philanthropic projects, a last step in creating a clean sheet.

Inessa went for mule rides, took long walks. There are pictures of her sitting with her children against rocky, cave-like backgrounds which could have been the setting of picnics. She took trips to Geneva, where there were many Russian exiles, and visited Georges Koukline's famous bookshop where Russian books and, it was rumoured, Russian passports could be bought or borrowed.[6] It was also a place of meetings and lectures, one of which she attended to hear Anatoly Lunacharsky, a young Marxist with star potential, whom in time she would come to know well.

She read *The Development of Capitalism in Russia* by V.I.Lenin, who was a new name to her although the book made a huge impression on her.[7] Later she was to write that it caused her to become a Bolshevik.

The timing was coincidental – Lenin had only coined this name for his faction in August 1903 – but important to Inessa's thinking. For the Russian Social Democratic Labour Party, the SDs, it was a period, too, that would be immensely important. These were still early days, of course, and the Party Congress in August 1903 was only the second to be held. It had been scheduled for Brussels in July but the Belgian police had intervened and the venue had been switched to London.

Three years earlier, in 1900, Lenin, Martov, and a friend, Alexander Potresov, had started a new journal titled *Iskra* (The Spark) which they hoped would form the tactical backbone of a cohesive SD party that until then had consisted of a series of independent groups, moving to Munich to produce it because of Okhrana activity. Martov had toured Russia, looking for agents, while Lenin had gone to Switzerland to seek the backing of prominent Social Democrats of the older generation, which was vital to the project.

But by 1903, the youthful close friendship between Lenin and Martov had faded with their differing views on strategy. Lenin believed the party should be a tight organisation of highly disciplined, full-time secret workers, controlled on a semi-military basis through local cells and area commands, by a small Central Committee, as spelt out in his pamphlet, *What Is To Be Done?* Martov was more of a Western-style democrat. He wanted a broad party, open to anyone who gave it 'regular personal co-operation'. To Lenin this was too mild to gain success, too open to compromise, too 'soft'. He wanted 'full-time dedication'.

On this membership question, the party backed Martov despite aggressive behind-the-scenes campaigning by Lenin. The division coloured the congress, and was reflected in other issues. The delegates split into 'hard' and 'soft' factions and eventually into Bolsheviks (Men of the Majority) and Mensheviks (Men of the Minority). Even the naming was clever opportunism, 'Bolshevik' being chosen by Lenin because of one issue in which his faction had won a majority vote. The fact that Martov accepted the minority labelling was proof of an attitude that was 'soft'. They were to remain political enemies for the rest of their lives, although they shared a respect for one another that was never to fade.

Attempts at mending the split were made repeatedly over the years, sometimes by Lenin for temporary tactical reasons, but they never succeeded for long. In fact the two factions represented different sorts of people, the 'hards' being militants while the 'softs' favoured debate.

So, just as Inessa was arriving in the mountains, Lenin had isolated himself from the rest of the party. Trotsky, after hesitation since he was an independent, had eventually gone with Martov, as had Plekhanov, the most prominent of the old Social Democrats. Lenin was to start building his Bolsheviks with only twenty 'hards'.

Rather oddly, shortly after Inessa left Switzerland in 1904, Lenin, who loved the mountains, arrived in Montreux, just up the lake from Lausanne. Had Inessa stayed another few weeks, she would possibly have met him, perhaps in Georges Koukline's bookshop in Geneva.

In October, 1903, Volodya's son, Andre, was born. And again Alexander behaved like a saint, granting the boy the same treatment and status as his own children, including his own patronym – registering him as Andre Alexandrovich Armand.

27

Inessa at last returned to Russia in May, 1904, with illegal litera-ture, doubtless obtained through Georges Koukline, hidden in the false bottoms of the children's luggage. This was to be the basis of a revolutionary library that she had planned with Volodya. Among the journals were old copies of Lenin's *Iskra*.

Naturally they were not searched at the Russian border, where they had to change trains since the gauge of the track was different. She was a lady of status, wasn't she? She was returning from a holiday in the Alps with her children and a nanny.

What Inessa had decided during those long months in the moun-tains was to devote her life to revolution.

The need, though not fully recognised by her, had long been there and is probably the key to all her relationships – including those with her children to whom she was devoted and whom she missed acutely whenever she was parted from them. Her letters, to the children themselves as well as to her husband and lovers, are marked by angst, a sense of loss, and filled with plans to be reunited. But the partings were her choice, a result of the life she chose.

For Inessa, revolution was to come first, just as religion or truth has come first for certain people throughout history, and, indeed, would become something she would be prepared to die for. In fact, it can be argued, she was to do just that. Now, because she had readied herself during her long months in the Alps and because the cause had suddenly become more immediate and therefore more demanding, she entered the fray. She was about to see the ugly side of revolt and gain a glimpse of its price. All the same, her internal conflict is fascinating: her letters are part wealthy middle-class mother and part revolutionary whom the police are watching like hawks. In some cases the letters are coded, the secret messages being in the references to the children.

Times were changing fast and so was the scope for revolution. Since February, 1904, Russia and Japan had been at war, started by a surprise attack by the Japanese Navy that had sunk much of a Russian fleet that had been sent east to impress them. Since that first brilliant assault the Japanese had won battle after battle in the field and at sea.

At first the war had inspired an outburst of patriotism

throughout the nation but this was now fading with the failures of the Russian forces and the reality of the trains bringing back the thousands of wounded. Social discontent, reflected for some time at Pushkino, was growing, and with it the nationwide rumblings of dissent.

Against this gathering darkness, Inessa returned to Pushkino with the children feeling, one suspects, a degree of trepidation. How had her behaviour gone down with the family now they'd had time to digest it? Eldigino was no longer her home and Alexander was in the Russian Far East in charge of medical relief for the Moscow Duma. She had always got on with her mother-in-law, Varvara Karlovna, but could hardly expect her to approve the break-up of a marriage with one son in favour of an unconventional liaison with another. Nevertheless, she was welcomed back, and for the time being the new baby took its place in the crowd of children that always swarmed about the Armand complex.

Inessa waited impatiently at Pushkino, taking the opportunity to organise the local SD network with the help of Dr Pechkin, his nurse Valentina Ethtekina and the local librarian, A. N. Rodd. Her aim was to link this network, amateurish though it was, with the hard-core networks in the city.

She made frequent visits to Moscow where she joined Volodya at his current apartment in Granatny Lane in the Arbat. While she had been away, he had at last committed himself, joining the Social Democrats, as opposed to the Socialist Revolutionaries. This had brought him under police surveillance, which meant a life of changing houses.

After a few weeks, as the winter came and snow covered Moscow, the lovers decided to settle, despite the police, and rented a house, 8 Ostozhenka Street, a big building with an archway opening onto a courtyard and, most important, with two exits! From a few yards up the street, if she needed a sense of history, Inessa could see the Kremlin in the distance, with its towers and cupolas and high walls that extended for a mile and half.

Inessa moved the children in with her and, to help with the rent, also took in Ivan Nikolaev, another student. Ivan – or Vanya – was in fact an SR and, since the SRs favoured violence as a tactic, carried weapons. Vanya's father had been an Armand serf, but the family, recognising the boy's talent, had funded his education and he was now reading medicine at Moscow University.

Inessa had put Vanya in charge of setting up her secret library. To help him with this, he had co-opted another student, Nikolai Druzhinin, the library actually being in the home of Nikolai's sister, an actress named Alvetina who was not a member of either party, so less likely to interest the police.

Nikolai would call at Ostozhenka Street every week to collect orders for literature which would then be passed to various SD cells in the city. The house also became a refuge for 'wanted' politicals, which confused the 'nannies', as the surveillance teams were known. Who, in fact, was living there?

All the time, the going was getting tougher. There was unrest in the universities in many Russian cities. The crisis year of 1905 was only months away, and as revolution began to make itself felt, so did the forces of restraint.

In September a student protest march in Moscow was broken up by police and there were many beatings. A few days later, a group arrived in the city from Vologda, three hundred miles up the line to Archangel, and there was a shoot-out with the police that ended with several people dead.

Now that there were members of both the SD and the SR parties in the Ostozhenka house, the Okhrana had put it under full-time surveillance. They had information that the two parties had agreed to join forces to create a revolution.

There were said to be 30,000 police on surveillance duties in Moscow at this time. Their reports draw a picture of their concern and method. They knew Volodya as 'Ipatievsky', after the Armand apartment, and often tailed him when he was with a girl named Alexandrovna Lipinskaya, known by them as 'Kurskaya', whose father was an adviser to the Court. One time, they traced the suspects to No 10 Basseinaia Street, the home of two daughters of the Gavrilovich family, where Volodya and Lipinskaya spent the night.

The next evening, they tailed Volodya and Lipinskaya with the

Gavrilovich daughters to the gardens of the university where they were joined by a thirty-year-old teacher, named as Bobrovaya, also daughter of an adviser to the Court. If suspects met someone else who subsequently left them, that person was followed by another agent. Every detail – what they were carrying, what they did, who they spoke to – was reported.

The following week the agents lost Kurskaya at the station but, by tailing Volodya, they found her again. Little of this had real relevance to what was going to happen, but it highlighted the growing tension. The Okhrana were preparing to act.[8]

Meanwhile, Inessa continued her maternal role. 'My dear Sasha,' she wrote in October to Alexander,[9] 'there is so much to tell you that I could write a whole book. The children were excited by the photos you sent them and want to reply to you, too. Varya loved you calling her a "rascal". Andrushka has been very ill with acute dysentery and the doctor told me that there was a danger he wouldn't recover. But he is now getting better all the time.

'For some reason Fedor [aged eight] has not been accepted by the gymnasium. I think it is a misunderstanding. I've placed him in a private school. Zalesskaya, the head mistress, runs it very well, but it is still only a preparatory and I still hope to get him into the best school in Moscow.

'Sasha [Alexander, ten] is doing well. There was a parents' meeting which I attended. He has so much to do this year because their standards are so high.'

Inessa is clearly staying at Pushkino, as she often did, for she speaks of sending the three boys – Sasha, Fedor and presumably Vladimir, her ward – to stay with friends. 'They were upset because I sent them with Dasha [presumably a nanny]. "So is she going to walk with us and hold our hands?" they complained.

'I went with Inochka [Inna, six] to Eldigino and it was snowing for the first time this year so we travelled by sleigh and she absolutely loved it. She wants to go again.

'For myself, I'm healthy and feeling much better than I have for the last two or three years, but still I don't work!'

She has been to the theatre, on one occasion with the children to see *Snowgirl* 'which they loved.' She's also been to a meeting of the Psychological Society and 'was so bored I almost swallowed my tongue.'

She tells him about the student demonstrations and the beatings. 'The police were helped by the porters and market-stall owners – those bourgeois who can be corrupted so easily.'

Now that she was living openly with Volodya, she felt guilty about taking so much of Alexander's money. She wanted to support the children and Volodya. 'I did write to you about our plans for Vanya Nikolaev and myself to give lessons at home here but there are problems.' [10] The police had approved, but the Okhrana had forbidden it, arguing that she 'was a member of the Armand family and well known for her political lack of loyalty ... the lessons are not recommended, given the propaganda that could take place there.'

She was advancing fast as a revolutionary, building her network and educating its members in politics, but the police were usually close behind. To outwit the police, they had taken to holding meetings with workers in the open fields with lookouts to warn of any approach by government agents – giving them time to disperse. The woods, the usual venues for such meetings, certainly nearer the city, provided too much cover for the police.

Early in January, 1905, Inessa was first exposed on a personal level to the dark side of revolution. In a protest march, Vanya was badly beaten by police, staggering back to the house, profusely bleeding and badly bruised, in front of the children. 'I cannot put into words my pain,' she wrote Alexander on 7 January. 'My children will never get over this sight.' [11]

She wrote also of the rising tension. 'There are spontaneous meetings on the streets and in the restaurants.'

Two days later, on Sunday 9 January, the new mood came to climax. In St Petersburg, a peaceful procession of unarmed men, women and children were led by Father Gapon, a priest of the Orthodox Church, to present a petition to the Tsar at the Winter Palace. This pleaded respectfully for better conditions for the workers.

As they drew near the Palace, the marchers were ordered to

disperse but they refused and marched on. Troops had been formed up in front of the Palace, although the Tsar was absent. The marchers streamed into Palace Square. The sight of the approaching crowd unnerved the officers. The order was given to fire. Hundreds of innocent people were killed and the whole nation was appalled. 'Bloody Sunday' was written into history and strikes broke out in all the major cities.

'Now [in Moscow] we have a sort of revolution, an unusual state of agitation,' Inessa wrote to Alexander five days later. 'Beyond the Moscow River everyone has stopped work. Not only the factories but workrooms and small companies like laundries. Also printers which means there aren't many newspapers left in St Petersburg, not a single one. And what do you say about the nomination of Trepov?' Trepov was Moscow's iron Police Chief whom the Tsar had ordered to St Petersburg to establish calm there.

'These days in the streets of Moscow there are notices that are really funny. The strikes, they say, are the work of the Japanese who are spending millions of roubles on provocative propaganda. This information is said to come from a Western Agency that, of course, does not exist. Isn't that the peak of stupidity?' [12]

She wouldn't be talking of 'funny' things much longer. On 4 February, the Governor General of Moscow, the Grand Duke Sergei, was murdered with an SR bomb by Ivan Kaliayev. It was his second attempt. On his first, he had seen two children in the carriage with the Duke and been unable to bring himself to commit the act. On the second, the Duke was alone. The police immediately reacted to the assassination by arresting radical students and known SRs such as Vanya Nikolaev.

At 4 a.m. they raided 8 Ostozhenka Street. 'I was woken up that night by a sudden noise,' Inna, then six years old, wrote years later, 'and found police searching our room, turning everything upside-down, even the beds of us children. Mother stood nearby, absolutely calm. She smiled at me and made a sign not to cry.'

Horrified, the child watched as they worked. Inessa had warned the elder children of this possibility. 'Do not show you are scared and do not say anything. If necessary look after the little ones. Varya and

Andre were crying. They didn't understand what was happening.'[13]

The police uncovered illegal SR literature and conspiratorial letters in Vanya's room. Then they searched Volodya and Inessa's room and, among her possessions, they found something that was far more incriminating – a revolver and bullets that belonged to Vanya.[14]

Inessa, being an SD, was presumably hiding them for him, but for her it was dangerous. It tainted her record and for years the police were to believe she was an SR. That night they arrested all three of them.

'Don't tell anyone I have been arrested,' Inessa whispered to Inna as she kissed her goodbye. For a six-year-old, this was asking a lot but, as Inna was to write, she kept the secret. It served her well, for three years later she was trusted to see Inessa several times when she was living illegally in the city and police were searching for her.[15]

Renee, who with Nikolai did not live far away, is mentioned in the police report of that first night. Someone had to take care of the children when their mother was removed. There would have been a nanny but a person of greater status would be needed for family decisions.

It was the start of the first big test for Inessa and, as she was driven away in the darkness of the police van, the sounds of the horses muffled by the snow of Ostozhenka Street, she must have been very aware of this.

THREE
Moscow Basmannaya Jail 1905

It was worse than anything Inessa had expected. 'I am among drunken men who scream and make a lot of noise,' she wrote to the governor of Basmannaya prison.[1]

She had been separated from Volodya and Vanya, who had been sent to the local Myasnitskaya prison. Basmannaya was normally a women's detention centre but, following the riots sparked by 'Bloody Sunday' in St Petersburg, the demands on all the prisons in the city were too great and men were also being held there.

Inessa was appalled to find herself being held in a large cell with other prisoners, mostly male, drunk and criminal. 'As the prison at Basmannaya is more than full,' she complained to the governor, 'I have been locked up in the drunkards' cell. I beg you to transfer me without delay to Miasnitskaya, my local prison, or to another place.'

Her request to move prisons appears to have been refused, since she was to remain at Basmannaya, but she was placed in 'solitary', probably for her own protection. The next day, she wrote to the governor again. 'I beg you to arrange for the return to me of the watch that was confiscated when I arrived here at Basmannaya. I also wish to be able to write and to have baths and to be able to take daily walks.'[2]

The writer, Ilya Ehrenberg, was in prison in Basmannaya for a time. 'The station was noisy,' he recorded. 'At night the drunks were brought in, beaten mercilessly and put into the "Drunk Box" – that was what they called a large cage of the sort one sees at the zoo ...

'When he saw me [on arrival], the head warder of the Basmannaya police cells bawled at once: "Off with your trousers!" A "personal search" began. From paradise I had come to Hell. A powerful clout over the ear soon introduced me to the new regime.

'In Basmannaya we announced a hunger strike, demanding transfer to another prison, I remember begging a cell-mate to spit on a slice of bread. I was afraid I wouldn't be able to resist just the slightest bit.'

Inessa had not, at this time, been charged with anything, but the revolver was damaging evidence. Technically, though, she was being held on suspicion, so her requests were not unreasonable. She was worried about Volodya, which was one reason why she wanted to be moved to the same prison, fearing that his fragile health would not be up to coping with a Moscow jail, well known for its cold, damp and minimally hygienic conditions.

She did her best in the interrogations to absolve Volodya of blame, insisting that she was an older woman, the mother of five children, while he and Vanya were just boys.[3] They had also arrested Nikolai Druzhinin who had arrived at Ostozhenka Street on his weekly call without knowing of the earlier arrests and been caught by waiting police. Unhappily, they found on him lists of much of the contents of Inessa's secret library. When they had confronted Inessa with him, she said she had never met him before – which Druzhinin confirmed.

There was much confusion among the police about which parties everyone belonged to. This did not surprise them since they had been informed that the Social Democrats and Social Revolutionaries had joined forces in the cause of revolution, but they also knew that the SRs were far more dangerous. At first, according to the reports, the police believed Volodya and the 'Armand woman' were SDs but they had been informed that Vanya was a member of a terrorist group 'attempting to make bombs and explosives' and involved with 'terrorist propaganda openly seeking the death of the Sovereign.'[4]

On the day of Duke Sergei's killing, according to the police report, some of the suspects had been seen near the Duke's usual route. One was found at the place of the crime half an hour before the assassination. It was at Vladimir and Inessa Armand's home that some of the hundreds of suspects 'were surprised and arrested.'

Inessa's concern about Volodya, and the effect on him of the cold, damp prison was growing. So was that of his mother who wrote to Inessa often, always in French, and spoke of Volodya's lungs as his Achilles heel. The fear, of course, was TB.

Inessa got regular news of Volodya through the prison grapevine, fed by prisoners in transit or warders who knew other warders. She was relieved to hear of his release, after a few weeks, together with Vanya's, though they were required to stay near Pushkino. But Volodya was now very ill.

For Inessa, apparent possession of the revolver made matters more serious. She was charged under Article 126 of the Criminal Code with 'belonging to an organisation seeking the overthrow of the existing social order,' and held in prison awaiting trial.'

Alexander, still in the Far East, was appalled at what had happened but she was allowed to receive his letters and found great comfort in them. 'Dear Sasha,' she wrote back, 'Thank you for your letter. I was touched by your loyalty and friendship. What a wonderful relationship we have.

'Sasha, about your offer to help with my release, don't do too much. If you want to talk to the General Major I don't know what to tell you. If it's the same for everyone, then perhaps it's all right to talk to him, but if it means treating me as a special case, then I beg you not to do it.

'At times I've felt a great need to get out but now I am under control. I feel fine. I am quite healthy. I am absolutely calm – probably because recently lots of prisoners have been released. And you see they will take a lot of money from you.'

Her light dismissal of her time in 'solitary' as a 'great need to get out' is impressive. Ehrenberg was to write: 'I tried knocking on the walls, but nobody answered ... I tried reciting poetry ... '

Solitary confinement has been described by many. You are an intelligent person so you do physical exercises, realising it's vital to keep active. You do mental exercises — recall the stories of books, attempt mathematical sums, play mental patience. You try not to sleep for then you won't sleep at night. Loneliness overwhelms you – worse, disorientates you.

Inessa would have been given a grey dress, a straw pallet to sleep on and fed on barley gruel, which only real hunger would have permitted her to eat.

However, she was spared the ways in which they could make 'solitary' worse – such as leaving the cells empty on each side so there was no scope for even minimal communication; or having the jailer, when he brought the meals, remain silent, refusing to answer even simple questions about the time or the weather.

Ehrenberg described the joy of release from Basmannaya: 'Coming out of the prison gates I was struck motionless. Cabbies, a young fellow with a piano accordion, a booth, Chichkin's dairy, Savostyanov's bakery, girls, dogs, a dozen alleys, a hundred court-yards. You can go straight ahead or turn left or turn right … That's when I understood, once and for all, what freedom is.'

In May Inessa became ill herself, informing the governor that she had 'developed anaemia and was in generally poor health.' She asked for more fresh air and contact with other prisoners, but the request was turned down.

With the approach of spring, she wrote to Alexander: 'You know, Sasha, there is something I want to tell you. When I was free with the boys, we had a plan to go down the Volga and also to visit the lakes in Finland. So if you want to, and have the money, this wish could come true.' She means, of course, that he should take them without her.

'I don't think they will release me, not for a year. There is this court hearing in a month and they say it can go on for four, five or six months. So you will have to go and return before my release.

'In prison, time goes very slowly. I am reading a lot but the last few days I haven't been able to concentrate because the weather is very good and I think about the meadows and the forests. But enough of my dreams. They say that defeat [in the war with Japan] is imminent. For the Revolution it is useful but when you think of the hungry people who must pay the price, then I have terrible fears and it seems to me that we are really heading for disaster. We have to shake off this terrible yoke [of the Tsar] as soon as possible. This is the only way we can survive.

'Thank you very much for the money. Now I am completely provided for and if I have need again I will tell you.

'So ask the children to gather flowers in the woods and meadows and send them to me in the same way as letters. Wild flowers, Sashechka. Something else. I was thinking of giving little history lessons to the boys. I've promised this for a long time.' To prepare for this, she asks for some books such as Ashley & Gibbons' *English History* and Guizot's *L'Histoire de la Civilisation Française*.[6]

The letter, with its revolutionary despair, would never have passed the censors and must have been sent to Alexander by the secret routes available in the jail. He had returned to Pushkino now and, despite her request for no special favours, the family influence was deployed to get her out of jail. On 3 June, some three months after her arrest, she was released, against guarantees by Alexander and his father, but still facing charges and under police surveillance until her trial.

The doctors' reports on Volodya were serious. He *had* contracted TB, they concluded, and must move to the temperate climate of southern Europe or the mountain air of Switzerland. The family urged Inessa to go with him but she had been deprived of her children for months and her revolutionary zeal had been hardened by her time in prison, so she was at first reluctant. Then, aware that every step she had taken since her release had been watched by Okhrana 'nannies', she decided it would be wise to stay out of view for a while.

It seems odd that, still facing trial, she was allowed to leave with Volodya for Nice, on the Mediterranean. Presumably the family bought permission for her, as they had for Kammer. Perhaps the police welcomed it as a form of foreign exile, often a regular sentence of the court, and were glad to see her go so far.

In July, at a time when the repercussions of 'Bloody Sunday' were looming larger every day, the couple left by train for the south. For Inessa, it would only be a pause in her work. She was becoming a veteran campaigner, well along the path she was later to describe to Volodya, her progress from right to left, from rich young wife to hardened revolutionary.

FOUR
Nice 1905

The news came in bits, partly because of the censors. Each day Inessa and Volodya scoured the newspapers. There were reports, mostly unconfirmed, of unrest in the cities – which was no surprise, given the state of the nation, with the rolling waves of revolt following 'Bloody Sunday'.

Nevertheless, it was a cause for anxiety. Pushkino – where the children were and, of course, Alexander and the family – was probably far enough from Moscow, the old capital, to escape serious danger, but it was on the railway line to Archangel and the railways would be a key element in any revolution.

In fact, as it happened, it was the printers who were to be the flashpoint – in Moscow, too, though St Petersburg was the seat of the government. In early October, 1905, the workers in twenty Moscow printing firms went on strike. Because they were located near the university, students flocked onto the streets in support of them. When the police acted, because these were illegal meetings, the students pelted them with stones. The workers in another thirty Moscow printers joined the strike and the Cossacks were brought up to control the crowd. They opened fire, killing ten people. The next week, in St Petersburg, the printers joined their Moscow comrades in a three day strike.

And so the crisis developed. In Moscow, the railmen closed the Moscow-Kazan line and marched to other yards to urge their colleagues to come out too. Four days later, there were no trains running out of Moscow, which was potentially catastrophic, for Moscow lay at the heart of the railway system running throughout the vast country that was Russia. And without trains, nothing was coming into the city – no food, no coal, no goods of any kind.

In St Petersburg, on 13 October, 1905, a workers' soviet, attended by deputies from most of the factories in the city, met for the first time, and formed a rough policy to merge their power, discovering quickly that the people would obey the soviet'srders.

In Moscow, meanwhile, there was an eerie silence. There was no gas or electricity. The trams had stopped. The telegraph system and the telephones were unusable. Post offices were closed. The water system was feared to be polluted.

On 15 October, General Trepov, the governor of St Petersburg, who now had wide powers, issued an ill-advised order which escalated the tension in the city. Police were to disperse illegal meetings. If crowds did not obey the police 'were *not* to use blanks [in their weapons] and *not* to spare bullets.'

This had defiant crowds heading for the streets in their thousands, especially around the university. And oddly the police and troops did nothing, despite the order. Two days later, the Tsar responded with a manifesto offering concessions that included freedom of conscience, speech, assembly and union, an enlargement of the franchise and the right of a new state Duma to approve laws.

This was greeted by jubilation throughout the nation, except by the revolutionary parties, who didn't trust it – and was in theory a huge gesture, not that far off being an offer of constitutional democracy. Leon Trotsky dramatically tore up the manifesto, on a balcony before a huge crowd at the university. The tiny Bolshevik faction of the Social Democrats declared that 'Tsarist freedom is the freedom of new Tsarist guards and the Black Hundreds to kill and rob peaceful citizens.'

The Black Hundreds were a civilian force who, campaigning under the banner of God and the Tsar, had often led the pogroms against the Jews, with the tacit approval of the police. Now they were ranged against anyone they deemed to be enemies of the sovereign.

But not many heeded the fears of the revolutionaries. A wave of optimism swept through the two cities. In Moscow a crowd of 50,000 people gathered in Theatre Square to hear speeches about the manifesto. Many wore red ribbons. A huge red flag was raised, bearing the words 'Freedom of Assembly' and all the men doffed their hats.

Someone started humming the *Marseillaise*, probably because they did not know the words. Others took it up. More joined them, with streaming tears, until soon the marching hymn of the French Revolution was echoing, in haunting tones, from that vast crowd, across that great square close to the Kremlin.

The elation of the two capital cities spread through the nation. Not many had expected success so soon, and they were wary. The St Petersburg soviet, still trying to find its feet, refused to call off the strike, fearing this would be seen as approval of the manifesto, which they still had to consider. But unplanned strikes of this nature are hard to maintain and already enthusiasm for it had started to wane. On 20 October, the soviet, fearing it could be wrong-footed, ordered the end of the strike, before it ended on its own, and urged workers to 'discuss' the decision in their factories.

From Nice, a frustrated Inessa wrote to Alexander. 'My dear Sasha, I started writing this letter a long time ago, but could not continue because Russia was completely cut off. We had neither letters nor telegrams.

'The news has deeply worried us but we are glad for Russia. We would love to be there and make to this great national cause our small contribution. At such great moments it is hard to be able to do nothing. We have a great joy for the common cause but we have been very worried for all of you – for you, for Vanya, for Boris and other comrades.

'I have had no news of Vanya. He was a nice, good person and, I heard, an energetic and valuable worker.

'I admire the way the working class have performed. They are real heroes. What strength and grandeur and what a splendid fight. And now in Moscow the Black Hundreds are acting. I am terrified for all of you – this systematic beating of the intelligentsia. Yes, I would love to be there, and Volodya as well, but [presumably because of his illness] we have to wait a little.'[1]

Two days after Inessa posted her letter, Lenin and Nadya arrived in St Petersburg from their home in exile, at that time in Geneva. He had planned that they should register under their real names and operate openly but, on detecting the Okhrana agents who were tailing them, he decided they should use aliases and they moved constantly, staying in various safe houses. He kept a low profile by contrast to Trotsky.

But, as always, Lenin was the tactician. Before coming back to Russia he had made fiery demands of his new Bolshevik faction. 'For God's sake there has been talk about bombs for more than a year and yet not a single bomb has been made.' He had urged the forming of detachments of workers and students who would kill spies, blow up police stations, and rob banks to gain the funds they needed for an armed insurrection.

Lenin had these *rages,* as Nadya called them in French, when his anger boiled over and his imagination ran wild. It hardly conformed with Marxist policy. It was what the Socialist Revolutionaries did. But he was soon back on course, though again changing policy, urging his followers to exploit the manifesto's legal avenues and put up Bolshevik delegates for the new Duma, only to be overruled by his comrades in conference as this would be collaboration with a hated system.

Lenin persisted, seeing the potential for greater influence, even proposing conciliation with Martov's Mensheviks, which astonished everyone in the faction he had created. For a year Menshevism had been a heresy and he had fought every suggestion of even minor collaboration, cursing the proposers as 'conciliators'. His whole drive had been to keep the two factions separate and, by this means, guard the purity of his own group. Anyway, his suggestion was only temporary, a kind of feint. Lenin was always one step ahead of his comrades.

Meanwhile, the revolutionary tension in the capital was easing and the tiger showed his claws. On 29 November, troops surrounded the St Petersburg soviet and arrested the President and several deputies. It looked like the end, but there was worse to come. In Moscow the SRs and both factions of the SDs had agreed to work together in a new uprising. Lenin himself had ordered the Bolsheviks to take part, and approved the funding. A civilian force of militiamen had been armed and, on 6 December, the Moscow soviet, also newly formed, called another general strike. Within two days 80,000 workers had responded.

In Pushkino, just up the line, Alexander, with a red ribbon in his lapel, had led his own workers out of the factory, which must have bemused the authorities in the city. He was supposed to be a hard-headed industrial boss who hired and fired his staff.

There was a short, tense period during which there were few casualties and both sides were holding back. Then the Governor General of Moscow ordered action, the revolutionaries responded, and the killing began in earnest. The troops began to use artillery, which was unusual in civil control, and the rebels responded with hand-thrown bombs and guerrilla tactics using small sniper units. These had orders to fire at officers and Cossacks but not ordinary soldiers, who might become supporters, nor the police – except those men known for their cruelty, who should be shot.

Barricades went up in the streets, strengthened with ice, and the battle developed. The rising confidence of the government was evident. The famous Semyonovsky Regiment arrived from the capital and poured shells into the Presnya textile district which had become the rebels' base area.

This truly was the end of the 1905 revolution and the cost was high with more than a thousand dead, including 137 women and eighty-six children.

'I remember that December,' wrote Ilya Ehrenberg, still a teenager. 'That was when I first saw blood on the snow. I helped to build barricades by Kudrin Square. I shall never forget that Christmas: the terrible heavy silence after the singing, the shouting, the firing. The ruins of Presnya stood very black.'

The events of 1905 were to serve as a dress rehearsal for future actions. The revolutionaries, and Lenin in particular, would learn good lessons in tactics and the psychology of reaction, both by crowds and the state. The soviets might have been closed down for the time being, but they had made their mark. They'd be back.

In Nice, the news of hope and disaster eventually filtered through. For an impatient Inessa the conflict was hard. She later wrote to her

friend Anna Asknazy that 'friction between personal and family interests and the interests of society [i.e. the revolution] is one of the most
serious problems facing the intelligentsia today.'

She stuck it out through January, 1906, and Volodya made good
progress in the Mediterranean climate. In February, when he seemed
well enough to leave, they returned to Russia, joining her children
and Alexander in Pushkino.

If the question remains as to why Inessa was allowed to leave
Russia, there is none about her return. The government was growing
skilful, using carrot-and-stick techniques. There was a political
amnesty, so Inessa was safe for the moment.

She was careful, too – so careful that there is little documentation
about her movements. The political climate was different after 1905,
and so was her sense of purpose. She became a serious revolutionary,
building networks, cell by cell, and tutoring them in political theory.
And the police were more vigilant, so she was in much greater
danger.

From the moment of her return, they were, of course, watching
her closely. According to the police records, she and Volodya moved
into an Armand apartment in Bolshoi Afanasievsky Lane in the Arbat,
but the lovers sometimes moved to other houses, presumably to
confuse the police.

At the same time, according to N.P. Bulanov, who was an SD
underground propagandist, Inessa was highly active in the Pushkino
area in March and April, reviving the old ring of A.N. Rodd, the
librarian, and Dr Pechkin, the local doctor. The organisation now
had a four-person executive that included Inessa's brother-in-law
Boris, of Kammer fame, and Alexander himself was also closely
involved.[2]

Illegal meetings were held either in Dr Pechkin's house or at the
Armand family home. The factory hectograph machine was used to
print leaflets which would be left at night by the village well for the
women helpers to find and circulate. In this way, so another worker
A. Shestakov reported, Inessa ran three circles in Pushkino and two
others in neighbouring villages, with a total of fifty-five members.

Despite this wide-ranging activity, Inessa had her children with her in the city when she was there – to the astonishment of Elena Vlasova, a young activist student, who could not believe how so hard a worker could possibly find the time to be a mother.[3]

The police did not delay long. On 10 March, barely a month after Inessa and Volodya had returned, they arrested Vanya Nikolaev at a Railway Union meeting where a strike was being planned. Then they raided his home in Novo Basmannaya Street, where Inessa and Volodya were sometimes to be found. The cook told the police that a number of people stayed there, sometimes sleeping on the sofas.[4]

In the raid the police found ten kilos of Marxist tracts hidden in a wardrobe, and various brochures and newspapers, still apparently forbidden, despite the freedom of speech clauses in the manifesto. Vanya and Tarasova, who had been arrested with him, were freed, since the police needed evidence more incriminating than this. But this arrest was linked to the watch being kept on Inessa and Volodya in Pushkino and the city, as they moved from house to house. Only weeks would pass before the police would act again.

In July, Inessa and the children – and possibly Volodya – took a holiday, which is still clothed in some mystery, on the lakes of Finland. This is mainly because it coincided with calls for a mutiny of the garrison of Helsinki fortress, organised by the Military Union of Soldiers and Sailors in Russia with the help of the local Bolshevik SDs.

In a letter to Alexander Inessa wrote, as usual with breathless wonder, of the beauty of the lakes.[5] But if anyone had been needed to check out the limits of the fortress from the water, then a tourist, doing what Inessa was doing, would seem to have been well placed. Certainly, the Okhrana came to suspect it. When they raided her Moscow apartment a few weeks later they revealed they were searching for links between her and the Military Union, but they found none.

On her return to Moscow, Inessa was put in charge of SD propaganda in the Lefortovo district of the city, although she was not yet formally a member of the party. R.C.Elwood has suggested that she won this role because she was older than the students and a woman, which was 'usually seen as an asset since a well-dressed lady was less likely in most areas to arouse police suspicions.' Also, male workers, who distrusted women activists since politics was men's business, 'were prepared to accept a well educated woman as their circle leader.'[6]

'Our meeting places,' wrote Elena Vlasova in 1920, 'were the Annenkova Woods and the Ismailov Zoo for daylight meetings and the banks of the Yauza, a backwater of the Moscow River, for more secret gatherings and this was where she and I used to meet.

'The workers in our district were from the sweet factories, bakers and textile industries ... Many were illiterate, living in great poverty. Inessa had a simple direct way of getting through the distrust and awakening their interest. She would talk about the differences between the Bolsheviks and Mensheviks and make them understandable even by the most ignorant of these people.'[7]

Inessa was a good communicator. She seemed able to simplify the Marxist theory, with an appealing enthusiasm and optimism, and to cross the social barriers without seeming to condescend. Already, too, she was revealing a talent for organisation within the networks that was to serve her well in her days with Lenin.

That autumn, taking advantage of the new admission of women, Inessa enrolled at the university, in the Faculty of Law, even though she would still be forbidden, being female, to practise. Most women were taking humanities and science courses, which could be put to practical use, but Inessa wasn't interested in being a lawyer, only in acquiring knowledge. It was a gesture really for, working long hours as she did, she had no hope of giving her studies the time they would need, but it was a gesture that was to have its uses.[8] She also revived her secret library, making it more akin to Georges Koukline's bookshop in Geneva, with borrowing and lending facilities, and a means of contacting other SDs.

At the same time, as winter approached, it was too cold for outdoor meetings and she became increasingly aware that she was followed every time she went near the Lefortovo district, where she had focused on the important railway unions that were still legal. She was also a member of the SD 'Lecturers' Commission', a pool of experienced propagandists.

48

With Volodya and the children, she had moved back to the Arbat. At the end of February, 1907, Volodya began to suffer new attacks of illness and he left Russia for his old sanatorium on the Mediterranean. It devastated Inessa to see him suffering, with constant coughing into blood-stained handkerchiefs.

But now that Volodya had left, and the children were back at Pushkino for a time, she was alone in the city. Inessa was never easy without people around, although oddly she seemed well able to stand her periods of 'solitary' in jail, which most prisoners find intolerable. Not that she was alone for very long in the Arbat. Like most of her previous homes, there were often political refugees staying with her, as there were when in April the police swooped again.

They found no suspicious literature and showed little interest in the other people in the house, but they arrested Inessa because they had her listed as an SR, and the discovery of Vanya's revolver in her room way back in 1905 remained on record.

They only held her for a few days, which clearly surprised Volodya. 'Thank you for your letters,' she wrote to him on May 11. 'I was so glad to receive them. Don't worry about me any longer. I have been at large for some time. I am rejoicing in the thought that you will soon leave there and come back to us. I don't understand why my letter from the police prison took so long to get to you.

'I work a lot. Sometimes I just don't feel my feet. I kiss you,' she finished off. 'Your Inessa.'[9]

A few days later, they arrested her again, this time for attending an illegal meeting, under the guise of a reunion, in the Sushchevskaya area and she was taken to the police HQ in the Arbat for interrogation.

She refused to answer banal questions about her children, husband, or parents, declaring simply, 'I haven't taken part in any meeting. I went by chance to the apartment where the office of the Steelworkers is ... I had met in the Ekaterininsky Park a friend who wanted to give some books to the [Steelworkers] Union library and invited me to accompany her.'

Ten days later she was released with a fine of 300 roubles.

With the spring, the children, who were at Pushkino with

Alexander, visited her often in the city. However, at last, she had come round to the view, fairly obvious to anyone else, that the constant danger of police raids to which her life exposed her, made an unsuitable background of fear for them. Discussing this with Elena Vlasova, the young girl urged her to move in with her, in an apartment in the Railway District.

'Quite a bit older than me,' Elena wrote, 'Inessa was an experienced revolutionary. Her political knowledge was very deep and for a young militant like me to know a woman like that was priceless. But we didn't have much opportunity for the happy moments I dreamed of. We had too much work and got back too late too tired to utter a word.'[10]

For Inessa, though, the omens were not good. The reaction to 1905 was growing stronger and the government were targeting even legal trade unions. And Inessa was more exposed than she realised. General Reinbot, the governor of Moscow, had been considering the evidence against her and decided that 'Elisaveta Fedorovna Armand [her legal name], wife of the Honorary Citizen Alexander Evgenevich Armand, is a danger to public order, deserving imprisonment until complete enlightenment about the circumstances of her affairs.'[11]

Her cause was not helped by a four-day strike at the Armand factory. When Alexander agreed to all but one of his men's demands, unusual for employers, this strengthened police suspicions of his confusing political sympathies. They arrested four of the local party members, and their watch on Alexander became closer.

In early July, the Okhrana, aiming to end SD operations, raided the party in the Lefortova district. They seized a printing press, leaflets and several workers, but not Inessa who was absent. A few days later, they had better luck when they raided another SD meeting in the area and arrested everyone there. This was being held in the offices of an employment agency, which gave Inessa, who arrived late, a chance to say that she sought only to hire a cook.[12]

It wasn't accepted, of course. Under interrogation she denied everything as usual and was allowed to write a statement, which did not really match her original statement: 'I have been retained as the result of a misunderstanding and with no official charge. I was arrested as I entered 30 Kolossov Lane to rent an apartment. But I am innocent.'[13]

This time it would be no brief visit. She was taken to Prechistenska jail where she remained unco-operative, keeping her eyes shut to make the police mug shots less useable. She lied about her age, saying she was twenty-eight, when she was, in fact, thirty-three and when asked for the names of her sisters, gave those of her children. The police noted that she had grey eyes, light brown hair and a sharp-featured nose. People who knew her, such as Polina Vinogradskaya, have described her eyes as green and hypnotic, her hair as voluminous and fair. Others have said it was auburn.

It would soon be summer and conditions in her new prison were a great improvement on Basmannaya in the winter of 1905. Volodya, too, was back, living in their old apartment on Ipatievsky Lane. 'My dear Volodya,' she wrote,[14] 'I am still waiting to hear from you. You've probably already been told the way to communicate with me and I hope I'll soon get something from you. I feel completely cut off and I don't know at all what is happening with you outside and sometimes the most crazy thoughts come into my head.

'I wonder if maybe all of you are ill and I don't know anything. Especially, I am worried for Andrushka. When we saw each other last time he was not well and you didn't tell me anything about him on the day when you were here. I am frightened that he is getting worse and you are keeping it from me. It is terrifying for me to have these horrible thoughts.

'My life here is not too bad. They say that in the autumn and winter the cells get very damp, but now we sit at open windows and eat well. We have quite a community and take turns to cook and wash the towels. On the day I was on duty I was very worried about my soup, but it was all right, though the vegetables were all half cooked. The whole day was very busy but this is better because then the time passes more quickly.

'In the morning I read until about 2 p.m. and at about 3 p.m. we have dinner and then French lessons. Then we walk (in the prison yard) for about an hour and a half. Then we have supper and, after supper, more French lessons, the last one devoted to "Conspiracy."'

51

Witnesses for her trial were being interrogated in the prison, but she claimed: 'My file doesn't seem to move. I was told I would be freed in three days but I'm still here.

'Volodya, I have a request. Please go where I spent the month of June (you understand) and ask there for Ida. It is best to find her about 5 p.m. and ask her in my name to ask the landlady for my passport. I'm worried about my passport. Again, I give many kisses to you and everyone.'

Meanwhile, realising that everything was different this time, she was displaying plenty of fight, writing to the prison governor: 'I have been imprisoned here for three weeks when I am completely innocent and have been arrested following a misunderstanding. On Saturday 7 July I entered 30 Kolossov Lane to rent an apartment. I rang the door bell of an apartment to enquire about the terms of the block when two police officers rushed out of the neighbouring apartment and forced me to follow them. Despite not knowing any of those present, I was arrested and brought to the Commissariat. Since nothing has been found on my person or in my home and I am innocent I humbly pray your excellency to return to me my liberty.'[15] Still nothing about the cook.

Her demand for provisional liberty was rejected and passed to the Moscow Gendarmerie for appropriate action. 'This close intimacy which had been denied to us as long as we were free, I was [now] able to savour fully in prison,' Elena Vlasova was to write. 'For we had been confined, several comrades and me, in the same cell as her. And at once she organised our communal life ...

'But this sojourn in prison made me understand the extent to which she was attached to her children. She missed them infinitely but she never spoke of them. But we knew that all the embroidery and knitting was destined for them.' The notion of Inessa knitting is hard to accept until it is remembered that her education, aimed at a good marriage, would have included such skills.

Meanwhile, the two men in her life fought hard for her release. Volodya had already had trouble in gaining visiting rights, being only a brother-in-law.[16]

He asked for meeting after meeting with the Gendarmerie captain in charge of the dossier. He spent entire days in the Chancellery. To the governor of the city he wrote: 'I have the honour to beg you to inform me of the exact grounds for the detention of my brother's wife, arrested on 8 July. Would you please explain why she has not been freed at the same time as others implicated in this affair.'

Alexander demanded her release, arguing that she was arrested when looking for a room to rent. 'Nothing was found on her. After one month, I was told she would be detained until her case had been studied but, during interrogation, she was told she was to be tried in three days time.'

But Inessa was up against serious opposition. They had no case, but they had a dossier. In fact, there never was a trial. The head of the Gendarmerie wrote to the Minister of the Interior on 1 September. For two years, he said, she had been engaged in agitation of the workers and communication with extreme parties. He asked that she should be exiled to a northern region for not less than three years.

The Minister agreed but reduced the period. In October she was told her sentence. Two years banishment to the Russian north, under the control of the Archangel authorities. The next day, when Alexander visited her, she passed on the appalling news.

Alexander wrote at once to the governor of the city and asked that Inessa should be allowed to serve her exile abroad. While waiting for a decision, suspecting that this would be adverse, he wrote again asking that she should stay in Prechistenska jail since exile would 'be prejudicial to the studies of our children who live in Moscow while my business keeps me at the factory in the country.'

At the same time, he appealed to a fellow member of the Moscow Duma to intervene, since he was close to the Minister for the Interior.

It was no use. Less than a week later a 'decision of the Privy Council' confirmed the sentence of Elisaveta Armand. The Minister was not opposed to her exile in Europe, but the governor wrote to him: 'I am advised that ... Citizen Armand will never give up her subversive activities. She will be less dangerous in the Archangel region than she would be abroad.'

And so on 21 November, Inessa, in handcuffs, entered Moscow's Yaroslavsky Station with two guards, to board a train. To her delight, Alexander, carrying a large bouquet, was there to see her off with all the children. Much moved, she was allowed to embrace them all.[17] Volodya, despite his frail health, was to travel with her.

Just over an hour later, the train passed through Pushkino and she most probably would have looked out of the window at the church of St Nikolai, with its pale blue cupola, where she had married Alexander and at the two tall red brick chimneys of the Armand plant.

The next day, the Armand workers struck again – this time in an openly political protest at the trial of SD deputies in the Duma. The police acted fast. Twenty-four workers were arrested and shortly afterwards they took Boris, Alexander's brother, A.N. Rodd, the Pushkino librarian and then Alexander himself. The family home was raided, as Rodd put it, 'like an invasion of barbarians'.

Meanwhile, as the train travelled to a frozen north, far colder than anything Inessa had ever experienced, Lenin was in trouble, too – not all that far away and for the same reason: the wave of reaction in November 1907 with the government growing ever harsher. It is interesting how the dramatic points of Lenin's and Inessa's lives tended to coincide.

In 1906, Lenin and Nadya had moved to Finland.[18] It was a cautious retreat from St Petersburg, since he could see the way the political wind was blowing. Finland was part of the Russian empire, but it was to some extent autonomous. Even so, the Okhrana had right of entry and during November, 1907 they were exercising it.

A message arrived at Lenin's home in Kuokkala that the police were searching the town. At once, he packed and left, making for Helsinki, 240 miles away, leaving Nadya with the help of several comrades, to move the Bolshevik HQ abroad. They burnt all the files that could not be transported and Nadya, who had lived this life for a long time, carefully buried the ashes, knowing they would otherwise cause suspicion. Meanwhile, the owner of their dacha hurried round to warn them that the police were getting close. In fact, the

Okhrana were hunting for an SR terrorist group. But it was an unpleasant moment.

Lenin's flight was typical. He would never in exile risk his life or security because of the destiny he believed was his. Lesser people, such as his wife, comrades or even, later, his mistress, might be exposed to any kind of necessary risk, but not the future leader of the world revolution.

It was a stance that was far-seeing, as well as arrogant, for at that time he had lost control of his own faction of the party, and had failed even to be elected to the Bolshevik Central Committee. The Moscow uprising had whetted his appetite as an outrageous revolutionary for whom nothing was barred if it served the Cause.

Early in 1906 he had persuaded the Central Committee of the combined SD party that defensive actions should be conducted against the Black Hundreds, who were dangerous in certain areas. Exploiting this vote, Lenin had set up a secret bureau and treasury within the party – secret, he insisted, because of the danger of Okhrana infiltration which, as would be discovered, was a real risk.

His Combat Bureau squads, under the control of L.B.Krasin, had mounted 200 'expropriations' alone in January and February, 1906, mostly in the form of bank hold-ups, attacks on customs houses and ticket offices, and train robberies. They had often used criminal gangs to work for them, thus providing these with a more respectable 'political' cover.

Much of this revenue had gone into Lenin's secret treasury, which he used to finance Bolshevik interests. Several raids were handled by a cross-eyed Caucasian bandit codenamed Kamo, a friend since boyhood of Josef Dzhugashavily (who in 1912 would change his name to Stalin). Kamo's most dramatic operation was to hold up a carriage on the way to the State Bank at Tiflis and take from it 341,000 roubles that he had then smuggled across the Russian border in a hatbox. But the notes were all of high denomination – 500 roubles – which could attract attention and be easier to trace.

To reduce this danger, Lenin thought up a clever plan. The notes would be presented in small quantities at a number of banks in different cities on the same day and time. As was to happen so often, one of Lenin's men was an Okhrana spy and the police were waiting, but not everywhere, so it still raised funds if not on the scale he had hoped.

The bank raid, and news of other raids, provoked a violent reaction against Lenin from the Mensheviks. 'How can one remain in the same party as the Bolsheviks?' Paul Axelrod asked Martov. Plekhanov declared that it 'was so outrageous that it is really high time for us to break off relations.' Lenin coolly shrugged off the attacks: 'When I see Social Democrats announcing ... "we are no anarchists, no thieves ... We are above that ... " then I ask myself: Do these people understand what they are saying?'

This method of fund-raising, however, had shocked many Bolsheviks, too, which is why Lenin had failed to gain election to the Central Committee of the faction he had created. The members were giving him a message. They knew they needed him, but there were limits, for them if not for him.

However, in November, 1907, while Lenin went into hiding in the village of Olgbu, near Helsinki, Nadya was still finalising party business back in Kuokkala, arranging the transfer of *Proletarii*, the Bolshevik newspaper, from Finland to Switzerland – and even returning to St Petersburg to set up new communication channels with local activists.

Lenin, still uneasy about his security, decided to move on to Stockholm, leaving instructions for Nadya on how to catch up with him. The plan was for him to take the ice-cutting ferry to Sweden from Turku, but Finnish comrades warned that the Okhrana were watching the boarding stage and advised him to pick up the ferry at its next stop at Nauvo island, twenty miles to the southwest in the Gulf of Bothnia.

He left Turku by carriage, switching to a boat to Kuusto island. From there he island-hopped to Lille Meljo island, from which he had to go on foot across the ice to Nauvo island. That early in the year, the ice had not settled and he had to keep jumping the gaps between the floes.

He had two local comrades to guide him, but they were both drunk. At one point the ice broke up beneath him and only by a huge, desperate leap did he manage to get onto a solid floe. 'What a stupid way to die,' he thought, or so Nadya recorded.

He reached Nauvo island, despite this, and boarded the ferry without detection by the police. The next day he arrived in Stockholm, where he was joined later by Nadya.

It would be ten years before he returned to Russia. By then he would have honed his Bolsheviks into a fighting force, able, as he was to claim to mocking laughter at the Congress of Soviets in June, 1917, of taking over the government of Russia. It would be a hard period, marked by frustration, poverty, furious arguments, and moving, always moving, from Geneva to Paris to Poronin, near the Russian border, and back to Switzerland, to Berne and Zurich – but always developing his vision, building his control, cheating when he felt he had to, for the end, for Lenin, always justified any means.

And for seven of those years Inessa would be working with him, loving him, sharing the tactics, doing the dirty work, going to jail, acting on his stream of letters when they were in different places, until even she rebelled, but still she obeyed most of his orders in the service of the party. For his vision of the future was her vision – a disaster, as some might say, considering the millions who died in its cause, but one that was to have a huge, continuing influence on the social and political development of the world.

Some three weeks before Lenin reached Stockholm, Inessa's train had drawn in at last at Archangel, Russia's only sea-going port until Peter the Great had built St Petersburg, and still an active trading town for timber from the vast forests that surrounded it, as well as for fish and flax. But winter had come. The sea was already frozen as was the Dvina River, which flanked the track. She saw a city cloaked in white as the train slowed and the Troitsky Cathedral with its five great domes came into view.

The dread at facing two years in this sterile country seemed intolerable. Two years! And she would not be remaining in the city. That much she knew. Her journey into exile would extend far further north, where the temperatures dropped to below minus 40°C, where even a cup of coffee would freeze in seconds. But the usual stoicism marked her letters – except for those to the authorities in which, as usual too, she demanded improvement of the conditions.

Inessa's gratitude to Volodya for coming with her, despite his damaged lungs, was immense. He was able to help, of course, because he was free and in a better position to negotiate with her captors, though in truth it did not achieve much. In fact, Volodya's efforts during this period of prison, both in Moscow and in Archangel, reveal a more definite personality than normally emerges from Inessa's letters and other evidence. Usually, he appears as a shadowy, rather colourless figure, an impression which she did little to correct. Her letters home would refer to 'I' rather than 'we' except when she is describing him doing something or accompanying her somewhere.

Later, Inessa is to thank Volodya effusively for his guidance into Marxism and clarity of thought, the suggestion being that she could not have matured without him. It is a strange relationship. She can, it seems, live for long periods away from him – even by choice – which suggests a lack of passion. But she appears totally content when she is with him.

She needs him, but he doesn't have to *be* there in person, providing she has other company. There was no sign, even during the far-away excitement of 1905, that she resented his keeping her from it in the tranquillity of the south of France.

If revolution was Inessa's religion, then it seems that Volodya was her priest – a very young one, but quiet and ideologically strong.

In Archangel, for the time being, while her onward passage was arranged, Inessa was held in a local jail, in what she called the castle. She was not in the holding cells where exiles were normally kept, but in solitary confinement, possibly for her own protection, in one of the only two cells kept in that prison for political prisoners. The other cells housed criminals. The conditions were worse than any she had so far experienced in prison.

Inessa had now learned that she was heading for Mezen, a small port more than 200 miles away, only just outside the Arctic Circle. It would be a rough, arduous journey by horse-drawn sleigh. At once, she wrote to the governor, claiming that she 'suffered from fever weakness and complete exhaustion and could not survive the long journey to Mezen. I am asking for a medical examination and to stay in Archangel or a nearby town.'

It was a good try but, as usual, it didn't work. And nowhere, in any of the reports or her letters home, is there any sign of a weakening in her beliefs or concern at the price they might demand. With the help, perhaps, of Volodya, she was still, and would remain, a fervent revolutionary.

FIVE

Mezen 1907

'In the second cell in Archangel,' Inessa wrote to Alexander, 'there was a girl who had been there nine months and was now a nervous wreck. She had hallucinations. She saw faces moaning and screaming. I was so sorry for her because, at eighteen, she was so young.'[1] It was a chilling reminder of what to expect. Although Inessa knew she would not stay long in the city, conditions in a remote colony like Mezen were likely to be worse.

For two weeks Inessa was held at Archangel. She wrote to a member of the Moscow Duma, saying she was imprisoned in the castle without the right of visitors, asking him to intercede on her behalf. Volodya, who had rented a furnished room locally, complained about the prison conditions to the Social Democrat members in the local Duma, though without much effect – possibly because such requests came too often. He appealed to the authorities that, because Inessa was ill, she should be allowed to stay in Archangel, presumably with a change of prison or in a nearby town such as Pinega or Kholmogory.

Volodya had caused some confusion because he was Inessa's brother-in-law rather than her husband, and this robbed him of authority. Normally, exiles were accompanied by their married partners. His complaints achieved nothing.

As Inessa requested, she was examined by a doctor. 'She is suffering from malarial fever,' he reported. 'She needs special treatment for a month.' The governor still took no notice. On 7 December, when she was despatched with Volodya to Mezen by sleigh, he wrote to the Mezen Chief of Police: 'She has agreed to pay for comfort on the journey by sledge,' adding darkly: 'I recommend that you watch her very closely on the convoy.'

The conditions of the journey were similar to those in the eighteenth century. Along the route to Mezen were 'stations' where horses were changed and the travellers could rest. But there was none of the welcome of the staging inns. 'All stations were the same,' Inessa wrote to Alexander. 'One sofa or double bed that were so dirty that we preferred to sleep on the floor.'

The journey made her yearn for 'civilisation' and appreciate the railways to an extent she never had before. However, the stations did have huge Russian stoves at which they could dry their clothes. These had ovens decorated in wood with semi-circular patterns in yellow and red. They also had steps so that people could sleep on platforms above them.

Washing facilities were limited, with no drains from the basins, copper scoops being used to get the dirty water out. Inessa was intrigued by the *malitsa* worn by the coachmen and later by the Mezen inmates – 'marvellous garments' of fur that were put over the head like a poncho.

That late in December, the sun was only above the horizon for four hours a day, from 10 a.m. to 2 p.m., presumably involving some travel in darkness, but Inessa was caught by the beauty of the place; the unbroken stretches of forest and the vast expanse of snow, blue in the northern light.

At every station they had to compete with the other travellers for fresh horses, sometimes having to wait for hours for replacements, and at one stop as long as twenty-four hours. In fact, despite the problems, she was impressed by their progress. Although it normally took seven to ten days, she told Alexander, her convoy made it in five – which, at over forty miles a day, with a twenty-four-hour hold-up, does seem remarkable in that type of territory. But sleigh travel in good weather on worn tracks, often along the course of frozen rivers, with frequent changes of horses, was very fast.

The journey, demanding as it was – especially for a person who was ill – perhaps eased the first formidable impact of that 'mean little town', as she described Mezen, sentenced to be her home for two years. Only one degree south of the Arctic Circle, it was excruciatingly cold, a country of dense forests stretching for vast distances, set close to the White Sea, with lakes and a river estuary. Wolves and bears roamed in the distant timber, though these rarely appeared to threaten the town. On the far sea ice were polar bears.

The long hard winter, with its white Arctic nights, lasted from October to May, when the sea ice would at last allow occasional ships to enter Mezen's little port for four months – though the thaw would, for six weeks, turn the land into a quagmire and floods, making sleigh travel impossible. This meant no post.

Inessa faced the harsh conditions of her sentence without making too much of it, though the depressions would come later. 'On the eve of our arrival,' she wrote Alexander, 'it was minus 37°C – warm by their standards. They were planning to send me even further (to Kodia, another colony, about seventy miles away) but I was unwilling to go. There were no politicals there – just criminals – and the whole village has had syphilis, which wouldn't be very amusing, would it?

'Up to now, I have managed to stay here where there are about a hundred politicals.'

Volodya telegraphed Archangel's governor, who had rejected all previous requests, asking that Inessa should remain in Mezen, where there was a hospital, since she still had malaria. This time the governor agreed. He also said that since she had no occupation, being the wife of an 'Honorary Citizen', she would receive an allowance of twelve kopeks a day, the rate being set by her background. Noble exiles got fifty kopeks and ordinary people received eight.

Meanwhile, Inessa made the best of it. Certainly, it was better than prison. 'To start with we had to share,' she told Alexander, who was at Pushkino, freed on bail, though she did not yet know of his arrest, 'and then we were given our own place. There is a local-style kitchen which I like – a big room with practically no furniture so it looks like a barn and a large larder.'

She was writing of the *isbas* rented out by Mezen's permanent residents, to supplement their incomes from fishing and forestry. They were roughly-made huts with ill-fitting doors and windows which let in icy draughts and had no running water. Theirs had three rooms including the big barn-like kitchen where they probably also slept.

'I cannot say much about my life here,' she continued to

63

Alexander. 'My thoughts still go back to Pushkino. I think of you a lot and all you have done to help me … I was delighted to find you all at Moscow station [on her departure]. It was a great joy for me. I am keeping your bouquet as a souvenir. I don't know how I will manage two years here without my children. But I hope I may be allowed to move to Archangel, where they could come to me.

'How did you settle down with the boys and Inna? I want to hear all the news. It's not worth writing about my moods. They keep changing all the time. When I was at Archangel I was very depressed which was worsened by the fever. At first, when I got here, it was good to be able to move around and see people … but now I'm not very happy. I can't complain, though. I'm better off than some people, but I do miss my children.'[2]

Volodya would get up first on those dark mornings, stoking up the stove, breaking up the ice in the water buckets and setting up the samovar. 'Strictly speaking,' Inessa wrote to her children, 'I should set up the samovar, but I am famous for being lazy. I get up late and … it always seems the samovar is ready.'[3]

She cooked but she wasn't very good at it, surrounded as she had always been by servants, even probably at a modest level before she married. She made blini with yeast and hoped they 'would be able to hack through it.'

In the afternoon, when it was dark again, they gave lessons to their comrades, Volodya teaching mathematics and Inessa tutoring them in languages. With so many 'politicals' around, they soon made friends. The range was wide, Social Democrats being outnumbered at that time by Socialist Revolutionaries and others, such as anarchists. Some were totally disenchanted with the revolutionary activity that had landed them in Mezen or with socialism altogether. 'Others drink and carouse,' Inessa wrote. 'In general hard drinking is very great here.'

In the general store, there was a piano which she was allowed to play.

Alexander received her early letters but by then he knew he too faced the possibility of prison.

Meanwhile, in December, 1907, Inessa wrote to her children, who were all still in Pushkino. It was a descriptive, cheerful letter, starting: 'Dear Sasha, Fedya, Inessa and Volodya [her ward],' she wrote, 'The road [on the journey] was very beautiful, hilly country and … we travelled much on the rivers.

'On clear days … the snow reflects many colours, such as rose and blue and green. Some places are such a bright blue that [at first] I could hardly believe my eyes.

'Mezen consists of two parallel streets with side streets crossing. It is not bigger than Pushkino, maybe 2000 inhabitants. But there's a school, hospital, post office and telegraph. The post comes twice a week.

'Today there was a more severe frost than we expected and we had let the stove go out. I told off Volodya, but it was probably my fault. Anyway, it was desperately cold and our hands were frozen.

'I dream about the summer, when you can come here because the ship arrives then. We also have a larder which in the summer can be used as a room. At that time we can hunt and fish, but (I am told) there are lots of mosquitoes.

'Andrushka you have mumps so you must be very careful not to get cold. What about you, Inessa [Inna]? Have you moved to Pushkino? And Volodya you do not eat gravy and are probably as thin as a rake. You're almost in the sixth form now, so what are you reading?

'[As for me], I love to curl up in bed at night cosy and warm with a book. If it is a serious book I fall asleep immediately. I implore you, though, not to follow my example. Only in this. In all other ways, as is well known, I am perfection.

'With lots of kisses – please kiss the young ones on my behalf, and don't forget to write about them.'[4]

In January, 1908, a new governor was appointed to Archangel Province who was, so the rumour went, hostile to 'politicals'. He soon proved he was 'a true cow'. An idea was mooted that the exiles should celebrate 9 January, the anniversary of 'Bloody Sunday', with a demonstration. Inessa and Volodya said they'd have nothing to do with it. Inessa, veteran by now, considered it stupidly provocative.

As it was, she did not escape suspicion, being sharply warned that, unless she took care, she would be celebrating the anniversary far away (in Kodia perhaps?). Her plea of innocence was eventually believed. 'The situation here is not suitable,' she said. 'It's like making war on war.'

Writing to her friend Anna Asknazy, she said: 'The locals here are quite wild. The men have dangerous and difficult professions. In winter they fish – when it is minus 40. They catch them with their bare hands. It is terrible to even think about it.'

The local women stayed at home, she explained. 'There is no respite for them, like the slaves of the past. Since there are no mills, they have to grind the grain by hand.'

She was still concerned by 'rumours that we are going to be sent far away because of the 9 January affair. The district police inspector has gone to pay respects to the new governor and discuss the new regime. The signs are that this is not good news for us.'

She was soon exposed to the reality of her situation, through an event that again was nothing to do with her – and was this time not provocative – but which brought her close to a man who was to become a valuable friend.

The number of exiles was rising fast, mainly because of the stronger government policies, and by February had doubled to 200. A meeting, attended by the new arrivals, was called as usual in the apartment of one of the local residents named Minkin, to decide where they were all going to live. Single people slept in dormitories and ate in a refectory, serviced by volunteer exiles, including Inessa, despite her poor cooking. Couples were normally given their own quarters and, helping to organise this, was a Polish exile, Saul Zubrovich.

At 8.30 p.m., long after nightfall, the meeting ended. The first six people to leave ventured into the evening dark and were horrified to find themselves facing a mixed detachment of Cossacks and police formed up in the street – visible presumably from the light of the moon and their lanterns. At once, they attacked the exiles, some of whom ran back into the room they had just left, only to be pursued by Cossacks who started hitting them until Minkin's shocked wife insisted they stopped.

According to Zubrovich[5] and a Moscow newspaper, *Rech*, the district inspector ended the street beatings, but now placed some of his men in two rows in the passageway leading to the front door, so that anyone leaving would have to pass between them. At the same time, other men were positioned outside the rear entrance.

The inspector entered the room, where the exiles were now very scared. Minkin told him that they had been having a regular housing meeting for new arrivals. The inspector appeared to accept this and ordered all exiles to leave. He promised no one would touch them but, in the passageway, they had to run the gauntlet between his two lines of men, who struck them as they ran.

Other men were waiting in the front yard of the house where the worst assaults were inflicted. The exiles panicked. There was terrified screaming. Some ran for the back entrance, only to find Cossacks waiting there, too. Others made for the attic, where they were cudgelled out of their hiding places. More still, like Zubrovich, headed for a nearby ravine, aiming for the concealment of deep snow.

Zubrovich was found later, stamped on, beaten unconscious and left with blood streaming from his mouth. He was carried to Inessa's *isba*, possibly because it was nearby.

'I came to,' he wrote, 'in a house I didn't know. I was bandaged, covered [with blankets] and lying on the platform above the stove. It was then that I made the acquaintance of Inessa [who had not been at the meeting].'

The reason for this violence remained obscure. Possibly the authorities believed the gathering had a political purpose, though housing meetings were officially approved. Perhaps the new governor had ordered an example to be made as a deterrent for the future. There were signs of a cover-up, of an official plan that had gone wrong. The most badly wounded had been taken to the hospital. On leaving, each had asked the doctor for a certificate they could pass to the district prosecutor. The doctor had refused, saying it was illegal for him to do this without police permission!

However, telegrams were sent to the new governor, Sosnovsky, in Archangel, with copies to the district prosecutor. And it would appear that it was seen as an error of judgement in official circles in Archangel, for the Mezen police were transferred to Kholmegory.

When a vivid account appeared unsigned in the newspaper *Rech*, sourced from Archangel, everyone believed it had been written by Inessa.[6]

By now, Inessa had heard that Alexander had been imprisoned in Moscow's Taganka jail together with A. N. Rodd, the Pushkino librarian, and Boris, Alexander's brother – part of the break-up by the Okhrana of Inessa's Pushkino ring.

She was appalled. 'I was so glad to receive your letter,' she wrote to Alexander on 16 February, 'but I'm sorry that it arrived only after you were sent to prison. Every day, I am waiting for the news that you're free. It makes no sense for them to keep you … There is nothing against you. Write to me please. What are your views? They have to explain your arrest. How is your health?

'Here, we live as before, the same grey life. The days don't pass but somehow imperceptibly slide by like pale bloodless shadows. We try to convince ourselves that there is life here.

'Of course I am better off than others because I am not alone. On the other hand, I am worse off because there in Moscow are the children I miss and worry about.

'What can I tell you about us?' They had produced some plays. 'Little pieces. I don't know what will come of it, but some of them are good actors.'[7]

Alexander was released after three months, in May, 1908, but banned for two years from the Moscow region and other major Russian cities. He tried to run his business from Dmitrov, some forty miles north of Pushkino, but found this impractical. He applied for permission to spend his exile abroad and opted for Roubaix, near Lille in France.

Roubaix was a textile town, where Alexander had done much of his training and he wanted to study the most modern methods of dyeing wool. Also, Inessa was keen that Sasha and Fedor should improve their French, so he took the two boys with him.

First, they had a holiday in Switzerland where, in August, six months later, Inessa was to write to him. 'I was so glad to get your

letter and little Sasha's. I am glad you are high up in the Swiss mountains with the healing winds …

'About schools in France, I agree it's important to be careful. Good
schools are [usually] only available [there] to rich children and could
be ultra-bourgeois. For the first year, while you are looking around,
it's better to keep the children at home with private lessons.

'I'm glad they are with you since they were missing us both in
Moscow. They are such affectionate, loving children.'[8]

Meanwhile, back in March, when the days were getting lighter, she
had established a routine. 'I do a lot of housework,' she wrote to
Inna, now nine, 'and I have two lessons, so up to 4 p.m. I'm usually
busy. In the evenings Uncle Volodya and I either read together or go
to see people or simply talk. Guests also visit us but we only have
three chairs and one bench, so when it is more guests than we can
seat … they have to sit on the floor, but no one seems to mind.

'I have portraits of some of my new acquaintances. When at last I
see you, I will show them to you. There are no photo studios … but
one of the post office staff has a camera, but charges a lot, probably
because he has a monopoly.

'Volodya brought his camera here but he has no paper or plates or
developing methods … With the last mail I received pictures of you
all and I was so glad that I cannot express it. They are not of very
good quality but all the others that I have on my desk are of when
you were little and they don't look like you are now.

'Thank you for your drawings … my dear sweet girl.

'I am so sorry Papa has been arrested. I don't think they'll keep
him long. Write to me if you've been allowed to visit him. He will be
dying to see you. Write and tell me how his health is, whether he
hasn't got cold there.

'I hug you warmly my dear Inushka. Uncle Volodya sends you
many kisses.'[9]

Inna had attached a letter from Andre, now three – written, of
course, by her. 'I don't kill bears,' Inessa replied to him. 'I don't have
a gun. There *are* bears but far away in the Arctic Ocean which is
covered with ice now, but we do have reindeer here. They are so
beautiful – brown, grey and even completely white.

'Ask Grandmother to show you the deer on the tapestry. They are harnessed into little sledges and they run very fast, not only along the road, but also directly over the snow.

'You say you have had a good haircut. I cannot see you, but I know you are my sweet boy.'

By April, the winter had caused a relapse in Volodya's health and he was forced to leave Inessa in Mezen. She dreaded his departure but she was delighted to hear from him in Pushkino, where he called on his way south. 'Thank you,' she wrote to him in May, 'for describing your meeting with the children. I so vividly imagined you with them.'[10]

Volodya's absence was made more bearable, she wrote Alexander, because she had found 'two new comrades she liked to have dinner with, so I don't have to cook myself any more.'[11]

One of these comrades was almost certainly Valentin Popov, a Bolshevik with whom Inessa was to work later. Zubrovich recorded that he was present at many of the talks she had with Popov, but couldn't understand much of what was said.

'She tried to teach me Russian,' he wrote, 'but I was lazy (and didn't study). So she would scold me. She wore her beautiful hair in long plaits and I'd respond by grabbing them. She'd scream but was never offended. If I had known what kind of family she came from I wouldn't have behaved like that, but it was only when I arrived in Moscow with her that I discovered she came from the most bourgeois of bourgeois. Among the Poles at Mezen were working class people and she got on well with them.'[12]

Zubrovich attended her study circles, even if he didn't do his prep. These were partly political and, since Inessa was very short of party literature, he arranged for some books to be smuggled into Mezen by a kulak he knew, together with some old issues of *Iskra*.

With Popov, Inessa formed an artistic group, the talent she discovered in her earlier efforts making her more ambitious with Anton Chekhov's one-act play *The Marriage Proposal*.

In May, Inessa made another plea to the governor to allow her to spend the rest of her sentence in foreign exile. She explained that she had been in Mezen since November, 1907 and provided official certi-fication that her conduct had been satisfactory, but her health was not. She attached a medical certificate confirming that she 'suffered from gastritis and malaria and that her state required a change of climate and a cure by thermal waters.'

This was met with yet another rejection – though the fact that, in a moment of rebellion, she had put this in the form of a demand and failed to address him as 'Your High Excellency' may not have helped.[13]

In April, 1908, when Mezen was still blocked by sea ice, Lenin was in the bright sunshine of the Bay of Naples – on the Isle of Capri. He was staying in the villa of Maxim Gorky, Russia's famous low-life novelist, where he went fishing and played chess with Alexander Bogdanov.[14]

He wasn't on holiday but was there with a special purpose. Bogdanov was Lenin's rival within the Bolshevik faction – and the only person in the party who was his intellectual equal if not his supe-rior – but their views on strategy were in total contrast. Lenin was still keen to use the existing institutions of the state, like the Duma, to extend their influence. Bogdanov opposed this, even insisting that all Bolshevik deputies in the Duma should resign or face expulsion from the party. His target, which took him to the fringe of Marxist historical theory, was armed insurrection by the working class, which would develop its own cultural development. To Lenin, this ignored political realities. Intellectual guidance was vital – which Bogdanov shrugged off as impossible because intellectuals were enmeshed in the bourgeois culture of the individual.

Lenin finally decided that there wasn't room for both of them in the Bolshevik faction. Bogdanov would have to go and the planning of this was why Lenin was in Capri playing chess with an apparently jovial cordiality – unless he lost, when Gorky would be astonished at his 'angry and childish' behaviour.

Lenin's decision was bold. Because of his criminal approach to the raising of party funds, he now had few important supporters among the Bolsheviks. He had not yet regained his position on the Central Committee – and the chance of this seemed remote.

Bogdanov, too, was finished with Lenin and bored by the endless conflicts within the party. After returning to Paris from Capri he resigned from the board of the Bolshevik newspaper *Proletarii* – as Lenin had planned. But he kept his place on the Bolshevik Central Committee – which, for Lenin, made him dangerous, given the mood of animosity in the committee.

Gorky had hoped that the meeting on Capri would ease the divisive tension between the two men. Certainly, he didn't think Lenin would split the Bolshevik faction. But this was exactly what Lenin had in mind. What made it possible was a new source of funds that shocked his comrades even more than the bank raids. The matter of the Schmidt funds would long echo throughout the party – and would, in time, involve Inessa.

N.P Schmidt, the nephew of a wealthy Moscow industrialist, and a revolutionary sympathiser, had died at the hands of the Okhrana in 1907, leaving a fortune to his two sisters. Lenin, seeing the potential, ordered two young Bolsheviks to woo the sisters, marry them and contribute their inheritances to the Bolshevik faction of the party.

Astonishingly, the plan worked – in part at least. The two men succeeded in marrying the girls. One then decided to keep the funds, but the other, Victor Taratuta, while retaining some of his wife's money, handed over a considerable sum – enough to give Lenin scope for independence.

The Schmidt funds, like the bank raids, were to cause Lenin a stormy few years of internecine fighting, which Inessa was to help him ride out, and frame the party that was to win success on such a scale that even Lenin may not, at that point, have believed it possible.

His response to the shocked flood of criticism was revealing. Victor Taratuta 'is good because he'll stop at nothing,' he said to one comrade. 'Tell me, could you go after a rich merchant lady for her money? No? And I wouldn't either, I couldn't conquer myself [because of his upbringing], but Victor could ... That's what makes him an irreplaceable person.'

But Lenin was deceiving himself – or his listener. He, too, would stop at nothing to achieve an aim that was worth it.

Mezen 1907

*

By June, when Lenin had returned to Geneva, the sea ice had broken up at Mezen and a white ship, named *Barty*, arrived in the port. Inessa was delighted to find Volodya on board.

This cheered her. 'The weather is very warm and sunny,' she wrote to Inna in July, 'and we walk a lot. We especially like to walk towards the Mezen River, which is about five miles. There are many lakes. The blackberries are already ripe and we got a lot yesterday. We plan to go tomorrow for the whole day. Maybe we will camp.

'For some time, it has been very light. At night you can read easily – and night is only different from the day because of the freshness of the air and the mosquitoes. You can't imagine how awful the mosquitoes are here.'

She had accepted now that her original plan for Inna to join them by ship was not practical, mainly because she had learned that the autumn weather was so bad, with 'sharp changes from very cold to very hot' and 'the wind whistles through [the huts] and it is easy to get cold – especially for you my fragile Inushka. I realised then that bringing you here was not a good idea.'

She added optimistically: 'Maybe I will be able to move to Archangel. The climate and conditions are better there.'[15]

By the next month she was gloomy again. 'We have just got through the six weeks "no road" period when we are completely cut off,' she wrote to Anna Asknazy, referring to the thaw, with its quagmires and floods.[16]

'And then I was ill with fever. Mezen is a town of the spiritually dead and dying; there is nothing particularly shocking or terrible here, as for example in penal servitude, but there is no life and people fade like plants without water. Those from the cities, with their intense life and richness of interests, cannot settle down and adapt themselves to this bog and they spiritually decline. It is sad to see how the comrades arrive here full of energy and life and then waste away. And it is unpleasant to notice the same process happening in yourself.'

In early September Volodya again fell very ill and it was obvious

FIVE

he could not spend the winter in Mezen. He was forced to leave her still facing the prospect of more than a year of her sentence.

After he left, she wrote to the governor again, this time with the aim of transfer, if only temporarily, to Archangel where Inna could join her. 'Further separation is completely inconceivable,' she had written to Inna. She complained to the governor of toothache, malaria and swollen glands. There were no dentists in Mezen. The police, she said, would confirm her continued good behaviour. Doubtless she addressed him this time as Your High Excellency but again, her request was refused. It made her feel desperate.

She had often talked to Zubrovich of escape — probably while Volodya was away. The plans, though vague, centered around one of the fishing boats.

Suddenly, however, martial law in Poland, under which many of the Poles had been exiled, was lifted. They were free to return home. 'Because there were so many of us,' Zubrovich wrote, 'we could hide Inessa and take her with us to Archangel. I told my friends about the plan and everyone supported it. So I hurried to Inessa and said "Get ready."'

'There were several women among us, so Inessa was not the only one. And we dressed her in the fur *malitsa* worn by the local women.'

They had 'documents and three sleighs' and, on the morning of 20 October, they set off over the early snows. It took a lot longer than Inessa's five-day outward journey of the previous year, but no one stopped them. 'Everyone knew that a big party of Polish exiles was returning to Poland and they didn't even count us.

'In Archangel, Inessa and I went to a former landlady of mine and waited until evening. Then we crossed the River Dvina to the station,' which was on the left bank, the town being on the right. They caught a train to Vologda, a junction station where several arterial lines merged. There, they changed onto another train to Moscow, arriving on 3 November – taking care because direct trains from Archangel would have been specially scrutinised.

They need not have worried. M. Lapine, the officer in charge of Inessa at Mezen, did not notice she'd gone until 8 November when the police reported her disappearance by telegram.[17]

Inessa did not underestimate her danger. As soon as her disappearance was noticed, she would be a wanted woman. The Moscow police would be searching for her and the national borders would be put on the alert. The last was not too serious because the Finnish border was notoriously easy to cross, but Moscow was a different matter.

A week later, on 10 November, she wrote to Volodya. It was a letter, almost childish in its colourful joy of freedom, and sent to him at Beaulieu in the south of France, where he was now in a sanatorium.

'My very dear Volodya, So I have managed to extricate myself from the ends [of the earth] to return to the centre at last. It is with great pleasure that I listen to the noise of the carriages as they rumble by, of the moving crowd. I look at the multi-storey houses, the trams and carriages and [think] my dear town, how much I love you. How closely I am connected [to you] by all the fibres of my being [sic]. I am your child and I need your bustle, your noise, your commotion like a fish needs water ... I am very happy and excited.

'I know you understand amazingly and are glad for me. I feel quite well in general and am quite joyful and excited in spite of the fact I've been here about a week, but I'm restless. It takes time. I think I'll stay in Russia until after the summer. Then it'll be apparent what to do next. I'll take the children with me. I haven't seen them yet.

'Tomorrow I'll be meeting Inna and I'm so emotional in advance and so rejoicing at the thought ... The other children I won't see yet for the reasons you know' – presumably because they were too young to be trusted with a secret.[18]

Altogether it was an excited cry, even if the Okhrana would be searching for her. That Inessa should feel euphoric after the long, dull, unpleasant months of Mezen was understandable, but it hadn't yet occurred to her, it seemed, that, with all her elation, she hadn't asked Volodya how *he* was. Also, her proposal to stay away from him until after the summer – some eight or nine months – can hardly have cheered him. Again, it is strange behaviour towards a lover – especially one who had shared her harsh Arctic exile, despite his deplorable health.

She may have been a Vera Pavlovna but she was no Anna Karenina. And, if she *had* been of course, it is unlikely she could have achieved the heights of influence that she did. However, as would soon be obvious, there is no question Inessa loved him.

She wrote to Volodya again the next day, perhaps nagged by a little guilt. 'I am writing again, my good one. All the time I am thinking about you. How are you? How do you feel?

'Up to now everything is going well [here]. Soon I will leave. I am in a comparatively good mood and I feel more alive because my social life is awakening.

'In my town I have found very big changes. It's more alive and it's becoming more important. In the evening in the streets it is so beautiful, so many lights, so lovely. I've got used to riding on a tram. I've been three times to the Moscow Art Theatre, twice to a cinema. I attended a lecture about Symbolism.'[19]

Although Inessa said she was thinking about Volodya and asked about his health, her excited description of her high life in the city, despite the dangers of arrest, cannot have been welcome news to a lover in a sanatorium. So he didn't reply. By the end of November she was getting worried. 'For a long time I've had no news from you and I'm afraid you are not getting my letters. I am still at the same address. Every day I am going to leave but something always keeps me … The last time I saw all of my family (though not the two youngest), which is a rare exception, they were all in good health and asking about you.'[20]

Meanwhile she kept a low profile, living at a secret address, reading and writing in the Rumyantsev Museum – safer than the university library which she would have preferred – and meeting women who had been co-prisoners in the Prechistenska jail. The news of some of them was not good. One had become insane, two others were in bad straits; a fourth had come out of the Butyrsk jail, still only nineteen, with wrinkled lips and a haggard face, probably due to severe dehydration.

Inessa was trying to form plans, her immediate intention being to move to Kiev with the children, believing presumably that a smaller city, where she was not known and the Okhrana were likely to be less intensive, would be safer. First, though, she decided to risk leaving Moscow for St Petersburg where she was due to meet Anna, her sister-in-law, to attend Russia's first All-Women's Congress. This had at last been reluctantly permitted by the SD leadership, despite the party being very anti-feminist. For all their ideas for social change and their nodding in the direction of Chernyshevsky, they still believed that women's place was in the home.

Alexandra Kollontai, destined to be both a comrade of Inessa's, and a rival, would be attending with a forty-five-member women workers' group and was certain to be prominent.

The police would be sure to be watching the congress, so Inessa had to keep a low profile – no speeches, even if she had been allowed to make one; no official position, since this would have been listed. Even without the fear of the police, however, it is unlikely she would have been playing much of a role. So far she had little status and, despite her work for the SDs, had still not formally joined the party.

Instead, she observed proceedings, interested mainly in the 'Women and the Family' sections and the discussions on 'Free Love' – the arguments hinging on the conflict between the need for freedom of love and the fact that most women had such small incomes that this was unattainable. 'They went around in this circle like a squirrel on a wheel,' she wrote Vladimir.[21] Still, it provided ideas that she would later raise with Lenin. In fact, it would further inflame their relations at a time when they were already sore.

The congress was not successful – and the women workers' section staged a walk-out over procedure. Anna and Inessa also felt they had had enough.

Anna left the city but Inessa decided to stay on in St Petersburg until after Christmas. Clearly it would be unwise to join the family at Pushkino, tempting though this was. Also, Kiev no longer seemed a good idea. St Petersburg had advantages. The city, huge enough to stay hidden in, was near the border and the party was well established there, with a good underground organisation.

So Inessa rented an apartment in Kolpinsky Lane, writing to Alexander in Roubaix that her plans had changed, though she couldn't find a large enough apartment for the children. 'To think,' she wrote, 'that for a year and a half I haven't seen them [the younger ones].'

It was not a happy Christmas for her. 'I had a terrible time,' she wrote Alexander. 'I felt absolutely lonely, completely despondent. I did not know such loneliness in the north as I have experienced here because, even after Volodya left, there was our circle which, through living together, became one big family.

'I quite understand how spoilt I have been by life and how used I am to being surrounded by people who are close to me. But when I found how hard it was I thought that there were so many people who were alone all their lives.' However, she was positive about the future, even if she was spoilt. 'I greatly hope something good will develop in my private life.'[22]

It was going to be a while before things got much better for her. 'The news I have of Volodya,' she wrote to a friend, 'is not very good. He is better, of course, but he has to stay in bed and he's bored. He was very pleased to get your letter.' She urges him to write again since several of Volodya's friends were out of contact for one reason or another. 'Send your letters to the old address, care of Anne.'

To Volodya, she wrote a deeply affectionate and grateful letter, reflecting on her gradual political ripening. 'During the last stages of this, you did so much for me,' she said. 'It is thanks to you that I came to understand so much better and quicker the different problems of Marxism because your approach to these was so true and so deep. Finally, it was because of this last reactionary year, when I lived with proletarians, unlike previous years, that I became stronger [in my beliefs] – and [also] because of you and your conception of the world that does not seem to have been dictated by any kind of obsession, but by mature reflection.'[23]

These were almost certainly the last words she ever wrote to her lover. A few days later, in early January, 1909, news reached her that Volodya's condition had suddenly worsened and he had been moved urgently to a clinic in Nice for an operation. Even so, the gravity of the situation was played down – as though it was 'like piercing an abcess.'

She had an anxious intuition, though, and left immediately for the south, crossing the Finnish border secretly to Sweden, first by train and then by sleigh over the frozen lakes.

By the time she reached him in the south of France, his operation was over but he was declining fast to the 'surprise even of the doctors'. Two weeks later, he died in her arms – possibly from septicaemia.[24]

She was absolutely devastated and fled to Roubaix, to Alexander and her sons.[25] Then, after a few weeks, she moved on to Paris where she had been born but which she had never visited before – alone, perhaps finding it easier to grieve on her own.

'His death was for me an irreparable loss,' she wrote to her friend, Anna Asknazy, 'because he was all the happiness of my life – and without personal happiness the path of life is so very hard.'[26]

Years later when Inna was eighteen, Inessa explained to her: 'I think, my dear Inochka, that everything ends with death ... You know, it seems to me that you only realise this when you lose someone. It is hard to believe that everything is finished and that you will never again meet the person you love. I remember that when your Uncle Volodya died how distressing I found this and how much I envied your Babushka [her grandmother, Varvara Karlovna] who believes in an after-life and for whom death is only a temporary parting.

'But in general, down here [on earth], it seems to me that this knowledge [Inessa's atheist belief] imprints on us the necessary spirit to fight and wrestle for a better life for us and for others.

'If you believe there is an after-life, it is easier to resign yourself to the adversities of existence in the hope of finding compensation in a better life beyond. But if you only admit to a terrestrial existence, then you want to make this as good as possible and, even if you cannot improve it for yourself, because of the time this may take, you can at least make it better for future generations.

'Life for most people is today so horrible that on arriving at the end of their time on earth, they can only think of it with bitterness and wonder why they have lived.'[27]

This, of course, is an argument for socialism versus religion – and Inessa was on the left – though it can be argued that the two are not necessarily incompatible. And it was written a long time later, when the scars of loss had healed.

Babushka, of course, had lost a favourite son, and doubtless did find her faith a consolation, but Inessa had developed as a socialist, as Volodya had too, and it is likely that she would have taken the same view even then, in 1909, when she was in desolate mourning.

Following family tradition, Volodya's parents gave ten thousand roubles in his memory towards the building of a biological station in Murmansk.

There has been some speculation within the Armand family that Volodya committed suicide, this being the reason he was rushed to hospital plus doubt about the wording and placing of the memorial plaque, but it has not been substantiated.

For Inessa, the future now seemed both dark and uncertain. She could not go home to Russia for fear of arrest. She was parted from her husband, as a husband, and now her lover was gone. She now faced a life in exile, but so far it had no emotional stability.

'On the question of work,' she wrote to Anna Asknazy, 'I'm doing nothing for it demands courage and energy and for the time being I have none. I drag along here. [For the present] I am living in a little French town until Easter. I have moved [my base] to Paris where I hope to find something to occupy me. I would like to get to know the French Socialist Party. If I manage to do this I will at least have got a little experience and wisdom for my work when I return to it.'

In Paris, she gravitated towards the Avenue d'Orléans to a café known for its Russian émigré clientele. There, she met Elena Vlasova, her fervent young friend, with whom she had shared both an apartment and prison in Moscow. Elena was shocked by how 'melancholy, pale and drawn' she seemed. In answer to her questions, Inessa explained, 'I've had a great sorrow. I have buried in Switzerland someone very close to me, who died from tuberculosis.'[28]

The café allowed its Russian customers to hold meetings in a large upstairs room and to hear speakers. And it was there, when she was attending one of these meetings with Elena, that Inessa at last met Lenin.

SIX
Paris 1909

Inessa had never met a man like Lenin. She had known young revolutionaries – and some older ones in prison, at Mezen, as well as Volodya's tutor at Pushkino – but none for whom revolution was his whole life; none who had Lenin's knowledge and intellectual powers; none who believed it was his destiny to reshape the world.

In a sense, Lenin was what she had been looking for from the start – the figure of authority and dedication for whom Volodya could be seen as a necessary predecessor, since he had given her the knowledge which had prepared her for Lenin.

Inessa was thirty-five; Lenin was thirty-nine – and an odd figure, either to be a world leader or a lover. He had a round head that was bald except for a ring of red hair; small, dark Mongol eyes and a short, pointed beard. Always, his clothes were crumpled, his trousers baggy and a little too long. 'To look at,' his friend Gleb Krzhizhanovsky once remarked, 'he is like a well-heeled peasant ... a cunning little *muzhik*.'

Most people found him unimpressive on first meeting, and later it was always his eyes, which sometimes narrowed into slits when he smiled, that gripped them. They gave to his face a mobility of expression that could display an exceptional scale of emotions, ranging according to Valentinov, an early comrade, through 'thoughtfulness, mockery, biting contempt, impenetrable coldness, extreme fury.'

'There is no such person,' said the Menshevik Fedor Dan, 'who is so preoccupied twenty-four hours a day with revolution, who thinks no other thoughts except those about revolution, who even dreams in his sleep about revolution.' There would soon be competition in his thoughts, although to love Inessa, as Lenin did, after his fashion and deeply, was probably a new experience for him, despite rumours of other women. It is trite to say they were made for each other, but the relationship was to have that colour. Certainly, she was the only woman, the only person, who ever made Lenin cry – even if, to achieve that, she had to die.

As it was, this first meeting, in company with others, seems to have had no great importance for Inessa – beyond showing her the man, whose works she had read and whom she probably knew of as a maverick of Social Democracy.

Certainly, Elena Vlasova, though writing of this first encounter after both of them were dead, when the Lenin hagiography industry was in full flood, reported no admiring comments.

Soon after this, Inessa left Paris for a holiday at Sables-d'Olonne, a resort on the Côte Sauvage in the Vendée, a province to the south of Brittany, where the Royalists had staged a strong, late resistance in the French Revolution – perhaps providing a revolutionary flavour for Inessa.

Alexander rented a large villa, named La Favorite, for the whole family. Possibly, with Volodya gone, he hoped Inessa might now return to him and live a family life, structured on more than deep friendship. It was a vain hope. He could not match what was now her basic demand of a man. He must be a revolutionary – ideally a totally professional committed one, which Alexander, though leftish in his views, could never be.

Before the end of the holiday, Alexander suggested she should come and live with him and the boys in Roubaix until his exile ended in 1910, but the thought of returning to that gloomy industrial town did not appeal to her. Instead, she proposed to take a course in political economy at the Université Nouvelle in Brussels, which was not far from Roubaix.

This would serve several purposes. Firstly, the course would concentrate her mind; secondly, she would be away from the émigré community where, in her present emotional state, she did not feel at ease. Thirdly, she wanted improve her knowledge of Marxist theory – that was important to senior Social Democrats and displayed by such female high-flyers as Alexandra Kollontai and Rosa Luxemburg. Inessa spoke much of the intelligentsia, of which she considered herself a part, but she knew she did not rank as a serious intellectual.

After the holiday, she moved to Brussels with the two younger children, Andre and Varvara, renting an apartment on the Avenue Jean Volders, not far from the university. This institution had only been founded fifteen years before and had something of a bohemian, radical reputation, attracting many foreign students. It was open to women and its faculty tended to be socialist.

Inessa cheated a little on the application form, suggesting that the few lectures she had attended in the University of Moscow were a year of full-time study.[1] She was accepted for a two-year licence programme, but she worked hard, gaining her diploma after only ten months on 30 July, 1910. A week later, she joined Alexander and the children for a celebration in the Hotel de Graeff in Brussels. His two years of exile were over and he was about to return to Russia. It would be some time before she saw him or her sons again.[2]

During her studies in Brussels Inessa had done some occasional work for the local Russian Social Democrats, probably using her language skills. She had also agreed to forward to Russia *Sotsial-Demokrat* and other party literature printed in Paris, since Brussels-sourced mail was less likely to attract the attention of the Russian postal authorities.

The eighth Congress of the Socialist International was soon to be held in Copenhagen and she wrote to her main Social Democrat contact in Paris, asking if he could arrange tickets for her. To her surprise, the response came from Lenin himself, who wrote to the organisers asking that Inessa's name should be added to the list of official invitations.

It was an important congress, attended by most of the European socialist stars such as Trotsky, Rosa Luxemburg, Martov, Lunacharsky, Plekhanov and Chernov. Inessa was probably joined there by Anna, her sister-in-law, who had been with her in St Petersburg and often attended such events with her.

Lenin was, of course, in Copenhagen and, although Nadya had planned to accompany him, he had eventually come to the congress alone – which has tempted speculation that this period, when they were both in the city, was when the affair with Inessa first started.

There is nothing to support this. Three years later, Inessa wrote to him of the awe in which she held him for the first few months of their meeting, rendering her nearly speechless even when he just came 'into the room to speak to NK' (Nadhezda Konstantinovna)[3] – though this seems oddly unlike the Inessa of insolent letters to prison governors; who shut her eyes to spoil mug shots. As it was, the relationship with Lenin does seem to have developed slowly — as it had with Volodya.

Certainly, in September 1910, Inessa returned to Paris rejuvenated. She was in her prime, in her mid-thirties, a pretty, elegant woman with luxuriant auburn hair – and an aura of confidence. She was dressed in stylish clothes and interesting hats, for which she had a special fancy, all presumably funded by Alexander. Her comrades spoke of her 'cheerfulness' and 'happy dynamism'. Some went further, maybe too far. 'Life in her,' reported G.Kotov, 'seemed to spring from an inexhaustible source.'

'I see her now,' wrote another comrade, quoted by Louis Fischer, 'leaving the home of our Lenins. Her temperament was impressive. She was a hot bonfire of revolution and the red feather in her hat was like … its flame.'

Paris was still in the Belle Époque and the writer Ilya Ehrenberg gave a vivid description of the city. 'I had never seen so many people in the streets … Cabbies shouted at their horses and cracked their whips. In the Boulevard de Sevastapol I saw a steam tram; it was hooting tragically … I was amazed by the number of "pissoirs"; on them was written "Meunier Chocolate is best" …

'The men wore bowlers, the women huge hats with feathers. On the café terraces, lovers kissed unconcernedly. There were bright posters everywhere. I felt as though I was at the theatre.'

Inessa joined the Russian émigré society in the Avenue d'Orléans, of which young Ehrenberg was a member. *Sotsial-Demokrat*, the SD party journal, was produced at No.110 and the Bolsheviks met at the Café des Manilleurs at No.11, sometimes retiring to the large upstairs room where Inessa had first met Lenin.

'I asked Savchenko [a comrade] what I should order,' wrote

Ehrenberg. "She said: "Grenadine. We all drink grenadine" ... red, sickly syrup to which they added soda water. Only Lenin ordered a mug of beer ... '

Ehrenberg heard Lenin's speeches. 'He spoke calmly without rhetoric or emotional appeal; he slurred his Rs a little ... His speeches were like a spiral: afraid that people wouldn't understand him, he returned to a thought he had already expressed, never repeating it but adding something new.'

Inessa was filled with a new exciting sense of purpose by a man she much admired – and even, as she said, came to 'love' although she wasn't 'in love with him then.'[4]

She soon showed her value with her languages and Lenin, whose French was weak, began to ask her to provide his translations – notably his oration later at the funeral, after their joint suicide, of Laura Lafargue, Karl Marx's daughter, and her husband Paul.

Inessa became close friends with Nadya and took over from her the correspondence with the party members in European cities, again using her languages, while Nadya concentrated on the contacts within Russia.

Inessa moved with the two youngest children – Varvara, nine, and Andre, seven – into an apartment in the Rue Reille, overlooking the Parc de Montsouris, not very far from Lenin's home in the Rue Bonnier, where he lived with Nadya, her mother and his favourite sister, Maria, who was ill at the time.

It is significant that Inessa, concerned as she was with the working classes, rarely refers in letters to the servants who must have moved with them, doubtless supported by daily locals and possibly tutors, enabling Inessa to live the life she did. In Paris, though, we do know from her letters that there was a Russian nanny named Savushka.

When Varvara went home to Russia, probably with Alexander, Inessa moved, with Andre, to a boarding house in the Rue Barrault, owned by a Russian émigré couple named Mazanov.

Meanwhile, for the first time, she joined the Bolshevik faction, being elected in due course to the Paris committee. She also became the Bolshevik representative to the French Socialist Party, which pleased her.

At a personal level, she used her fluent French to help new arrivals find work and accommodation. At that time, in early 1911, Russian exiles were flocking into Paris, which had become the heart of émigré activity, from all over Europe.

During the nine months after the Copenhagen congress, Inessa became close to the core of the Paris Bolshevik community through Lenin and his two lieutenants Grigori Zinoviev and Lev Kamenev – known with him as 'The Troika' – and through Nadya, who shared her strong feminist sympathies.

Then, in June, 1911, she played her first major role in Lenin's life – and in the most serious fight he'd ever had within the party. And, of course, without the party, or at least *a* party, he was powerless.

At first sight, with all the factions and conferences and conflicts – like Lenin's with Bogdanov – this little world of exiles had a Lilliputian quality. Few people, even in Russia, had ever heard of Lenin. The émigrés were almost all poor and frustrated – one even drowning himself in the Seine – and lost in fierce, passionate arguments in the street cafés about the new society that the revolution would create. *If* it ever came.

That, however, was the one thing they could all agree about, as they had to, that it *would* come, but not, of course, about its form. The events of 1905, though six years before, had given them new hope, coloured always by sentimental dreams of home. What some people might regard as failure in 1905, since the government had regained control relatively fast, the exiles saw as a standard for what *could* happen. But the 1905 upheavals had not been planned, they reasoned, so they could never have been truly exploited.

Next time, Lenin would argue, they must be ready for the opportunity when it came, and learn the lessons of the earlier revolution. 1905 had 'taught the masses ... to fight for liberty ... The second revolution must lead them to victory.' He had even flung himself into a study of military tactics, poring over General Cluseret's *On Street Fighting* and von Clausewitz's *On War* – and was to deploy what he learned in the street fighting in July, 1917.

Many of the more prominent characters in this tiny, taut community would achieve great power in the Russia that was to be created in 1917 – or die in challenging it. What Lenin did in Paris, together with his associates and his ever-growing number of opponents, would in time be reflected in his success in the revolution and, through that, on the world political stage.

The Okhrana, at least, did not underrate the émigrés. The year 1905 had been a shock for them too. There was a Paris surveillance bureau set up, that reported to St Petersburg with a running account of the conflicts in Paris plus useful information about the parties' counterpart organisations within Russia, legal and illegal. The Okhrana had several well-placed spies and, as it was to be discovered years later, were supporting Lenin – unbeknownst even to Lenin – because he was a divider and division was police policy.

In Russia, though, censorship was easing. Left-wing party newspapers could be published, providing they weren't provocative, although conversely the parties themselves remained illegal. Lenin was not slow to take advantage of this and plans for a newspaper were forming fast.

In Paris, though, he was in severe trouble. While Inessa was still in Brussels, Lenin had faced a showdown with the Social Democratic Party, with many Bolsheviks lining up against him alongside the Mensheviks.

At a meeting of the united SD Central Committee, even with Bolsheviks in the majority, he was ordered to close down his faction's Paris Centre. The Bolshevik journal *Proletarii* was to cease publishing. The leadership of the party was to be switched to Russia. The Schmidt funds, gained by the comrade who'd married into money, were to be handed over to a group of trustees, accountable to the Central Committee.

Never before had Lenin been so diminished – and it is interesting that Inessa should have come into his life at a time when he was still surveying the ruins. Not that he appeared to be in disarray, apart from lashing out as usual at 'The Liquidators', as he called those who were disenchanted with the conflicts and wanted to concentrate on legal activities. He knew what must be done. He would create a new Bolshevik party with the make-up and discipline that he wanted

– whose members would do what he ordered – though he didn't actually admit openly that this was his purpose.

His first move in what was an elaborate scheme was to set up a revolutionary school in Longjumeau, a few miles south of Paris. And the comrade entrusted with its organisation was Inessa.

There had been two similar schools before, controlled by others – in Capri and Bologna. Lenin's purpose was the same as theirs – the training of inexperienced workers in propaganda, agitation and illegal organisation. But Lenin's aim was also to create more Bolsheviks, screened and brainwashed to his specific view, to add to the small group of supporters that still remained with him – before moving on to the next stage of his plan. This was Inessa's first step in an escalating series of assignments, many of them linked, each more important than the last. As it was, her involvement at the school surprised many comrades.

Longjumeau was in the valley of the Yvette River – 'a straggling French village stretching along the high road,' as Nadya described it, 'over which cartloads of farmers' produce rumbled all night to fill the belly of Paris.' Lenin knew it well because he was a great cyclist and had often escaped there on weekend jaunts. Accommodation would be cheaper than in Paris and surveillance, by his party rivals as well as by the Okhrana, would be harder in a village than in a crowded city.

Inessa, with the usual help from Alexander, rented a house in the Grand Rue, where everyone ate food prepared by Katya Mazanova, her Russian landlady in Paris, in a communal dining room. It also provided bedrooms for Inessa and Andre, and three students, including Sergo Ordzhonikidze, who was to rank high in the party after 1917 and to play a special role in Inessa's own life. She also rented a metalwork shop next door where classes would be held. Inessa provided the furniture and took over the organisation of the school programme, supervising the daily curriculum.

The school opened on 11 June, in weather that Nadya described as 'unbearably hot', with only eighteen students – one of whom, Georgi Safarov, was to become a close comrade of Inessa's, and almost as many lecturers, if you included the part-timers, some of whom came for little more than a day. Still, among them were figures who were to become eminent. Meanwhile, the locals were 'surprised' that 'our teachers would walk around barefoot.'

Lenin and Nadya, as she points out carefully in her *Memories of Lenin*, lived at the opposite end of the village, but dined with the others in Inessa's house. Nadya seemed to have very little to do with the school, returning often to Paris to keep up with her main activity of correspondence with Russia. And she gave Inessa full credit for 'the comradely atmosphere which was created.'

Lenin and his lieutenant, Grigori Zinoviev, were the two main lecturers but the surprise was Inessa's role as the only woman teacher, although her university diploma from Brussels and her solid experience of illegal activity in Russia provided some background for this.

Lenin always gave the day's opening lecture at 8 a.m., on aspects of Marxism, the party – *his* party, of course – and political economy before often leaving for business in Paris. Inessa would then run a class discussion about what he had said.

She also gave lectures on political economy, in which she had gained her diploma, and various other subjects though Lenin would not allow her to speak, as she wanted, on prostitution or the organisation of women workers, despite the fact that Alexandra Kollontai had run a similar course at the Bologna school. Women's interests were not a priority for Lenin, certainly not at this point of a new campaign.

It was not all work. 'Some evenings,' Nadya wrote, '[the students] would go out into the field where they would sing or lie near a haystack and talk about all sorts of things. Sometimes Ilyich would accompany them.'

At weekends students and some of their lecturers sometimes 'took cycling trips or walks through the hot countryside, went swimming in the Seine, or made excursions to Paris where they saw the landmarks of the French Revolution.'

The closest group – 'Ilyich [Lenin], Armand, Sergo [Ordzhonikidze] Lunacharski – went to a theatre on the outskirts of Paris,' to see avant-garde or proletarian plays.

If Lenin had been growing close to Inessa during the spring, working together at the school was to bring them closer still.

To the comrades, although there had been suspicions in Paris, Longjumeau was where the affair with Inessa developed. Several historians have put it earlier, without much evidence. Inessa has given her own version when writing to Lenin in early 1914. 'At that time [the early months in Paris], I was terribly in awe of you. I wanted to see you but I would have died on the spot before entering your study and, when you came into NK's room, I did not know what to do with myself. I felt awkward and stupid. I envied those brave people who just walked in and talked with you.

'Only at Longjumeau in the summer and the following autumn when I did your translations did I get a bit used to you.

'I loved to listen to you and especially to watch you as you spoke. Firstly, your face was so animated and then you were so absorbed that you did not notice me observing you.'

In the same letter, she wrote, 'At this time, I was not in love with you, but I already loved you very much.'[5]

Her dating may not be exact, for she wrote this letter, in a state of deep and desolate sadness, very soon after their first big parting – as lovers, anyway – in late 1913. A degree of self-delusion has to be suspected, as has already been noted, for this picture of timid restraint hardly fits the Inessa of 1911 who was already a confidante with responsibility, as testified by her appointment as a teacher at the school.

By that autumn, they may not have been lovers, but Lenin was engrossed with Inessa. The French Socialist Charles Rappaport commented on how they would go alone into the cafés in the Avenue d'Orléans and 'Lenin with his little Mongol eyes gazes all the time at this little "Francaise"'.

Nikolai Valentinov, another associate, reported that the affair was 'never a secret for [Lenin's] old comrades such as Zinoviev, Kamenev and Rykov.'

Stefan Possony wrote of contemporaries who saw him drinking alone with Inessa in a bistro in Longjumeau, where the prices were too high for most émigrés. They noted, too, 'at lunch at the school how Krupskaya's mother manifested open indignation whenever Lenin conversed with Inessa.'

Alexandra Kollontai told Marcel Body that Lenin 'had been very much attached to Inessa,' and that Nadya knew of the affair and offered to leave him 'in the summer of 1911.' It was not the only time she did this, but he always asked her to stay.[6] However, according to Lydia Fotieva, one of his secretaries, Nadya gave up sharing his bedroom and moved in with her mother.[7]

Over the years, during the periods they lived apart, Lenin was to write more letters to Inessa than to anyone else, often several a day, usually about politics, since politics was his life, but also about personal concerns. When Inessa died his grief at the funeral astonished several of his female comrades and the romantic Kollontai even suggested that the loss of Inessa contributed to Lenin's own death, four years later.

Inessa was the only person, other than his family and Martov in their early days, whom Lenin ever addressed in letters or verbally by the intimate pronoun 'ty' (thou) instead of the usual 'vy' (you) – equivalent to the French 'tu' and 'vous'. She addressed him in the same fashion. Even Zinoviev and Kamenev, his two nearest comrades were 'vy', as indeed were their wives, whom he saw several times a week.

Certainly, Lenin came to rely on Inessa at times even more than his lieutenants in the Troika. She was, of course, a veteran revolutionary. They had all been in jail but not as often as she had, and not in near-Arctic exile. Nadya had shared his passion and his vision but in a plodding kind of way. She understood him completely and provided him, in their endless travelling, with a solid base. Inessa touched this passion, made it flare both intellectually and emotionally, reducing him at one level to a normal man but enlarging him at another by providing him with another voice, eventually taking his place on the platform under tight briefings, using her fluency in languages. Longjumeau was the first display of her organisational and speaking talents, ensuring a closeness with Lenin that was both emotional and professional.

In September, 1911, Inna and Varvara arrived back in Paris and Inessa needed more space than she had with Katya Mazanova; so she rented an apartment at 2 Rue Marie Rose which was next door to the

Lenins' new home at No. 4. Both Nadya and Lenin enjoyed the company of the three children, who would often pop next door. Polina Vinogradskaya, a post-revolution comrade, suggested that they were even a surrogate family to the childless couple.

The story is told in Armand circles of Lenin coming across Andre, then aged eight, and a friend as they played. 'You're a Bolshevik,' he told Andre. 'And you,' he said to the other boy, whose father he knew, 'are a Menshevik.' After Inessa's death when, of course, Lenin and Nadya lived in the Kremlin, they became informal guardians of Andre who was then sixteen and in poor health, and Nadya retained a close friendship with Inessa's two daughters.

Inessa's relationship with Nadya is almost as intriguing as that with Nadya's husband. For, despite the affair, the two women appeared to get along. Nadya came from the same sort of background as Lenin, with parents who were minor nobility. As a young girl, she had heard of his Social Democratic group, run with Martov, and joined it.

When Lenin was exiled to Shushenskoye, near the Mongolian border, Nadya applied to join him, saying she was his fiancée. He didn't argue. The taunt later was that he married her for her copper-plate handwriting. She had never got on with his mother or his sisters, something that was not helped when she failed to bear him children.

She was a year older than Lenin and by 1911, she had become plain. She had put on weight with middle age and she had bulging eyes, because of a thyroid condition, and this caused Lenin's sister Anna to comment that she looked like a herring.

The marriage had always been a working relationship – marriage anyway being deprecated by revolutionaries as bourgeois – but they shared a common sense of humour as well as common ideals and it was not unhappy. Their relationship lacked passion, and there is little personal emotion in Lenin's letters to her, but they shared a deep need for revolution.

If Lenin's relations with Inessa came to a head at Longjumeau, it would seem he convinced Nadya that he was not going to leave her – possibly because of a lingering bourgeois past or out of a belief that a broken marriage was undesirable in a future statesman. Maybe, too, he was comfortable with a wife who provided a stability that at times he lacked.

At any rate, Nadya clearly accepted Inessa in their life and, for the next five years until 1916 – when there was nearly a total, if temporary, break from Lenin – Inessa was to have homes that, while not always next door, as at Rue Marie Rose, were very close. Inessa shared the Lenins' holidays and, until the war, they shared her children on their frequent visits.

This then was the situation in the autumn of 1911 when Lenin, on his return to Paris, was planning his next move, and again Inessa was put in charge of organising it. Incredibly, he proposed to seize control of the whole Social Democratic Party.

To achieve this objective it had to be agreed by vote in an SD Party conference – where, on the face of it, there would be no chance of success. Not only was Lenin at odds with all the leading figures in the SD movement, but many of his own Bolsheviks were now opposed to him. His tactic was to keep the attendance thin and to load it with his supporters – especially Longjumeau students, who had been exposed to the Lenin philosophy.

There were Social Democratic groups in cities all over Europe. Some were split into Menshevik/Bolshevik factions; some still operated as one party. And until Longjumeau it had been Inessa's job to maintain contact with them – which was to have its uses now.

Lenin's plan was to call a party conference in January 1912, in Prague – which was not the easiest place to get to and required a passport, something not then needed in all countries. He gave very short notice and just shrugged off criticisms that he was rushing it for no good reason, though Lenin's reasons were always suspect. And why Prague, in midwinter, for heaven's sake?

He persisted. And Inessa made arrangements. She was skilful, ensuring a pro-Lenin Bolshevik majority by only sending invitations to a few Mensheviks who were sympathisers and 'forgetting' the more critical of the Bolsheviks.

Trotsky, who edited his own newspaper in Vienna, saw what was happening and angrily announced his own conference to be held later, which suited Lenin and Inessa because many Mensheviks, who might otherwise have come to Prague uninvited, opted to wait for Vienna instead.

In the event only eighteen people attended Lenin's Prague 'conference' and eight of these had been 'indoctrinated' at Longjumeau. Only two Mensheviks turned up. Even there in Prague, despite his huge majority, Lenin did not have too easy a time. He was opposed in some issues – especially by Sergo Ordzhonikidze, who lived in Russia and believed the leadership should be sited there. He was supported in this by most delegates. But Lenin achieved his principal aim: a big majority empowering him to appoint a new Central Committee – all Bolsheviks except one.[8]

There was outrage throughout the movement, but it was technically – and therefore, he argued, legally – a party conference decision. And it would have its own journal, to be named *Pravda*.

Prague was not really accepted as a fully legitimate party conference. Lenin's opponents knew exactly what he had done and how he had done it. But the fact is that it survived.

Lenin expected the Mensheviks to wither, which never quite happened, but they did lack the disciplined virility of the Bolsheviks, and had no strong leader. It was dirty work that Inessa had been doing for Lenin, but, although the new party faced a shaky few years of challenge, it would be there for good.

One of the members of the Central Committee of the new party was Roman Malinovsky, whom Lenin much admired. But Malinovsky, though he would soon be a Duma delegate, had also become an Okhrana spy. This, in fact, aided Lenin during this period, though naturally he didn't realise it, for the Okhrana was backing his breakaway policy, divide-and-rule being an old, effective technique.

Now, the Okhrana increased Lenin's control of the Central Committee by arresting those members of it who were opposed to him. With each arrest his influence grew – as did Malinovsky's – since this gave him an opportunity to replace them with activists he could rely on for support.[9]

A few weeks later, in March, Inessa wrote to Alexander in a curious way. She enclosed a letter to a lawyer named Malyantovich, who'd had past contacts with wealthy industrialists. 'Please read this,' she instructed him, 'and intercede with the two people mentioned in it ... and take it yourself to Malyantovich and tell him that this letter is from Lenin and that he has signed it as Ulyanov only for conspiracy purposes in case the letter falls into the wrong hands ... Say that the affair will go forward in the very near future – i.e. between March and May ... '[10]

One 'affair' which took place between March and May, R.C. Elwood speculates, was the launch of *Pravda* on 22 April, adding that the Central Committee had been informed that 'the heir of a certain factory owner' had promised 3000 roubles. 'It is reasonable to conclude ... that Inessa's husband was actively involved in raising money for the paper.'

'Goodbye my dear Sasha,' she ended rather intriguingly, 'write to us quickly ... Anya is worried about your acquaintance and she would like to know what is going on with her. We read your letter two or three times. And, because we are women with imagination, we have two interpretations and they are radically different.' Could this be Anna Arbels, the widow of a friend of his, who became his first post-marital companion? Or his sister Anna, who was often called Aunt Anya?

By now, Lenin was making plans to leave Paris which, with all his angry party critics, was becoming uncomfortable for him at this time. The furious arguments, which he excelled at and so often provoked, were becoming tedious. In June he moved his base to Cracow close to the Russian border. Once the capital of the Kingdom of Poland, it was a beautiful city that was now in Austrian Galicia. Zinoviev, with his wife Zinaida and their little son Robert, moved with them. Kamenev remained in Paris.

There were other reasons for the move. Lenin was better positioned to exploit the fact that, though the party itself was suffering from arrests, party newspapers could, with care, be published in Russia. As planned, *Pravda* had been launched in April.

Correspondence, too, was much easier. 'Peasant women from Russia,' Nadya recalled, 'would come to market in Cracow and for a small fee would take our letters across [the border] and drop them into the letterboxes in Russia.' Without foreign postmarks, the Russian police ignored them.

Also, the comrades could cross the border with a *polupaska* – special semi-passports permitting locals to cross from both sides. At the frontier the names of the passengers were called and each had to answer 'Present' in Polish. A comrade, Nikolai Krylenko, who lived at Lublin near the border, supplied addresses they could go to on the Russian side. 'Once, we got Stalin across that way,' wrote Nadya.

Perhaps the best thing was that, unlike the French police, who co-operated willingly with the Okhrana, the Polish police 'did not spy on us, nor intercept our correspondence and ... had no contacts with the Russian police.'

Which is not to say that Lenin was without problems. The editors of *Pravda* were not carrying out his orders, or observing the decision of the Prague conference for a separate Bolshevik party. They were not publishing some of his articles and were changing the slant of others.

Someone would have to go to the capital to persuade them to change their policy to conform with the new party line. Lenin decided to send Inessa, his troubleshooter, even though this would expose her to extreme risk since she was a 'wanted' woman in Russia. With the Okhrana infiltration that was always feared, the chances of her arrest were very high.

But, as expected, Lenin would not allow personal considerations to guide party decisions. Inessa had not moved with him in June but arrived in Cracow in early July with Georgi Safarov, a young Armenian who had been at Longjumeau, to support her.

Lenin briefed her on her mission which went way beyond dealing with the *Pravda* rebels. He wanted her to repair the St Petersburg committee, the most important in Russia. This had been badly fractured, in terms of numbers and morale, by Okhrana activity. He also wanted her to take charge of the plans for the elections to the Fourth Duma. Again, the local Bolsheviks were joining forces with the

Mensheviks in Social Democratic campaigns. Didn't they know that this was forbidden, and again in contravention of Prague?

The best person to have taken on all this was, of course, Lenin himself but, as usual, no physical risks could be expected of the future leader of the revolution. With the aid of Nadya, who handled contacts with Russia, he gave Inessa and Georgi addresses and contacts in St Petersburg. And Inessa did not hesitate. She was proud to be asked to take on such an important, top-level duty for the cause, reflecting as it did, Lenin's trust in her, and as big a task as fixing the Prague result.

With Safarov, Inessa crossed the border with a passport in the name of a peasant woman named Frantsiska Kazimirovna Yankevich, that stated she was twenty-eight (not thirty-six!) – and dressed for the part in old boots and a tattered shawl.

Lenin was fully aware of the dangers. He wrote to Kamenev: 'The two of them are already on their way. If they are not arrested, this will be useful.' He had calculated the risk. She was good but maybe she was a party comrade he could spare rather than other senior members, who, of course, were men.

Their orders were to contact Nikolai Krylenko in Lublin, who would provide what help they needed to get to the capital.

They reached St Petersburg without trouble but there was no chance of their avoiding arrest. Already an Okhrana dossier had recorded the return from abroad of Elizaveta Armand, her legal name, together with her assumed name and her disguise as a Polish peasant.[11]

But they didn't arrest her. At least not then. She could be a useful lead for some time yet.

SEVEN
St Petersburg 1912

There was something quaint, even farcical about this clandestine venture of Lenin's two recruits as they crossed the border into Russia. They were doomed before they started, given the Okhrana's information, and, though Lenin didn't know this, his decision to send them – *either* of them – is still strange.

Lenin was clearly very worried about what was going on in St Petersburg. The city party was in a total mess as a result of Okhrana raids back in May, provoked by strikes. These had also eliminated many of Nadya's secret addresses for correspondence or foreign-printed party papers. Even bringing the dissenting Pravda editors into line would require a firm hand.

Yet, to deal with all these big problems he sent a boy of twenty-one and a woman, elegant though she was, dressed as a Polish peasant. Single women were never taken seriously by the chauvinistic Russians, and Inessa, long wanted by the Okhrana, was dangerous to anyone she met. Neither of them had any formal ranking in the party beyond being sent by Lenin, whose current standing, after all the internal party turmoil, was under question.

However, they reached the capital without any dramas which, since the Okhrana was waiting and watching, was not strange. It is not clear where they stayed. They probably moved often. Georgi Safarov's father, an architect of some note, lived in the city, though his home might have seemed a dangerous place to go. Safarov, too, had been condemned to exile two years previously, though he had been allowed to spend this period in Europe.

Safarov had, as has been seen, attended the Longjumeau school and he and his young wife, Valentina, had become close friends with Inessa. The Okhrana drew conclusions, since the two of them were travelling together, and recorded that Inessa was Georgi's mistress. It was an area in which their judgements were often faulty.[1] They did not link Inessa intimately with Lenin until 1916, by which time she had withdrawn from him for a time, in an almost total break.

Still, a sexual relationship with Safarov was possible, given the dangers they were sharing, and the fact that Inessa clearly liked younger men; but there is no evidence of it. Certainly, on her return to Galicia the following year, she was still deeply in love with Lenin, as she would be for the rest of her life.

Georgi and Inessa faced serious obstacles in their mission. The police raids had broken the party underground into a series of individual cells that lacked links with one other. They also found that many of the Bolsheviks they met were critical of Lenin's manipulation of the Fifth party conference, arguing that there were many advantages to Social Democratic collaboration. Lenin, they doubtless reasoned, was too far away to understand their life in the capital and they did not sympathise with his need for rigid control of the party.

So there was resistance, Safarov recording that for a couple of weeks they 'wandered about Petersburg in vain and at considerable risk,' dressed in old, worn boots and clothes, 'far away,' as V.I. Malakhovsky, a comrade, put it, 'from the Paris fashions' of Inessa's past life in Moscow, which would seem to be overstating the case.[2]

Inessa wrote to Alexander, thanking him for money that 'arrived just in time since I was down to my last kopek … The weather lately has been very poor. Everywhere is damp … I have a bad cold and a fever … I take quinine … in a few days I will be all right.'

Almost certainly at an early stage the two emissaries met A.M.Korelkov, although Safarov doesn't mention him.[3] It was, however, he who had re-established underground cells in three areas including, most importantly, the Narva industrial district. This included the factories of the great Putilov Corporation, the biggest engineering complex in Russia, handling government orders for ships and artillery.

Korelkov, too, favoured a united party rather than Lenin's new and suspect creation. Even so, he gave the couple something of a free hand. They were allowed to address Putilov workers about the Duma elections and many were reported to be impressed by Lenin's position following the Prague conference.

This brought Inessa and Safarov into touch with the left of the party in the Narva district which gave them a foundation for their work. From this, contact was made with cells in other areas which, after some months, developed into a newly formed St Petersburg committee, as ordered.

By and large, it was hard going, though they were making a degree of progress. They had far greater difficulties with *Pravda* – which was ironic if Alexander had indeed provided some of its funding. The editors refused to talk to them and, according to one report, an associate of the paper 'threatened to kick them down the stairs.'[4]

Inessa, opting for a more indirect approach, made contact quietly with Konkordia Samoilova, secretary to the editorial board, who was to become a leading feminist Bolshevik. Samoilova arranged a meeting with the editors, but this achieved little. They still refused to print many of Lenin's articles.

The shadow of the Okhrana loomed over Inessa and Safarov wherever they went. 'The police watched us constantly,' recorded Evgenia Adamovich, a close comrade. 'We were well hidden, but the circle was getting tighter.' The agency even knew that Inessa had attended a dentist named Rogovin and, on 27 August, its operatives, in the form of Technical Group 1143 of State Security, accompanied her by train to Moscow. Their report mentions visits to the Moscow apartments of Renee, Inessa's sister, as well as Alexander's brothers Boris and Sergei.[5]

They make no mention of her seeing her children but since that was certainly the reason for her trip to Moscow, there is little doubt that she met them, possibly hidden from street surveillance by Renee or one of the others.

Back in St Petersburg, Inessa and Safarov held Sunday meetings of workers – sometimes more than a hundred – in a field near the rail track, rich with mushrooms, which they could all pretend to be picking if the police appeared – as they did. 'The Pharoahs [mounted police] tried to interfere but they didn't succeed,' reported Safarov. He didn't explain why, though the rail track might have caused problems for the horses or maybe the police thought they truly were picking mushrooms.[6]

By this means, interfering in the capital's complex electoral process, they were able to influence the decision to allow six Bolsheviks to stand for election on a separate Leninist Bolshevik slate, instead of being multi-faction SDs, to the Fourth Duma. And one of them made it to the Duma in due course, which was a minor coup, though there were other Bolshevik deputies who were not of the Prague persuasion.

This process, too, was marked by setbacks, and Inessa had rather desperately called a meeting at the Women's Mutual Aid Society on 14 September with the aim of raising the pre-election pressure. The Okhrana decided to trap them there, surrounded the building and arrested the fourteen Social Democrats inside, including Inessa.

Inessa was held in solitary confinement in the city's police prison. For two weeks she was constantly interrogated, denying she was anyone but the Polish peasant she claimed to be. But at last agents who knew her arrived from Moscow with photographs and there was no longer any point in pretending she was not Inessa Armand.[7]

Once she had admitted her real identity, she insisted she had entered Russia under cover only to arrange her children's schooling, but again it wasn't believed. It was all irrelevant since she had long been 'wanted' for her escape from Mezen.

This time, it became apparent that she was going to stand trial, which until then, of course, since serious evidence had always been lacking, she had never had to face.[8] Again, until then, she was to be kept in 'solitary', this time for six months, and again she had to work to keep her sanity, her identity, her health, but now she was a veteran, she doubtless displayed her usual stoic acceptance of the situation. None of her letters from this period have survived, except for requests to Inna for books. She was allowed occasional visits from Alexander.

The winter, in a damp prison cell, in freezing temperatures, began to damage her health. She became ill with the early signs of TB. Her handwriting suggested deep fatigue. At last, on 20 March, 1913, Alexander obtained her temporary release on health grounds until her trial, scheduled in five months time, against bail of 5400 roubles.[9]

This was a huge sum for bail. Safarov's bail, by comparison, was only 500 roubles.

For the time being, however, it meant Inessa could return to Pushkino, and her beloved children, to recover before a prolonged trip with them down the Volga and on to Stavropol in the Caucasus, where they were joined for a time by Alexander. 'How pretty is the Volga,' she wrote later to Inna, recalling especially 'the early mornings at Stavropol. I remember when Sasha and I went to meet Fidia. It was still dark and then dawn gradually came. When we arrived at the quay it was already light and the river and the sky were an unusually tender shade of pink. I loved our time at Stavropol.'[10]

At the end of June, she wrote to Alexander that she was awaiting summons to trial, had appointed a lawyer and witnesses, two of whom were Alexander and Anna, her sister-in-law. She was looking forward to Alexander joining them in Stavropol.

On 4 August, some five weeks later but still at Stavropol, she wrote that the term of exile had been shortened and would end on 6 August, though quite why is not clear. However, by then she had also received the summons for her trial on 27 August. 'As you will see, I give you the pleasant news first and the bad news last. I hug you. Did you get back all right? It's so bad without you.'[11]

She did not stand trial. By then she had crossed the border illegally, as she had in 1909, and was in Finland, having jumped bail. Sending Alexander an undated card, in August, she wrote: 'I am in a rush to drop you a line. I have been a bit ill, but generally things are going all right and the doctor assures me that by Monday I will feel well enough. I kiss you hard – and everyone.' An archivist's note says that this is code, indicating she is delayed a bit but hopes to be across the Finnish border (into Sweden) by Monday.[12]

From Stockholm a few days later, she sent another card, this time bearing a picture of a nude lady in a body stocking. 'I have been here for two days already, but I haven't been to the Post Office since nothing could have arrived from you yet. I am waiting for news impatiently ... I am concerned about a lot of things I cannot mention. I will only stay here a few days. I am writing to you now for the third time. Have you received the rest of my cards?'[13]

It was September when Inessa next wrote to him. She had joined Lenin and his group in Poronin, a village about eighty miles from Cracow, in the Tatra foothills. 'My dear, I am already in Austria and will probably stay some time … At last I have received your telegram. I have been terribly worried. I couldn't understand why there was no news from you … There is not much to write about yet. I am staying in mountains of 9000 feet … streams are running just below my window. It is raining all the time … I think you are likely to be in Moscow … Has Fidia passed his exam? What about Varya and Inna? Have they started studies with Nikolai Evgenevich [Alexander's brother]? I regret a lot that I obeyed [you]. I kiss you hard. Please kiss Mama [presumably staying in Russia now] and my sisters.'[14]

'Obeyed' him, presumably, because he had urged her to cross the border to escape her trial – at great cost to the family. It is part of Armand legend that the family had to sell a large area of woodland to raise the cash when the bail was 'called in'.

Inessa had arrived at Poronin while there was a 'summer' party conference in progress, with Bolsheviks from various parts of Poland and Russia, including most of the Central Committee; but, as Nadya put it, 'Inessa flung herself into party work with her usual ardour,' adding that 'Malinovsky was in a terribly nervous state; he would get drunk night after night, would become maudlin and complain he was mistrusted.' With good reason, of course, though Lenin would never accept this until at last, after the February revolution, it was forced on him with the opening of the Okhrana files.

They stayed in Poronin for two weeks after the conference. 'We walked a good deal,' wrote Nadya in her 'memories', 'and visited Czarny Staw, a lake of extraordinary beauty. All of us became very much attached to Inessa. She always seemed to be in good spirits … It seemed cosier and livelier when Inessa was present.'

Nadya's memories of this period appear strange, but the date of such writings – in this case a 1933 publication – is often relevant. 'We had known her [Inessa] in Paris, but there was a large colony there, whereas in Cracow we lived in a small, comradely, isolated circle … She told us a great deal about her life and about her children; she showed me their letters and in speaking about them she seemed to radiate warmth and ardour.'

Are they strangers then, these children who lived next door to her in the Rue Marie Rose in Paris, who dropped in often to see her? Was Longjumeau not a small circle? She makes a point that Inessa rented a room in the house where Kamenev lived – distancing her from Lenin's house.

'Ilyich, Inessa and myself did a lot of walking. Zinoviev and Kamenev dubbed us the "Hikers' Party". We usually took walks along the meadows outside the town. The Polish word for meadow is Blon and it was from this that Inessa assumed the pseudonym of "Blonina"' – and, indeed, this is why Varvara's daughter is named Blona.

Nadya writes of Inessa's music. 'Ilyich was particularly fond of Beethoven's "Moonlight" Sonata and he always asked her to play it.' In fact, although Lenin liked Inessa to play to him, he was not a great music-lover and was bored by the concerts she made them attend in Austria. Also, he distrusted music because he believed its effect was weakening. He confided to Maxim Gorky, after listening to Beethoven's 'Appassionata' that it 'is amazing, more-than-human music. I want to utter gentle stupidities and stroke the heads of people ... who can create such beauty.'

It was all superficial, this recital of pleasant sunny memories. As Nadya surely knew, there was a dramatic undercurrent, which can be glimpsed in Inessa's letters. By the end of September, her earlier plan of staying in Galicia was changing. She wrote Alexander that she was wondering where to go, considering Paris 'but most of the people I used to know have left Paris or have died.' She wanted to settle soon and have the children with her. But her mood seems good. 'Spoil me a little please. Send me "chewing" candy and even some red caviar if the season is not over yet ... We can get it duty-free up to a weight of twelve pounds.' She asks for a book. William Morris's *A Dream of John Ball* and for her 'graduation certificate that Renee has.'[15]

A little while later, she wrote to him again. They were now back in Cracow. She said that the children should now be sent to Vienna, subject to finalising plans, and asked for some money to be forwarded in Nadya's name.[16] Soon she was writing again, with another change.

She had decided to stay in Cracow. What was his opinion? She had received the parcel, she said, presumably of caviar, but not the money.[17]

Then on 22 November, as can be seen with hindsight, there were signs of serious trouble. Inessa asks Alexander to delay sending the children until Christmas. She has not arranged to rent a flat, although – as Nadya wrote in her memoirs – Nadya had been helping her to look for one. 'Thank you for the money,' Inessa wrote. 'So please bring the children, but not before Christmas, since it is not possible to make arrangements before that.'[18]

But the children would not be going to Cracow at all. Three weeks later, Inessa had fled to Paris. Nadya explained that 'there was nothing in Cracow which could provide Inessa with an outlet for her abundant energies,' as a reason for her sudden departure, but this was clearly a colossal understatement. Inessa and Lenin had been locked in the second big crisis of their affair, if the early stages after Longjumeau, when Nadya offered to leave, are seen as the first.

It is clear that during this period following her return to Galicia the affair acquired a new dynamic. Stefan Possony has suggested that all that walking was not done as a threesome, as Nadya implies, but as a couple. Nadya had only returned to Poronin from Berne in August, after a three-hour goitre operation without anaesthetic , and without any proper convalescence, and would hardly have been up to such athletic exercise by the time of Inessa's arrival.

Whether or not Possony's speculation is correct, the affair would seem to have extended beyond walking and to have escalated. This, it appears, became too much for Lenin, who decided to end it, as is spelt out in painful detail in a long letter Inessa wrote over a kind of lost weekend, using the intimate 'ty' (thou) pronoun.

Paris, Saturday morning.

Dear one,
Here I am in La Ville Lumière [City of Light] and the first impression is most repugnant. Everything irritates me here – the grey of the streets, the overdressed women, the casually over-heard conversations and even the French language.

106

When I arrived at the Boulevard St Michel and the Avenue d'Orléans etc, memories were seeping from every corner. I became so sad it was scaring. I was remembering old moods, feelings, thoughts and was desolate that they would never return. Everything seemed so 'green'. Perhaps this is a stage that we have already passed and anyway it is sad to think that one will never (again) be able to think like this, to feel like this, to approach reality in the same way and then one regrets that life is passing by.

It was sad because Arosa was so temporary, so transitory. Arosa was so close to Cracow while Paris is, well, so final. You and I have parted, we have parted, my dear, and it is so painful. You'll never come back here again! I know it!

When I gaze at these places I know so well I realise more clearly than ever how big a place you occupied in my life here in Paris, so that almost all activity has been bound by a thousand threads to my thoughts of you ...

Even here I could cope without your kisses if only I could see you. To talk with you sometimes would be such a joy for me – and this could not cause pain to anyone. Why deprive me of that?

You asked me if I am angry with you for 'carrying through' our separation. No, for I don't think that it was for your own sake that you did it.

In Paris my relations with NK were very good. Only recently, in Galicia, she told me that I had become dear and close to her and I myself have loved her from almost the first meeting. She has such charm and softness. Her comrades and friends trust her implicitly with their confidences.

When I was in Paris I liked coming to see her in her office. I would sit by her table and talk about party matters first and then stay later talking about all sorts of things.[19]

This is the first part of a letter to which she would devote many hours, and which became a valuable historical document, confessional in nature, covering her relationship with Lenin and other matters. Nevertheless, it contains a riddle, or rather, several riddles.

Firstly, there is the reference to Arosa, which is a Swiss mountain town, with words that are significantly emotional. Inessa says it is 'close' to Cracow which, geographically, it is not. Clearly, it seemed, when the letter was released into the archives, she meant 'close' in time or, just possibly, in heights of passion. The impression was that Lenin had been with her in an idyllic, stolen few days in the mountains, unlikely though that seemed. It had always been hard to pinpoint a date when both Lenin, whose movements have been closely charted, and Inessa could have been there together.

There was then no mountain railway and it took some seven hours by carriage to reach the resort from the nearest mainline station at Chur, which itself was some three hours from Zurich, so this difficulty of access would have put even greater limits on such a meeting.

There were other theories: that Arosa was the name of a village or a hotel or was even code for somewhere else that *was* physically close to Cracow.

Professor R.C.Elwood found the answer, several years after his biography of Inessa was published, while himself taking a holiday in Arosa.[20] There, he was loaned by a resident some old copies of the *Aroser Fremdenblatt*, a weekly newsletter naming the guests staying in the resort. Inessa was listed in the issues of 23 December, 1913 and 1 January 1914. She *was* accompanied – but by Anna, her sister-in-law, not by Lenin.

The emotional tone, the words Inessa uses when she writes about Arosa still invite speculation, however, that Anna was a 'cover'. It is unlikely, though, that Lenin spent Christmas and New Year away from his wife or that, having broken off the affair, he would renew it so quickly or dramatically. But in love affairs, of course, ends are not always ends and lovers can be resourceful.

It seems, therefore, that Inessa was referring to a period of coping with the parting, of absorbing what was clearly a devastating blow, and deciding where the future lay. Her return in January to Paris with all its memories did not make this any easier.

Then there is the mystery of the letter itself. It was clearly written in January, since she refers in it to her stay in Arosa, not December as it is dated on the original in pencil in the archive. Certainly, Lenin never referred to it – not even in the postscripts of letters in which he did sometimes make apologetic allusions to the pain he had caused her or to the anger he had inspired.

A few months later, in June 1914, he ordered her to bring 'our letters' (i.e. *his*) – presumably for fear of future compromise[21] – insisting that she did not send them by registered mail, since he didn't trust the postal authorities. He wanted to destroy the letters, as would have been the fate, for the same reason, of any sent to him by Inessa – *except*, it is apparent, this letter from Paris, which would seem to have survived because she never sent it. Presumably Inna found it among her mother's papers after her death.

Without question it is genuine. Anyone researching Inessa's life, and reading so many of her letters, will know her writing and her voluble phraseology, *and* the way she wrote in her small, sharp hand, to the extreme edges of the pages. On her favourite tinted paper, too.

But where does it take us? Well, it *is* a love letter supporting what the comrades already knew, even if never sent. Also, Inessa's insistence of a warm affection for Nadya suggests that she would have accepted an open *ménage à trois*. Cynics might see this as a feminine ploy, a step on the road to something more. This, though, would be out of character. Inessa was never devious or clever in this kind of way. A *ménage à trois* would have been acceptable to her.

If Inessa proposed this to Lenin verbally, which is doubtful, or in some other way, he clearly turned it down – again probably because it would not have looked good for a statesman in that period, or out of concern for Nadya. In Russia after the revolution, his special relationship with Inessa was known at the higher levels – and indeed this provided her with a unique influence – but it remained surmise.

In this long letter she was concerned also with other things, though this, too, is odd. She returned to Paris, it seems, still troubled deeply by her possible role in the suicide of a young girl comrade.

Saturday night.
If I am sad it is because my anguish torments me when I think of Tamara. Yes, Tamara's death was a horror that I can't get over and at the same time it had something tantalising in it – as some

people are affected by passing trains – finding them both frightening and tempting [to leap onto the line?]. And the most awful part is my suspicion that I have some guilt for her death. I want to tell you how it happened.

I got to know Tamara in Paris and we were attracted to each other from the start. She visited us every day, spent holidays with us, becoming something like an elder daughter.

She was a lot younger than me and my feeling for her was maternal. That's certain.

She was very lonely and enjoyed my tenderness. She'd ask me to caress her and it was like caressing my children. And in her affection for me, there was an element of adoration. We liked spending evenings together. The children go to bed. Savushka retires. And the house is totally silent. We are in my room. More often she is sitting in my armchair; I am on the carpet close to her and we talk sometimes until the early hours of the morning.

At times, our conversation was very intimate. We argued, discussed different questions. And these were making us even closer. But then one evening the harmony was broken.

The children and Savushka were away visiting and we were alone in the house. It was a winter evening and the brazier was on, with the doors open. She was squatting by the fire and I was next to her on a log basket. We were talking about what the life of Social Democrats should be like. She assured me that they should give up everything for the sake of the cause.

I was a bit irritated by that because I thought for her it was only words … Words which very often vary from deeds. And it was painful for me to see this in Tamara.

From that day peace was over between us. I found myself repeating often 'these are your words and these are your deeds.' I teased her unmercifully. 'You are staying abroad without real need.' Our discussions became coloured by irritation and anger …

And then the decisive moment came when the words could be turned into deeds. Tamara decided to go back to Russia but in Paris there was a man she was in love with but who could not go with her [an exile possibly]. It was a hard conflict: to stay in

Paris and lose her self respect [as a revolutionary] or to lose a man she loved.

And that conflict broke Tamara and who knows, if it had not been for my interference, maybe that vague dream would have remained a vague dream ... I didn't understand that Tamara was a very beautiful but very fragile and tender flower. 'Life' was already too hard for her and she just needed to be petted. Then probably the flower could have been supported (and allowed to bloom) ... I am afraid that I only helped 'Life' to put a greater burden on her, because I assure you I loved her so much and when this thought comes into my head, and it came in Cracow, I am horrified. I hate myself.

Inessa's words matched *her* deeds all right, but two other aspects of the letter are particularly remarkable.

Here she is grieving for her broken affair with Lenin and yet she chooses to speak of this unhappy memory which clearly still troubles her. Even now she is afraid it will bore him and she marks the start and end of the Tamara story with crosses, saying he can skip straight to the end section if he wishes. But why hasn't she mentioned it to him before?

It is the sort of secret worry that lovers discuss, so why has she concealed it? Possibly because of the shame she mentions. Also, there is a hint of a lesbianism which Lenin, ascetic and at heart prudish, would not have approved of, though there is no other such indication in her life. She emphasises that her feelings were 'certainly maternal' as if, even now, checking any suspicions he might have.

Why, however, should her break with Lenin, as a lover, require her to declare it at this time?

She is in a highly emotional state, more or less alone – though in the Mazanovs' familiar boarding house. It would seem that she has a great need to confess it to Lenin, almost as though her lover is a father figure.

On Sunday morning, she continues with the letter – the same letter, still using the word 'ty' – though this section is about business. It is emotionally important because it indicates to Lenin that she

111

wishes to continue to work for the party. This is what *he* wants, too. He already relies on her heavily – as shown by Longjumeau, Prague and the mission to St Petersburg. These were important assignments attended by much risk and carried out with no hint of complaint. But he cannot continue with the affair in the form which it has now acquired, because it interferes mentally with the purpose to which he has devoted his life.

Inessa is indicating that she is prepared to go along with him on this, and she means it. But she *is* human and he cannot rid himself of all emotional interference. At least not for ever.

She reports on people she has met on her return, seeks political guidance – or orders – before adding: 'All right, my dear, enough for today. I want to send this letter off. There was no letter from you yesterday. I am so worried that my letters are not reaching you. I have sent you three letters (this is the fourth) and a telegram. Have you not received them? I have various crazy thoughts about it. I also wrote to NK, to "brother" [Kamenev's cover] and to Zina [Zinovieva]. Hasn't anyone received anything? I kiss you hard. Your Inessa.'

If it was doubtful that this long emotional letter reached him, it may have been because it could serve no purpose. Only a few days after she returned from Arosa, Lenin arrived suddenly in Paris with Malinovsky and they, too, stayed in the Mazanovs' house.[22]

EIGHT
Paris 1914

'Leaders are made and developed in the struggle,' wrote Nadya. 'It is from the struggle they draw their strength.' Lenin, she said, furiously resisted any attempt to 'back out' (of the proletarian cause), dubbing it 'opportunism'. 'He would break off relations with his closest friends if he thought they were hampering the movement; and he could approach an opponent of yesterday in a simple and comradely way if the cause required it ...

'The years of exile ... drained much of Lenin's strength. But they made him the fighter the masses needed.'

What room was there in such a man for love?

In the last few days of that December of 1913, the letters to Paris came fast, though it is doubtful if Inessa was still there to receive them. Whether or not Lenin ever saw Inessa's long commentary, he was acutely aware of their crisis. He had instigated it, and was probably suffering for it, too. And he quickly established their new situation, writing between December, 1913 and August, 1914, more than forty orders or screams of rage (at others, not at her – not yet), but touched occasionally with soft notes of concern for her and what had happened between them – and all, until August, 1914, using 'ty'.

People only write letters when they are apart and it was not until he moved to Galicia that he was parted from her for any length of time – except after he despatched her to Russia when, if he did write, which he probably didn't for reason of caution, no letters have survived. And she was in no position to serve the cause!

His first letter following their crisis is dated 18 December – i.e. two weeks or so before she started writing hers. 'What's happened to the Central Organ? ... Enquire and get an explanation please.'[1]

113

In another note, he is furious with Kautsky, the German Socialist leader, because he has written in a journal the 'rotten phrase that there is no party' (referring to Lenin's new one). He orders Inessa to organise a protest campaign.

Interestingly, his next letter, dated the end of December, lacks a few lines at the start, being torn off in mid-sentence, and also at the end – always suspicious, but not normally the practice of Soviet censors who simply omitted what should not be printed.

In the first, he wrote of 'the campaign for the working masses in Russia. The majority are for us!' How has that been achieved? 'By "cunning" forms of the underground.'[2]

And he displayed more cunning, urging her, in a final sentence, to 'set about the women's journal super-energetically!' knowing this would please her. He had long given this a low ranking, like other men in the party, and, in truth, still did, but it was a sop to her that would also appeal to other feminists.

The plan for a women's newspaper, to be called *Rabotnitsa* (woman worker), had long been discussed by the party's senior women, ranging from Nadya, Lenin's sisters Anna and Maria, to such personalities as Lyudmila Stal, Zinaida Lilina Zinovieva, and Konkordia Samoilova, who had tried to help Inessa with the *Pravda* impasse in St Petersburg.

And there was much logic to it. The number of women working in the nation's factories had overtaken that of the children, but their wages were only half that of the men – which made them popular with employers. Already they were a substantial part of the work-force.

In January, 1914 Inessa got to work with Lyudmila Stal, who was also living in Paris, planning the paper. But it soon became obvious that Lenin didn't want her to waste much time on it. He had other plans for her.

He was devious. 'Put me down on the list of speakers of 9 January [Bloody Sunday] if it is useful for your success – financially – but with my right to let you down. Privately, I declare that even if I am in Paris on 9 January, I won't go.' Not with 'such a bunch of assorted animals as the SRs and Leder & Co.'[3]

Inessa's father, Theodore
Stéphane, an opera singer

Inessa, aged 5, with her
maternal grandmother

Inessa, aged 6, with her Aunt Sophie, 1880.

Inessa, aged 6.

Inessa, aged 10, 1884.

Inessa (bottom right) at 18 in playful mood with Renée (top left).
Others unknown, 1892.

Inessa, aged 15.

Inessa, aged around 19, 1893.

A portrait of Inessa, taken the year of her marriage, 1893.

Inessa and her husband Alexander Evgenevich Armand,
soon after their marriage, 1893.

The Armand family home at Pushkino.

The Armand family on a verandah at Pushkino.
l–r: Andre, Inessa, Maria Armand, Evgenni Armand (Inessa's father-in-law),
Varvara Karlovna (her mother-in-law), Vera Armand and Vladimir Armand.

Eldigino, Inessa's first marital home, pictured today.

Anna Konstantinovich, Inessa's sister-in-law and close friend.

Inessa in 1902, reading in Moscow.

Inessa aged 30, in the Swiss mountains, pregnant with her brother-in-law's child.

Inessa on horseback, in the Swiss alps, 1903.

Inessa with Inna (on her knee) and Varvara, others uncertain; but probably her mother-in-law and her aunt Sophie.

Inessa with Inna and Varvara.

Inessa with André, her son by
Vladimir Armand (her brother-in-law).

Inessa, aged 36, in 1910 with her
five children (André, Varvara,
Fedor, Alexander, Inna).

Vladimir Armand, her lover
(and her husband's brother).

Inessa in exile in Mezen, 1908.

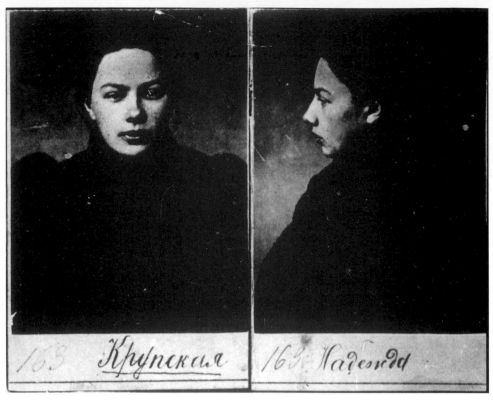

A police mugshot of Lenin's wife Nadya (Nadezdha Krupskaya) when young.

Alexandra Kollontai.

Lenin in cap, 1917, aged 46.

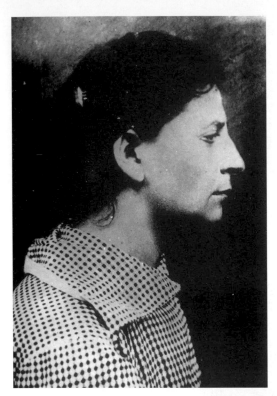

Fanny (Dora) Kaplan, who so nearly assassinated Lenin in 1918.

Grigori Zinoviev in 1917.

Street scene in St Petersburg during the mayhem of the revolution, 1917.

Lenin and his sister Maria, Moscow 1918.

Lenin, 1919.

Lenin, 1920.

Lenin addressing the crowd, 1920.

Felix Dzerzhinskiy, head of the Cheka, with his chiefs, 1920.

Inessa, 1920, shortly before she died.

Inessa's coffin lying in state, with a female Guard of Honour.

In another letter, he warned that 'the conciliators of all shades [who wanted a unified Social Democrat party] are out to catch us. Bon! We'll catch those scoundrels, those ridiculous mountebanks, They're getting stuck in the mud ... Our tactic is: Give [them] time to sink deeper into the mud. That's where we shall catch the scoundrels.

'Meantime we've got ... to learn as much as we can. Paris is convenient for finding out things and for "diversions."'[4]

It should be remembered that all these 'scoundrels' were political exiles, too, and wanted broadly the same revolution as Lenin did. At heart his fury was over method, strategy and, of course, control by *him*.

Lenin and Malinovsky stayed in in the Mazanovs' boarding house in Paris for a week in January, with Inessa there, too. This, though, was probably too close to their parting for anything to have changed much. Lenin was there primarily to help her whip in the Paris Bolsheviks and the Foreign Organisation, who were being far too lazy. He enjoyed the visit, writing to his mother that 'there is no better or more lively a city to stay in for a short time.'

Which was surprising, for he had a rough time politically. Malinovsky was 'heckled by a large and hostile audience' – as usual, about splitting the party – ending with 'Malinovsky in tears and the crowd chanting "Lenin, Lenin, Lenin".' At a personal level, though, the visit would have given Lenin and Inessa a chance to try out their new relationship, after the debacle in Cracow. It was successful, in the sense that, whatever else she may have wanted, Inessa could live with it in this changed form.

Back in Brussels for a meeting, Lenin wrote to her in her role of confidante. After he'd gone, she had written him a letter that must have pleased him, for he rushed off a brief note about a conference he had attended – 'Victory! Hurrah! The majority are for us'[5] – before responding to her at length, starting, 'Dear friend, I was terribly glad to receive your nice, friendly, warm, charming letter. I am inexpressibly grateful to you for it.'[6]

He confided that 'things here have gone worse.' *Pravda* was in trouble with a dropping circulation. The 'Conciliators' had not been stuck in the mud yet but, from his appalled view in Brussels, had gained ground and would now 'have it all their own rotten way.'

It is tempting to wonder if the 'warm, charming letter' that he was so grateful for was a shortened and edited version of the long, sad draft she wrote before his surprise arrival in Paris.

Two days later he wrote to Inessa once more, with the first two pages missing from the original – i.e. not just a censor's judgement.[7] Excited by a new way of getting literature into Russia – organised with Belgian seamen by Ivan Popov from Mezen – he demanded that she should arrange publishing and printing in Paris *and* find the money to do so.

And Inessa took on the job, as she had taken on others, without complaint although she had no official position as she was no longer on the Paris committee, and deployed 'her speciality' as a fund-raiser, seeking money for the party in America and Switzerland with some success. By May, the Bolshevik faction had developed a new dynamism with more than ninety members.

Lenin's capricious relationship with Inessa was marked by a slight change. 'My dear friend,' he wrote from Cracow in late February in a letter that was censored, 'You answered my sad letter but I have completely forgotten when how or why I wrote anyway. This is the inconvenience of corresponding from afar, but I will continue talking to you in spite of the distance and time.'[8]

What could have made him sad? Sometimes he got battle-weary, for his letters were nonstop, to a large range of people. Maybe he was just missing her.

Soon however, Inessa was hankering for her children, who still had not arrived, though Christmas was long past. 'What an awful daughter you are,' she scolded Inna, now nearly sixteen, for not writing, 'I think I did not beat you enough [when you were little]. I am glad you have kept your word [studying hard] and not going to the cinema until Christmas. As for dancing, why should you stop it? Losha's circle is not right for you, though I understand very well. You feel as bold as a lion there, but [swaggering] cavaliers and coquettte mesdemoiselles are not worth much. With time you will find your own company in which you may not a feel a lion, but you *will* feel comfortable – and not just for dancing.'

She wondered if Sasha and Fidior can dance, sadly guessed that 'too much time has gone by' for the much-loved dog to remember her and complained that no one writes. 'My dear Inushka I am very upset – nothing from either you or Papa. From no one. Except for a postcard.'

It was an old refrain, but then she cheered up. 'You'll be coming to me soon.' She was still living at Katya Mazanova's but would move when the children arrived. 'Tell me where you would like to go in the summer – the sea or the mountains? I think sea is better. What does Papa think?'[9]

Soon she was writing again. 'I have found a nice apartment. I will have a piano and I really want to play, especially in the sad moments. It's so soothing. I hope that Andre and Varya will not be bored here. I have already fixed up lessons ...'

She dreamed much of Russia but was pleased that Inna had a good new friend. 'Friendship is very important and should be valued. What do you mean by saying your friend is an idealist?

'Are you still reading Belinsky? Did you read the argument between Gorky and other writers about Dostoevsky's *The Devils*?

'I see that you are a terrible hunter. I did want to say intrepid [in English] ... I wouldn't like to see a hare in its pre-death convulsions and hear it screaming. It seems to me a little cowardly for six dogs and as many hunters to chase after one poor hare. This is slaughter.' And, indeed, it seemed a strange activity for a young girl in 1914 even if she did live in forest country. 'This year Tolstoy, yes?' Inessa ends.[10]

Meanwhile the letters from Lenin kept streaming in, often breaking into English and sometimes French. He issued a whole range of orders – draft a letter, get someone to sign it; find Popov, who's disappeared with a woman; get contacts to write to the Ukraine to start organising a new party there.

He shared with her his delight at the new *Pravda*, now Kamenev was running it – 'It's getting to be a real beauty!'[11] – and his despair later when 'We're having hard times since Kamenev left.'

He often offended her, claiming on one occasion that she was behaving like 'the Holy virgin' then apologising profusely. He was, like Marx, an atheist. So, of course, was she.[12]

In a letter about Malinovsky that was held in the secret files he ended, writing in English, with a rare mention of the past: 'If possible do not be angry against me. I have caused you a great pain, I know it ... '[13]

Repeatedly he asked if she was still angry with him and in one letter defended himself against her wounded anger: 'Never have I written that I esteem only three women [from whom presumably she felt excluded]. Never!!! I've written that fullest friendship, absolute esteem and confiance [using the French word] of mine are confined to only 2-3 women. That is quite, quite another thing.'[14] He suggested they discuss it when they met, though the difference must have seemed marginal to a woman who surely only wanted assurance that she was one of the three.

Meanwhile, Roman Malinovsky was proving a great worry. The only senior Bolshevik with a working class background, he had risen high in the party hierarchy and was now on the Central Committee in Russia and the Bolshevik spokesman in the Duma. Lenin, as has been seen, was a great admirer of him and was embarrassed by rumours circulating Moscow that he was in the pay of the Okhrana.

'It is very hard to see him,' Lenin wrote to Inessa, 'so useless and helpless now ...' in the face of the 'infamous campaign of slander. Wiring [sic] with Brother [Kamenev] and small understandings ... Generally he is very good, excellent – but ... in such crisis a little too weak.'[15]

Later that day Lenin wrote again: 'The Malinovsky affair is warming up. He is not here. Looks like "flight." Naturally, this gives food for the worst thoughts.' He added that Russian newspapers were accusing Malinovsky of being a provocateur. 'You can imagine what it means,' he said, switching to English. 'Very improbable but we are obliged to control all "oui-dire" [rumours in French].'[16]

Lenin was forced to set up a Central Committee Commission of Enquiry, loaded to give him control, consisting of Lenin himself (who would be compromised when Malinovsky's Okhrana links were proved), his long-time comrade Ganetsky (Jacob Furstenberg), and Zinoviev – but the situation remained explosive. After several oppressive sessions, the Commission ruled that the case against Malinovsky remained unproven. 'Scoundrels,' Lenin was to write later, 'were letting blackguards and vermin and skunks, ignored with contempt by the working class, root around in all this.'

Inessa, meanwhile, was anxious about her relations with Nadya who, she suspected, was still resenting her. 'You haven't written [to] me for ages, my dear,' she wrote, using 'thou'. 'Aren't you ashamed of having forgotten me ... Please write soon. I have received a letter recently from Inessa [Inna]. I am sending it to you. It's very interesting and I hope to share the joy in it with you ... I strongly, strongly embrace you.'[17] Was she using the emotional appeal of the children?

Nadya was being cool with her even though she had seen off the competition – for a while, at any rate – but perhaps she was still scarred from the December crisis. Clearly Nadya was in no hurry to rebuild any damaged fences. Two months later, Inessa wrote to Nadya again from Trieste, en route for an Adriatic holiday with the children. She had heard from her, though it hardly helped.

'Dear NK, I was pleased to get your letter, although I did not like it too much. It was very business-like and didn't tell me anything about yourself. I would like to know all about you. What are you reading? What are you interested in? How are you feeling? Do you go walking? Please write, my dear.

'I am again in Trieste with the children. We are stuck here because the children have colds and Andrushka has had a very high temperature. I thought it was typhus, but today his temperature has dropped ... Thank you for your copy of *Rabotnitsa*.'[18]

Rabonitsa, the women's journal, had been published in Russia with the help of Armand money and other sources, but its priority continued to be down-rated by the male Bolsheviks, the first six issues appearing without any articles by Lenin, which would have given it some authority.

Inessa, who had been its leading advocate, seemed to have lost interest, locked as she was into the stream of demands from Lenin, which came to a head in July with the biggest task he had ever asked of her – to take his place on the platform facing some of the most important figures in the socialist movement, most of whom would be hostile.

He was again playing games, twisting and turning and pretending to support issues that, in practice, he was against, Inessa being his mouthpiece, partly for her languages, but also because she was not *him* standing up there. The difference was subtle, but significant.

At any other time, she would have been flattered if scared, but she was on a rare holiday with four of the children in the Adriatic town of Lovran. Alexander was joining them with his new companion, Anna Arbels, the widow of a great friend, and Anna, her sister-in-law was expected. Announced in late June, the conference had been scheduled with less than three weeks' notice and clashed with Inessa's holiday. While she did not agree to go, she didn't actually say 'No.'

Organised by the International Socialist Bureau, this was intended to be a 'Unity Conference'. Lenin, the great divider, was not against 'unity' – providing, of course, it was unity of the kind *he* wanted and of which *he* was in charge, but he knew that this conference would not advance 'unity' of that kind.

For once, however, after years of declining influence, he was 'dealing from a position of strength … The Bolsheviks had scored gains in the elections to the 4th Duma; *Pravda* had won a vastly greater circulation than the Mensheviks' *Novaya Rabochaya Gazeta*; and his party was steadily taking over … the top positions in formerly Menshevik trade unions.'[19] And he was planning the sixth party conference for August, which, unlike the Prague sham, would be properly attended and provide him with unarguable legal status.

Despite more cheerful prospects for the party, Lenin was vulnerable personally – still facing the Malinovsky scandal, continuing problems over the Schmidt money, and a furious quarrel with Camille Huysmans, the Bureau secretary – all of which would be exploited with some glee from the platform by his enemies.

Lenin was probably surprised by Inessa's resistance to attending the conference in Brussels. He understood the value of the children in her life, but they were now getting in the way of the party. So he put on the pressure. There wasn't much time, of course – only days really. He wrote at the start of July, asking her to 'consent to be a member of the delegation ... if you have the slightest chance to fix up the children for 6-7 days ... or even less.' He reasoned that she was well up in the business, spoke perfect French and read *Pravda*. 'I don't want to go "on principle" ... You are more sure of yourself now ... and could carry this through perfectly ... Consent, do!'[20]

He wrote again, saying he was 'extremely glad that you are well [i.e. able to attend],' remarking that Lilina Zinovieva was 'still in hospital [i.e. ruling out the Zinovievs].'[21]

Only hours passed before he wrote once more. 'I am terribly afraid that you will refuse to go ... You see, it's extremely important that the main report should be read really effectively ... Excellent French is definitely needed' and an understanding of 'essentials' *and* 'proper tact ... You are the only suitable person.'[22]

And so it went on, in letter after letter, and in telegrams, flattering, cajoling. Meanwhile, he was planning around her. Ivan Popov, found at last, was to go with her as well as her St Petersburg friend, Georgi Safarov, as secretary.

At last the campaign worked, though Inessa was still reluctant. He was like an excited boy. 'My dear and dearest friend, Oh, I would like to kiss you a thousand times ... I am fully sure you will be victorious.' He used 'toi,' of course, and this letter was censored.[23]

A week later, Lenin was worrying again. 'I am sure that you are one of those people who develop, grow stronger, become more vigorous and bold when they are alone in a responsible position – and therefore I obstinately do not believe the pessimists, i.e. those who say that you ... can hardly ... Stuff and nonsense! I don't believe it! You will manage splendidly! With your excellent French you will lay them all flat and you won't allow Vandervelde to interrupt and shout.'[24]

He had already asked her to come to Poronin after the congress and 'Bring when you will come [bring with you] all our letters.' He told her not to send them by registered mail since 'the packet can very easily be opened by friends.' (He didn't mean 'friends' of course.) 'Please bring all letters,' he repeated for a second time.[25] This explains why no love letters to her have survived. Not 'thou' this time. In fact, the wording suggests much concern that the letter might fall into the wrong hands. It also explains the torn pages and part-pages from other letters. For these, too, could have been compromising in the future, yet the political pages should, as usual, be conserved, to take their places in the history of a man of destiny. She did not go to Poronin, but could have obeyed his order when she next saw him in Berne.

And then came the briefing. 'Plekhanov likes to disconcert comrades of the female sex with "sudden" gallantries. You must meet these with quick repartees: "I'm delighted, Comrade Plekhanov, you are quite an old spark" to take him down a peg or two.

'Everybody will be very angry (I'm very glad) at my not being present and will take it out on you. But I am sure you'll show them your "nails" and deliver "cold, calm and somewhat scornful snub[s]."

'Plekhanov will heckle ... Cut him short immediately ... "will you please not interrupt me ... " turning it into "an attack upon him."'[26]

Lenin urged that, if she was brought under pressure, she should just quote the party's resolutions, which 'they don't like'. Rosa Luxemburg, he said, would challenge the validity of the Prague Conference, as would others. Answer: quote the Party Resolutions. 'We are an autonomous party. Keep this firmly in mind.'

In follow-up letters he expanded on the theme, changing his mind on tactics – in one decreeing they should 'agree to nothing, walk out' and, in another, that they should 'not walk out' under certain circumstances.

He ordered that she should attend as 'Petrova' – since it was not advisable to let the liquidators know the name, Inessa. Why not? Surely the rumours would have reached them, too.

And so she went, with Popov and Safarov and two other comrades, into the fire – with Rosa Luxemburg there as anticipated and Trotsky, Axelrod, Kautsky, Plekhanov and Vandervelde.

Ten Social Democratic groups were represented and everyone was indeed angry that Lenin was absent. Stubbornly, Inessa and Popov insisted they were there by the decision of the Central Committee. And the anger grew as they abstained in vote after vote. Inessa started to read Lenin's report, in a voice so low that many could not hear, and was warned she was running out of time. She was allowed to give Lenin's agreement to unity *providing* they agreed to fourteen conditions which, as he had forecast, were considered 'monstrous'.

'The majority of the delegates were greatly disgusted,' according to one report. The cold tone makes it all sound like nothing, but it certainly wasn't that. Inessa was standing alone on the platform with no formal senior role in the party. Before her was an audience that was growing increasingly impatient and outraged. Once she started to read out the conditions there would have been murmurs, building to interruptions and cries of shocked amazement.

For the conditions were truly absurd – one even demanding the closure of all Menshevik newspapers that competed with the Bolshevik press – and had no hope of being accepted, as Lenin well knew.

Plekhanov complained that they were 'the articles of a new criminal code'. Kautsky called them 'a demand for self-destruction'. Vandervelde said it would 'be impossible to breathe' if they were accepted.[27]

Inessa kept her nerve, though, and continued doggedly to read them out. But the moment when she finished, and faced those furious faces with a defiance she did not feel, must have been beyond anything she had endured for Lenin before, short of prison.

Even so, the conference debated the conditions for the rest of the day. At last, the next morning, the secretary, unwilling to accept that Lenin had successfully sabotaged the conference, introduced a resolution so mild and vague that anyone could sign it. But not Inessa. Lenin had told her to agree to nothing. 'We abstain,' she announced, no doubt provoking another roar of anger.

She had carried out Lenin's orders and he wrote several letters thanking her. 'You have rendered a very great service to our party! I am especially thankful because you have replaced me … You handled the thing better than I could have done. Language apart, I would probably have gone up in the air … would have called them scoundrels. And that's what they were waiting for. That's what they were trying to provoke.' Lenin seems genuinely to have seen them as the provocateurs, not himself, though his letters make it quite clear that *he* was.

'Are you very tired?' he asked, 'very upset? Are you angry at me for having persuaded you to go?'[28] Inessa was certainly fed up. She had done his dirty work and hurried back to her children at Lovran.

'A very likely result' of the party's behaviour in Brussels, Professor Elwood has written, 'would have been the expulsion of his [Lenin's] party from the European Socialist movement.'[29]

But that didn't happen. In fact none of it mattered – or seemed to matter – for much longer. The world was about to fall off the cliff. Archduke Francis Ferdinand had already been murdered in Sarajevo. Ten days after the conference closed, Austria declared war. 'The idiot Brussels Conference can be forgotten in such times,' Lenin wrote to her. 'Best greetings for the commencing revolution in Russia.'[30]

He saw it as opportunity. All year Russia had suffered strikes. The volcano within the nation was rumbling again. Now there would be a war between the greatest imperial nations in the world that – so Lenin believed – the participants would be unable to end. Only by transforming the conflict into a class struggle, he declared, would it be terminated.

He was wrong, of course. It would end in the usual way, with winners and losers. But it would certainly provide the scope he forecast for revolution, and all this political manoeuvring – in France and Belgium and, during the dark years to come, in Switzerland – would acquire a new meaning.

NINE

Berne 1914

Weeks were to pass as nation after nation, bound by alliances, declared war. Inessa and her children were in Austria as citizens of that country's major enemy, which was already mobilising.

She moved fast, took the children by train into Italy, which would remain neutral for some time. At Genoa, they boarded a ship bound for Archangel. It was the end of a holiday that had been a great success. With a mood that was 'frivolous' and rewarding, as she wrote to Inna, 'We wanted to do everything together – the sun, the sea.'

Then Inessa returned to Lovran to tidy up the villa she had rented. She did not know it then but she would not see any of the children for the best part of three years.

'I went back with a sore heart,' she wrote to them. 'It was so empty and I was sad to see the bare table in the dining room, and not to hear your jolly voices and your laughing. I was sad to look at the things you left behind, sad to enter your rooms now so empty ... '

Still 'wanted' by the police in Russia, she headed for Les Avants, above Montreux on Lake Geneva, near her old Swiss territory of 1903. From there, she wrote to the children again, saying that she had started to write the day after she was in Lovran 'but that letter started to upset me so much I decided not to send it, so as not to upset you, too.

'I am planning to move to Berne ... Today it is very beautiful here. Snow has just come to these mountain peaks, Rochers de Naye and Col de Jaman, and at sunset it was all pink ... I kiss you hard, my darlings. PS: My word, how happy I'll be when I learn you have made it all right and that you are healthy.'[1]

Inna wrote to Inessa on the voyage, while anchored off Cardiff in

125

Wales. 'We arrived last night, but we couldn't enter harbour because the waves were too great and now we are waiting for high tide.

'We left [Italy] on 9 August about midday. The wind was strong and there was some pitching and tossing. Andrushka, Varya and I were all very sick … On the third night we passed Gibraltar and were still unwell. Sasha and Andrushka [presumably recovered] looked after us very well, bringing us tea and bread. We are all getting better now.

'We are now entering harbour shouting Vive l'Angleterre, Hurrah! Hurrah! And the English (the Welsh?) have been responding enthusiastically.'[2]

The letter made Inessa 'awfully happy' but she was worrying in her response whether their woollen clothes would be adequate for the cold of the Arctic Ocean. She knew what it could be like at Archangel.

'Already I am [eagerly] expecting a letter from Russia. Letters come perfectly well but they are a little delayed … '[3]

By then, she had heard from Zinoviev that Lenin had been arrested as an 'important spy' since, unlike Inessa, he had not moved out of Austria fast enough. In fact, it was a great shock for Lenin and Nadya to find suddenly that they were on enemy territory and victims of the high emotions that wars inspire. 'We witnessed a horrible scene … ' wrote Nadya in *Memories of Lenin*. 'A train had arrived from Krasnik bringing dead and wounded [Austrian] soldiers. I heard some peasant women coming out of a Catholic church … Even if the authorities released the spy [Lenin], the peasants would put his eyes out, cut off his tongue etc. It was clear we could not remain in Poronin.'

With the help of the Austrian socialist Victor Adler, and money raised in Berne by Inessa and telegraphed to Lenin, he was released and they joined her in that city, renting an apartment at 11 Distelweg, while Inessa settled into a house at 23 Drosselweg, some ten minutes walk away, near the Bremengartenwald.

There, Nadya drew the usual picture in *Memories*, if not of a *ménage à trois*, then of three close friends living serenely together in the autumn landscape. 'We used to roam for hours along the woodland paths, which were bestrewn with yellow leaves, Vladimir Ilyich,

Inessa and myself ... Sometimes we would sit for hours on a sunny wooded hillside, Ilyich jotting down notes for his articles and speeches ... I studying Italian ... Inessa sewing a skirt ... She had not quite recovered yet from the effects of her imprisonment [in St Petersburg] ... In the evening we would gather at Grigori's [Zinoviev's] tiny room ... '

It was hard to imagine that some 250 miles to the west the guns would soon be pounding the trenches of Picardy. This thought would not have bothered them. The war had produced a new and far deeper division of Social Democracy than all of Lenin's wildcat strategies.

The socialist patriots believed their countries' armies should be supported while Lenin's Bolsheviks, though some disagreed, saw the defeat of Tsarist Russia as the 'lesser evil' and urged that the aim should be to 'transform the present imperialist war into a civil war' – leading in time to the long-expected revolution. In his new world, of course, patriotism would be irrelevant.

Soon, a new idea was forming in Inessa's mind. During the summer holiday with the children, there had been mealtime conversations when the girls, sixteen-year-old Inna, in particular, had questioned her about marriage and love and their emotional environment. Inessa was an ardent advocate of the freedom of women, well experienced in the impact of passion and the arguments which she had described in St Petersburg in 1908 as going 'round like a squirrel on a wheel.'

The girls' interest had stayed with her and she decided to write a pamphlet on love and the family which, as she told Inna, 'your questions were largely responsible for spurring me on to write. If it comes out I'll dedicate it to you and Varya.'[4]

In January, 1915, travelling alone, she left Berne for the mountains to start work on the pamphlet. She sent some of it to Lenin for his comments, and was shocked to receive a sharp retort from the man who still occupied her emotional life, advising her, among other criticisms, to 'entirely throw out the "demand [by women] for free love."' What did she mean by it? He listed ten possible meanings ranging from prejudices about religion or society, to 'paternal injunctions,' and 'possibly adultery.'[5]

Inessa defended her work angrily – angrily because of who was criticising – and Lenin was 'astounded' by her 'attack'. He repeated her words: 'Even fleeting passion … is more poetic and pure than the loveless kisses exchanged as a matter of habit between husband and wife.' Loveless marital kisses were, he agreed, impure. But what did she pose as the opposite? A 'fleeting' passion. Why 'fleeting' which, he suggested, was by definition loveless? 'It follows logically [in her argument, he said] that these loveless kisses, since they are fleeting, are the opposite of loveless kisses exchanged between husband and wife … Strange!' She was not, in other words, comparing like with like, he argued. Loveless kisses, he implied, were loveless kisses. How could they be the opposite, as she suggested?

Lenin, whose kisses had clearly not been loveless, had a logical point, but he seemed to be discounting the fact that sexual passion may indeed be 'fleeting'. He did concede reluctantly that she could add 'if you simply must, that a transient liaison may be vile or pure,' but he would prefer that she didn't. It muddied her argument.

Some commentators have supported Inessa, attacking Lenin for 'prudish' nineteenth-century views. Others, siding with him, have pointed to her lifestyle with two known lovers, and others rumoured, as evidence of promiscuity, although there is no proof of this. But she was on shaky ground. After all, marital kisses were not necessarily loveless, which was his point; but she, of course, saw marriage as oppressive (though this hardly applied to hers) – as indeed *he* did in theory, while in practice clinging on to his own.

What she was trying to put, it seems from further letters, was a case for the freedom of women throughout all aspects of family life – including making love or *not* making love. However, the quarrel with its underlying note that her pamphlet lacked intellectual quality – something to which she was most sensitive – left a note of sourness that was to remain with her.

Inessa had already written at length to Inna about love. With a side reference to the Greeks who 'worshipped beauty' and 'looked freely at love', she wrote that 'love is also a product of culture and civilisation. Animals and savages do not know love … ' She spoke of 'today's society' with its background of the highest 'manifestations of love', but warned that 'there are people who in love feel completely like savages ... the majority ... Everyone marries or indulges in lust but very few love or have loved.'[6]

Quite what Inna, at sixteen, made of this is not known. Her mother seemed to be arguing that there is a higher level of love, denied to all but a minority. Most people, she implied, have to be content with lust.

Inna had, as usual, been slow to satisfy her mother's great need for letters. 'Of course you're a pig,' Inessa charged, 'because you haven't written ... You asked me to be critical so I hope I won't have to call you a pig again. Mostly, I want to hug you.

'I think you are strong,' she reassured Inna, 'and you were never a coward as you call yourself. You don't know yourself well enough yet or know your own strength ... In your femininity and softness there is charm but this is also strength. You do not [yet] know how to use it ... how to direct it.

'I remember when you were small that you could keep a secret. You can remember the circumstances of that [presumably her arrest at night when Inna was six years old] ... I think such firmness in a child is a rare thing and you were certainly a little hero.

'As for strength of will, this should be developed by exercise like any other muscle.'

In another letter, she urged emotional freedom. Inna had said that she was afraid of falling in love with someone her mother didn't like. 'Inushka you must be independent and make your own decisions.'[7]

The year 1915 was marked by socialist conferences, three in Berne in the few weeks straddling March. Inessa attended them all – one, a youth conference with her old friend Georgi Safarov, and another for women in her new platform role of the previous July, once again under briefing by Lenin.

A difference in her was emerging, however. In a Bolshevik 'foreign' assembly she stoutly opposed Lenin over a manifesto aim he had promoted, to form a 'republican united states of Europe'. This was impractical, she said, because of conflicts of interest among the nations. Tempers rose in a fierce argument. Lenin attacked her 'as an anarchist' – this on the floor in public – and she fought back with that special knowledge of people who know each other well, alleging he was 'an opportunist' which was close to home, being what he was always calling other people.

Lenin shrugged off this flash of independence. He asked her to work with him and Zinoviev on the re-drafting of his main resolution – and actually backed down on the united Europe proposal. This showed his regard for her – though, with Lenin, there was always a feeling about any concession that his eyes were on the future. Still, the vigour of Inessa's fight was a sign of a new attitude. She was not just doing what he wanted any more.

In June, Lenin and Nadya left for their long summer break at Sorenberg and Inessa soon joined them. It might seem that they all spent a great deal of time on long summer vacations, while Lenin was pleading poverty, but these were in effect working holidays and Lenin had found to his delight that he could order books by post from public libraries in Berne and Zurich.

It must be remembered, too, that most people were permanently worried about their health. When they said 'How is your health?' they meant it. It was not simply a greeting. People often fell ill – Lenin, in fact, suffered from frequent headaches – and they all believed that mountain air had therapeutic qualities.

'We would rise early,' wrote Nadya in *Memories*, 'and, before dinner which was served at 12 o'clock, each of us would work in different nooks of the garden.

'During those hours Inessa often played the piano and it was particularly good to work to the sounds of the music ... . After dinner we sometimes went to the mountains. Ilyich liked to get to the crags of the Rothorn toward evening when the view above was marvellous and below the mist was turning rosy ... '

Inessa spent much of her time there working on her pamphlet on Love and the Family, though this was never to be published. She was missing the children as usual. 'I cannot adjust to the fact that you cannot come to me this summer ... ' she wrote to Inna. 'It is very hard for me to live by myself ... I have been torn away from everything that is dear ... We must meet and talk and somehow I must make this happen ... '[8]

130

She had plans to meet Inna, and presumably the others, in Sweden. 'I have asked a friend who is going to Moscow to talk to you about this,' she wrote later though the plans were to come to nothing.

At the time Inna had other concerns. 'Your jealousy towards Varya,' her mother insisted, 'has no basis. You're a funny little cuckoo. I love you both deeply, though a little differently because you are different individuals … Mothers strive to see in their children something better than in other children, but mothers are not blind. They see their children's shortcomings through a magnifying glass, sometimes with pain. None of you has given me this pain … '[9]

During 1915 which, isolated as they were by the war, was a trying time for them all, Inessa showed further mild signs of disenchantment with Lenin – or, rather, with Lenin's view of her – though some historians have suggested that there was a renewal of their affair. Certainly, the mountain life, with its long walks, and doubtless long talks might have brought them closer – especially since Nadya's health was still not up to much walking. But there is not a scrap of evidence of the renewal of their sexual relationship.

In early September, however, Lenin left Sorenberg with Inessa, to attend the Zimmerwald conference, and Inessa suffered another blow to her self-esteem. The conference was called in secret by Robert Grimm, a middle-of-the-road Swiss Social Democrat. The thirty-eight delegates met at the Volkshaus in Berne to board coaches that would take them the nine miles to the village of Zimmerwald. Grimm had claimed they were members of an 'ornithological society'. The Russians were permitted only eight delegates, including a mere two Bolsheviks, the others being spread among Social Revolutionaries, Mensheviks and other factions.

Lenin had intended Inessa to be a delegate, but this limitation forced him to exclude her, choosing Zinoviev and himself as the two Bolsheviks. She may have felt he did not try hard enough, but he did his best to make amends. An International Socialist Commission was to be set up in Berne and Lenin named Zinoviev as the Bolshevik representative with 'Comrade Petrova', her new name, as an alternative.

The conference had raised Lenin's status. Now he was seen as head of the 'Zimmerwald Left', as part of an international group, reaching beyond party, even though, in this small world, there were only eight members! It would grow, though, and, as usual with Lenin, make an impact far beyond its size.

Inessa was being a mother once more, reassuring Inna again that she 'had always been a strong character ... ' She added that 'We are watching intensely and emotionally what is happening in Russia now ... We can see something bright which is filling the heart with hope.'[10]

Inessa was probably referring to workers' strikes for the party news was dreadful. The Okhrana had arrested most of the Central Committee, *Pravda* and the journals had been closed down and the networks had been broken up. With a war on, the police wanted no trouble at home.

By the end of 1915, Lenin was keen to build on his new Zimmerwald Left but the French Socialists were firmly against him, taking the patriotic line, so he decided that Inessa must enter the fire again – this time by crossing the border illegally, even though she was French, with a false passport in the name of Sophie Popoff.

Inessa was reluctant. The will to show her paces, which she had displayed in her dangerous return to Russia in 1912, was no longer there. Perhaps she felt the war made a difference, but she went to Paris, responding somewhat wearily to the call of the cause.

'Crossing international borders with forged documents,' as R.C. Elwood wrote, 'and preaching defeatism in wartime to a party favouring defensism was at best a risky venture.'[11] The Okhrana's Paris bureau soon picked up her trail in early January, 1916, but, as usual, sat back and waited.[12]

Alphonse Merrheim and Albert Bourderan, the French Socialist leaders, whom Inessa knew well, would have little to do with her, refusing to allow her even to address their members. She tried an associated body that was pacifist, only to find that it was not as pacifist as Lenin would have liked, but she did better with the old French Bolshevik workers, persuading them to spread anti-war literature in the factories.

Lenin, as expected, was growing impatient. 'Not a scrap of news,' he wrote on 13 January, 1916. 'We do not know if you have arrived.'

Two days later he wrote again. 'I'm rather surprised that there is no news from you. Let me confess, while I'm at it, that the thought occurred to me for a moment that you might have taken offence at my not having gone to see you off the day you left ... But I dismiss the unworthy thought ... ' A few lines earlier, he had spoken of the sunny day and a walk they had all taken a few weeks back. 'I kept thinking of it and was sorry you were not here.'[13]

On 19 January, 1916 he complained that 'this is my third (unanswered) postcard to you, this time in French to make the work easier for the censors ... You are causing me great anxiety.' Lightly, he ended 'Sincerely yours, Basil.'[14]

Again Inessa did not answer him but on the same day Nadya heard from her. 'The mood in the streets is sombre and there are many women in mourning.' She judged it would be hard to achieve anything in the short term.[15]

Was Inessa making a point? She didn't write to Lenin until 25 January, nearly a week later, but *he* wrote to *her* – in answer to her letter to Nadya. She obviously wasn't getting his letters to her poste restante address, he said, so suggested a code. 'If you underline the date twice, it will mean that you are receiving my letters.'

Inessa's behaviour is interesting. A resentment has crept in, possibly stemming from the time in Brussels in 1914, when she may not have liked what she was asked to do. Or perhaps his response to her pamphlet still rankled. Perhaps she is disheartened at her lack of progress. Also, in Paris, she is once more in a highly dangerous position and she suspects she won't be given appropriate credit. She will be thanked profusely, as she was after Brussels, but she won't be ranked.[16] Lenin, sensing her discontent, maintained the light tone for a while, at least in the endings to his letters. 'Salutations Cordiales!' were the last words of a letter in February.

Then suddenly, Inessa had some success with a youth group and two trade unions. She impressed the Okhrana, who reported that she 'won the confidence' of her young audiences 'by virtue of her command of the language and enticing manner.' Certainly, she was pleased, writing to Lenin that she had won some allies for the Zimmerwald Left, not from above, but from below.

Lenin's response was frigid. He was unimpressed by youth groups and urged her sharply to try harder to cause a split in the main French Socialist party organisations. In response she sent him an 'angry postcard' and he replied on 19 March that 'nothing is accomplished, even in a fit of temper, by using rude words … this is not an encouragement to further correspondence.'[17]

Inessa could hardly believe what she read. She didn't want to be in Paris in the first place – under a cover name at that – and reckoned she had achieved a lot in very difficult conditions. The French, still touched by the old glamour of Napoleon, were not natural pacifists. Even Lenin had second thoughts, writing on 31 March, twice congratulating her on her success. It was very late – certainly for two people who had been lovers and were still linked by deep emotions. If there was resentment, his calculated 'use' of her could only intensify it.

When Inessa went to an Internationalist committee, organised by the French Socialist Party, and urged it to 'foment unrest in the French army', she alarmed the vigilant police of a nation already shocked to its roots by the long horror of trench warfare. Inessa only just avoided arrest for treason by slipping across the border the next day. For Lenin it was just another little quarrel that he was always locked in with someone or other. For her, it was far more.

Two weeks after leaving Paris Inessa attended the Second International Socialist Conference at Kienthal as a formal delegate, but she made no speeches, simply translating for Lenin and Zinoviev. Lenin's Zimmerwald Left made progress, its numbers rising from eight to twelve – which, despite the absurdly low numbers, he used like an advance commando unit, hammering at each weakness in the proposals.

Then Inessa left Lenin, but there was no great scene, just a vacuum of sorts. Lenin and Nadya had moved to Zurich, but Inessa did not join them there. Instead, she stayed on for a few weeks in her old home in Berne near the Bremgartenwald.

When they moved, as usual, to the mountains for their summer break, this time to Flums, there was no Inessa. Instead, she went with Zinoviev and Zinaida to their favourite resort at Hertenstein, not far from Lucerne, before moving on her own back to the same old hotel at Sorenberg until the end of the season.

In November, 1916, she headed for Baugy-sur-Clarens, near Lake Geneva, and not far from Les Avants, her earlier refuge of 1914. She rented an apartment opposite Nikolai Rubakin's Russian Library, which gave her scope for study.

There were other Russian revolutionaries living nearby. In fact, acting with her, the 'Baugy Group' would be a power in Russia after 1917. Led by Nikolai Bukharin who lived in Lausanne, like her they were on the 'romantic' left wing of the party. But if Inessa saw much of them, as she must have done in the library, she does not seem to have written of them to Lenin.

But Inessa was behaving strangely again. She had always needed company and she had written to her daughters about the importance of friendship. Now she seemed to have condemned herself to a remote existence in a way that was quite out of character.

Lenin refused to acknowledge any kind of break. He maintained an active contact after Inessa's escape from France, with some fifty letters as well as speaking to her on the telephone and sending telegrams.

In fact, Inessa continued to work for the party, but she only did what she wanted to and she also started to challenge some of Lenin's views and Marxist interpretations, with the help of the Russian Library, now so close. He didn't like this, but he still commanded the relationship, though sometimes, being Lenin, he lost patience with her.

The war was now more than two years old and more horrific than anyone had forecast. When Inessa moved to her new apartment in the Swiss mountains the battles of the Somme and Verdun had come to a terrible end, with the death of nearly two million men, yet little had truly changed. Millions, too, were dying on the Eastern Front and in other parts of Europe. To Lenin, who saw the whole war as a capitalist imperialist conflict, it held hope for the future. When it came to its ghastly end would the survivors in the trenches, mostly workers in civilian life, just go back to their jobs? It seemed impossible.

In Russia, famine was threatening the nation with winter

approaching. The bread queues seemed endless. Within only a few weeks that huge nation would explode but, if Lenin or Inessa or any of them had been told this in late 1916, they would not have believed it possible. Meanwhile, they continued with their little lives, their little quarrels, their tense relationships.

Back in July, when Inessa had been with the Zinovievs, Lenin had again written of her success in France, speaking of the 'great influence on the French', leaving 'enduring marks', which he thought might cheer her up. He had hoped, as he confided to Zinoviev, to persuade her to go back into Russia for him but, in her present frame of mind, she wasn't going to prison for him again. But he knew her vulnerable side and suggested she should go to Norway to replace the Bolkshevik Central Committee's representative in Scandinavia. She could meet the children there, couldn't she? And, since Russia would then be so accessible, via Finland, he was reckoning she might be persuaded to risk occasional visits there for the party.

Inessa was tempted but cautious, knowing who she was dealing with. She hadn't got a passport, so he tried to get her a false one with the help of Olga Ravich, a comrade who lived in Geneva. Then, when this failed, he suggested she took Nadya's. He urged her to consider going to England as a stopping-off point, and even offered to lend her money.

Then, when at last Inessa rejected this, he decided she should help run a publishing business – the Bolshevik official publisher in Switzerland – but she wasn't very taken with the idea, knowing she would be the dogsbody overseeing printers, correcting proofs, with Lenin doing the writing.

In January 1917 Lenin decided that Switzerland, at present neutral, could be drawn into the war. The French would at once occupy Geneva. So to be in Geneva would then be like being in France and contact with her ally Russia would be much easier. He had decided, he told Inessa, to transfer the party treasury to her 'to be kept on your person. In a little bag.'[18] She was quite keen on this because it underlined her value to him. And then, as with the other plans, he seemed to lose interest.

All the time, amidst his demands and suggestions, Lenin showed care for her. 'Don't stay in Sorenberg,' he had urged earlier. 'You'll freeze.' On 20 November he had written: 'Of course I also want to correspond. Let's continue our correspondence,' as though there was some question of not doing so. 'How I laughed over your postcard. I really had to hold my sides, as they say.'[19]

In November 1916, he had written, in a letter that was censored, that he 'felt like saying a few friendly words to you and pressing your hand very tightly. You write that even your hands and feet are swollen from the cold. That's just terrible. Even without this your hands were always chilly. Why bring it to that?'[20]

On 17 December 1916 he had asked in a letter to her in Clarens: 'Do you go skiing? You really should! ... It's good in the mountains in winter ... and smells of Russia!'[21]

A few days later, he wrote, again in a letter that was censored, that 'Your last letters were so full of sadness, and these ... stirred up such pangs of conscience in me that I simply cannot compose myself. I would like to ... urgently beg you not to sit in virtual solitude in a little town where there is no social life ... and shake yourself out of it.'[22]

Then he spoiled it with another letter. 'I urge you when choosing your place of residence, *not* to take into account whether I will come there. It would be quite absurd, reckless and ridiculous if I were to restrict you in your choice of a city ... '[23]

He still demanded translations in his old lordly way. 'Still no article ... What is the meaning of this? I demand that you send it immediately.' And then, when she did send it, he didn't use it.

What Inessa really wanted was to set herself up as a writer – again because writers, in the party and the socialist world, acquired status. She had written two articles for *Rabotnitsa* and one for *Sotsial-Demokrat*. She was expecting to be assigned a piece on women workers, but it went instead to Lilina, the pseudonym used by Zinaida Zinovieva, who was becoming a literary rival. When Inessa prepared a paper, *Who Pays For The War*, it was not published but another by Lilina was – but then, Lilina was the co-editor's wife!

Lenin 'had to choose his words carefully or sometimes lie,' wrote Alexander Solzhenitsyn of his dealings with Inessa. "What could I possibly have against publishing your article in the Sbornik [*Sotsial-Demokrat*]?" Lenin replied on 20 July, 1916. Then afterward he would pretend that unforeseen circumstances had prevented it.' Lenin was like a ringmaster, handling the horses, but he would constantly take great trouble to keep Inessa in the ring.

In January 1917, Inessa became deeply depressed and Lenin felt for her, way up in the mountains that can be so gloomy if the winter weather is poor. 'I know how terribly bad you feel and I am eagerly anxious to help you in any way I can.'[24] It is easy to see Inessa during these months as sulking, but this would be unfair. She was trying to re-plan her life. She had bound herself to Lenin, without reservation, seeing him as a bastion of her future, willingly going to prison for him. But she had fallen deeply in love with him, as was almost certainly mutual – if not, for him, so intense. Her desolation when he had distanced himself in 1913 had been profound.

The cause, though, was crucial to Inessa, sacred in its quality, so she had continued working for the leader who she truly believed, rightly as history was to show, would conduct her, and everyone else, to what she thought would be the Promised Land – and, when he did, she never doubted that this was what it was, as she confirmed in her journal, only days before she died.

It is not surprising Inessa was confused. Her love as a woman and her devotion to the cause were totally merged. She knew that Lenin confided in her more intimately than he did in any of his male comrades. But she was not alone in feeling undervalued. Rosa Luxemburg and Alexandra Kollontai shared her view and her experience with the revolutionaries in their lives. Kollontai even wrote a novel about it, *A Great Love*, which was widely believed to be based on Inessa's life with Lenin, but could well have been about her own life.

For Inessa, the one good thing about their terrible isolation in Switzerland was that she could challenge the status quo without harming the cause. And it developed into a recognisable man-woman conflict. Lenin, too, was to some extent confused. He saw her at party level as an extremely good personal assistant, useful for her languages and any dirty work or dangerous missions he might need, but who could also be trusted to take his place on the platform before a hostile audience. What kind of an assistant was this? Not, he felt instinctively as an old-fashioned chauvinist, one in the top rank. In later years, though, when he was a head of state he was to give her free rein. She would become arguably the most powerful woman in the capital but still not as powerful as the top ranking men.

During these last few months, Lenin's and Nadya's lives had been reduced by poverty. They lived in a single room at 14 Spiegelgasse, a steep, cobbled alley of close, tall houses that was so exposed to the smells from a local sausage factory that they had to keep the windows closed. It was a bitterly cold winter and Nadya had been ill for much of it with bronchitis and the effects of Graves' Disease. Their bare room had no heating and they shared a small kitchen with their land-lady, Frau Kammerer. Often for lunch they had only oatmeal that Nadya was always scorching, not being a natural cook. 'We live in grand style, you see,' Lenin joked to Frau Kammerer. 'We have roasts every day.'

'I need to earn,' he wrote to Alexander Shlyapnikov, 'otherwise, we shall simply die of hunger … ' He urged Mark Elizarov, who was married to his older sister Anna, to find him work as a mere trans-lator. 'We shall soon be coming to the end of our former means of subsistence,' Nadya wrote to Maria, his younger sister.[25]

The year 1916 had been bad for them. Lenin's mother, whom he had adored, had died. His sister Anna had been sentenced to exile in Astrakhan, though released under controlled conditions owing to illness. Even his confidence in his future role in history showed signs of fraying. 'We of the older generation,' he told a young audience in January, 1917, 'may not live to see the decisive battles of this coming revolution.'[26]

It was only a moment of depression, but significant. In little more than a month he would be proved wrong. Revolution would break out in St Petersburg and – with the toppling of the Tsar – ripple throughout Russia. With the arrival of 1917, Lenin felt trapped. Nadya, conscious that there was 'no outlet for his colossal energy', recalled a visit to the zoo when they were living in London, and watched a white northern wolf. 'All animals,' explained the keeper, 'get used to their cages in time. Only the white wolf from the Russian north never becomes accustomed to the cage and day and night bangs his head against the bars.' Lenin, she knew, was a white northern wolf.

Lenin fought with everyone. Zinoviev, Rosa Luxemburg, Bukharin, Olga Ravich, the lover of Vyacheslav Karpinsky who produced *Sotsial-Demokrat*. He would be overwhelmed by an almost childish loss of temper and, if provoked by political opponents, this would be in the form of violent fits of hatred. At these times, according to Valentinov, a comrade of earlier days, he 'wanted to smash their faces in ... Following an attack ... his energy would begin to ebb, and a psychological reaction set in: dullness, loss of strength and fatigue ... He could neither eat nor sleep. Headaches tormented him. His face became sallow, even dark at times.'

It was against this setting that Inessa, from her mountain seclusion, was presenting him with a growing challenge, marked by the acute sensitivity of an unhappy lover, playing the game of being slow to answer his letters, or ignoring them altogether. But, to be fair to Lenin, he allowed few of his many problems in Zurich to colour his long correspondence with her.

'Apparently,' Lenin wrote in a censored letter on 9 January, 1917, 'your failure to reply to several of my last letters reveals on your part ... a somewhat changed mood, decision or state of affairs ... I don't know what to think, whether you took offence at something or were too preoccupied with the move [to a local boarding house] or something else ... I'm afraid to ask because I suppose such queries are unpleasant for you ... and, of course will not repeat [them].'[27]

This restraint was not always evident. 'You did not take offence, did you,' he queried incredulously in March, 'at my writing about your not having gone over the French text? Incredible! ... Is it conceivable that anyone can take offence at such a thing? Inconceivable! And on the other hand the complete silence ... is strange.'[28]

Perhaps not so strange, given that Inessa was in serious and barely believable revolt, considering the reverence in which she and the others held Lenin – and achieving this, what is more, at an intellectual level, with the help of the Russian Library.

What she was doing was changing the balance of power in their personal relations. It was *she* who failed to reply to his letters so that he, while not quite pleading with her, was asking why. It was *she* who was tossing in the odd firework, knowing how he would react. The point is that she was doing this to a man who, within two years, would be one of the most powerful figures in the world.

Her change of mood initially emerged quietly enough. 'On occasion,' R.C.Elwood wrote, 'she would suggest a point to be added to something she was translating or she would question a particular phrase or term. Sometimes Lenin accepted these suggestions but more often he ridiculed her idea.'[29]

In January, 1917 Inessa refused to translate a few words because 'they made her blood boil.'[30] 'Thanks awfully ... ' he wrote back. 'As regards the censorship to which you have subjected my French article, I am surprised really ... '[31]

She had already gone far, far further, but at a different level and softly. This was a climax in their declining relations. She had challenged him intellectually, suggesting politely that the master was being inconsistent on political theory.

Marx, who condemned patriotism, had stated in the *Communist Manifesto* that 'the worker has no fatherland.' So why, Inessa asked, was Lenin constantly arguing against the use of the slogan 'Defence of the Fatherland' in the current war?

The argument was complex, but it illuminated the new Inessa. Lenin, unaccustomed to such questions from his assistant, replied that there were some exceptions, such as the colonies of the warring imperialist nations who were being encouraged to fight for their independence – i.e. for their own identity or 'fatherland'. And he sent her one of his articles explaining this more fully.[32]

Inessa found this at variance with his earlier work. He was shocked, accusing her of 'apparently wanting to establish a contradiction between my present writing and that of an earlier date. Why? Where precisely? What precisely?' She told him. An article written eight years before seemed to contradict his present position on 'defence of the Fatherland'.

Simplistically, he explained that 'you have taken one quotation from the Communist Manifesto ... to the repudiation of national wars.'[33] But Inessa wasn't letting up and, if Lenin discussed this esoteric quarrel with Nadya, she must have smiled to herself. She was always on the side of the women, even if she had gone through some unpleasant moments with this one. And times were bad enough anyway with Lenin in that dark winter.

He was getting very irritated with Inessa. Two days before Christmas, he wrote: 'I would find it extremely unpleasant if we should differ on this.' He said that the international background in 1891 differed from that in the current war – and explained why. 'Think about this,' he said as though she was a child.[34]

Inessa didn't like his tone and went back into action. 'We are talking past one another,' she wrote, but argued he was being illogical when he said that Germany's defence of the fatherland was justified in 1891 but unjustified in 1914.

And so it went on. It wasn't what the argument was about but the fact it was happening at all. This woman he loved had become a terrier, hanging on with her teeth. Eventually he fell back on a regular male taunt. 'You must be in an excessively nervous state. This is my explanation for the number of theoretical oddities in your letters.'[35] Oddities, rather interestingly, that would crop up a year later when Inessa and the Baugy Group became the core of the Left Communist opposition.[36]

In fact, it was amazing that this aspect of the correspondence, which lasted months, mixed in with Lenin's concern and his orders, was continuing at all.

For ten days earlier revolution had broken out in Russia.

TEN
Zurich 1917

On 15 March, 1917 Inessa was, as usual, in the mountain village of Baugy-sur-Clarens, now staying at the Pension Lergive. It is doubtful if she had received the news of revolution. Montreux, where the newspapers would doubtless have carried the telegrams, was close, but down below on Lake Leman. Perhaps there were rumours, maybe from tradesmen or even exiles from Bukharin's group who might have come up on routine visits to the Russian Library.

It is possible that Lenin's letter was the first she knew of it – a letter, not a telegram, because he was still unsure if it was all a hoax, and not mentioned until his third paragraph.[1] 'We here in Zurich are in a state of agitation today. There is a telegram in the *Zürcher Post* and in *Neue Zürcher Zeitung* of 15 March that in Russia the revolution was victorious in Petrograd[2] on 14 March (1 March, Old Style Russian calendar) after three days of struggle, that 12 members of the Duma are in power and the ministers have all been arrested.

'If the Germans are not lying,' he cautioned, before adding: 'I am beside myself that I cannot go to Scandinavia!! I will not forgive myself for not risking the journey in 1915!'[3]

No letters from Inessa have survived from this period though she is certain to have written to her children. Like the other exiles, she had been waiting so long for revolution that doubtless she found it hard to believe. It seems she did not immediately reply to Lenin, relations between them having reached a kind of nadir. Perhaps she needed time to think.

Even Lenin needed that, as his letter showed. The news had taken him totally by surprise. An excited Polish comrade, Mieczyslav Bronski, had pounded on their door just after lunch. Nadya, as she wrote, was washing up and Lenin was preparing to return to the

143

library. 'Haven't you heard the news?' asked Bronski, according to Nadya. 'There's a revolution in Russia.'

Bronski's excited announcement was so completely incredible to Lenin that he was totally 'bewildered', as Nadya was to describe it in *Pravda*, at the sudden tantalising glimpse of what they had worked for all their lives.

In fact, he refused to believe it, but the young Pole insisted that special editions of the Zurich newspapers, only just on the streets, carried telegrams from St Petersburg.

It was easy for Lenin and Nadya to imagine the scenes in the city. The crowds surging through the streets. The Cossacks formed up to charge; the drawbridges raised over the Neva – which the Tsars had always used to divide this city of a hundred islands. The bridges were not much help this time, for the Neva River was frozen and the workers in the Vyborg factory area had crossed over the ice into the city centre. Lenin had forecast that Europe, after three years of war, was 'pregnant with revolution', but he had not believed it would happen yet and he had not expected it to break out in Russia, with its millions of peasants, who were unresponsive militant material, and an industry that, despite substantial pre-war growth, was still old-fashioned. Germany and Britain, with their big working populations, had seemed far more liable to social explosion.

Lenin and Nadya hurried down the familiar lanes of the 'Old Town' to Bellevue Platz on the edge of Lake Zurich, glistening that afternoon in winter sunshine. There, Swiss newspapers were on display beneath an awning. Surrounding the stand was a crowd of barely credulous exiles. Lenin and Nadya shouldered their way through the throng and, still dazed, confirmed for themselves that what Bronski had told them was true.

Lenin was still suspicious, fearing some kind of German master-plan, as he'd suggested to Inessa. But three days later his doubts had gone. 'We are all dreaming of leaving,' he wrote to her, concerned that once again she had not replied to him, though surely it was different this time. 'If you're going home, drop in to see us first ... I would very much like you to find out for me in England discreetly whether I would be granted passage.'[4]

On the same day Inessa did write back and also spoke to him on the telephone. Not that she pleased him. 'I must say I'm keenly disappointed. In my opinion everybody these days should have a single thought – to rush off ... I am sure I will be arrested or simply detained in England if I go under my own name ...

'I was certain that you would rush off to England, as only there could you find out how to get through and how great the risk is ... ' He assumed, he added, that she was planning to go to Berne to see the consul, 'but you write that you are undecided and want to think it over ... My nerves naturally are overstrung. No wonder! To have to sit here on tenterhooks. Probably you have special reasons ... '5

Then came the orders, in this and succeeding letters:

Find some Swiss or Russian in Clarens who would agree to give Lenin his passport, 'without them knowing it's for me.'

'Run to the German consulate. Be energetic. Pay Zurich lawyers.'

Get Anna (her sister-in-law) to go immediately to the Russian Embassy in Berne to get a visa in order to find out the procedure for re-entry into their own country.

Get some Russian Social Democrat in Clarens to ask the Germans to allow for the passage of a railway coach to Copenhagen for various revolutionaries. 'You will say perhaps that the Germans will not give a coach. I bet they will! Of course if they learn this idea came from me or from you, then the scheme will be ruined.'6

On 23 March Lenin was in despair. A comrade had been told at the British Embassy that 'there is no passage at all through England. What if no passage whatever is allowed either by England or by Germany! And this is possible!!'7

He considered going across Germany in a plane, but realised that this was impractical, presumably for reasons of refuelling or being shot down. Then he toyed with using the passport of a dumb Swede – dumb, of course, so that he would not be required to speak Swedish. 'You'll fall asleep and see Mensheviks in your dreams,' Nadya teased, 'and shout "scoundrels" and give the whole conspiracy away.'

It was on 25 March, in the midst of all this high emotional activity, that he found time to write to Inessa about 'the worker has no fatherland', describing it as her 'theoretical oddities', continuing the argument that had already lasted months. She must, he alleged, be in an 'excessively nervous state'. Who was talking, she might have thought? And at what a time! He even ended this letter: 'Probably we won't manage to get to Russia!! Britain will not let us through. It can't be done through Germany.' This was after hinting that 'someone with free time … should collect all the press telegrams in all the foreign newspapers about the revolution.' Could he mean her, still in her secluded spot? Despite all the orders![8]

He didn't speak of his real problem to Inessa, though he didn't have to. The Russian reaction to his travelling through an enemy country already responsible for thousands of Russian deaths was certain to do him huge political damage, unless he could find some way of making it acceptable.

In fact, the Political Section of the German Foreign Office had been planning to provoke a revolution in Russia ever since 1915 – 'revolutionising', as the policy was called – since the resulting mutiny of the army would enable them to switch the million troops engaged there to the Western Front.

Their main contact had been Alexander Helphand, an astonishing character who had been close to Lenin in the days of the first party journal *Iskra*, but had since made a fortune by dubious means in Turkey. He had become a millionaire Marxist and suspect to every socialist – a fat, caricature capitalist with an enormous car, a string of blondes, thick cigars, and a taste for champagne at breakfast.

But he knew everyone, even if they didn't like him, and he now ran a company, in Copenhagen, of which he owned fifty per cent, selling chemicals, medicines, and even condoms, by means of sales teams within Russia – which would be useful for getting money into Russia and communicating, under cover of legitimate business, within her borders.

For two years, Helphand had been insisting that the man the Germans needed to back to achieve their object was Lenin, though Lenin would have nothing to do with him.[9]

These were crucially important days for another reason. Before the Russian Revolution in March, Arthur Zimmermann, the German

Secretary of State, had taken a huge gamble. In order to starve Britain and France, he had ordered the German U-boats to sink all shipping bound for their ports – including neutral vessels. On 18 March, the US people learned to their fury that three American ships had been sunk. War was now certain to be declared. Zimmermann's gamble now depended on one issue: could his U-boats weaken the Allies fast enough to gain victory, before US troops could be deployed in Europe?

Suddenly, the revolution – or, rather, its direction – became urgent to Germany's broader strategy. Alexander Helphand took centre stage, seeing himself as a kingmaker. Oddly, Jacob Furstenberg, Lenin's old friend, who had partnered him on the Malinovsky Commission, was the manager of Helphand's company. He cabled Lenin, offering him transit for two people.

Lenin was cautious. 'Uncle wants to know more. Official transit for individuals unacceptable,' wired Zinoviev. Lenin had hoped to reduce the immense political risk, firstly by travelling with an all-party group of exiles rather than just Bolsheviks; secondly, by seeking prior approval from St Petersburg.

The last was a dubious hope. Both Paul Milyukov, the new Foreign Minister, and Alexander Kerensky, a potential high flier as Minister of Justice, were patriots. Without question, they would not want Lenin and other anti-war socialists in Russia, making trouble.

Martov, in fact, had come up with the same idea of a multi-party group but, as expected, no approval had come through. On 31 March, 1917, with Martov insisting on waiting, Lenin decided they would go anyway, but not with Helphand's direct help.

Contact had already been made by a Swiss comrade with Gisbert von Romberg, the German Minister in Berne, exploring the possibility of passage by train. Now Lenin confirmed the request by wire. His condition: it should be 'sealed', and have the extraterritorial status of an embassy. No Russian would even speak to a German during the trip and to avoid this, Fritz Platten, a Swiss Social Democrat, would be in charge of the party and do any talking that might be needed.

Then Lenin wrote to Inessa. 'I hope we shall be starting out on

Wednesday – with you, I hope. I trust you have received the money [100 frs sent that morning by express for her and Alexander's sister, Anna]. We have more money for the journey than I thought, enough for 10-12 persons. The comrades in Stockholm have been a great help ... We shall fight. The war will agitate for us. A thousand greetings. Au revoir.'[10]

Three days later, on 2 April, Romberg was ordered from the Wilhelmstrasse to expedite arrangements. The next day, Lenin wired his sisters in St Petersburg: 'Arriving Monday 11 p.m. Inform *Pravda*.' It was optimistic, but on Wednesday, as soon as he heard that Romberg was trying to contact him, Lenin told Nadya to pack. They were taking the first train to Berne.

Fritz Platten called on Romberg and demanded that 'safe transit' of the exiles should be guaranteed, insisted that no names would be given, just numbers, with everyone paying their own fares. The minister agreed, but Lenin was nervous. He was placing himself completely in the hands of his stated enemy, Kaiser Wilhelm II, at a time when revolution had toppled his cousin, the Tsar.

On 6 April, Inessa joined Lenin and Zinoviev and seven others at the Volkshaus in Berne to negotiate a formal list of conditions under which they were returning to Russia. Inessa translated them into French and German. Bolsheviks were alerted in the main Swiss cities.

Meanwhile, Lenin's train was causing wide foreign concern. From Berne, British ambassador Sir Horace Rumbold reported that a group of Russian socialists and anarchists, in favour of immediate peace with Germany, were about to be given safe transit. From London the Foreign Office cabled the news to Sir George Buchanan in St Petersburg, asking if the new government 'intended to take any steps to counter this danger.' Lenin, despite his fears, was unknown in British high circles except as one of many names on a list of anti-war revolutionaries.

In Halifax, Nova Scotia, Trotsky and his friends, who had been in America, had been arrested on the way home on a British ship. Would London please discover, requested local officials, if the Russian government would like them to proceed?

There was reason for anxiety in London. A big new Allied offensive was planned for 9 April, 1917.[11] While telegrams were being exchanged between the various embassies, troops were moving up into position, with artillery and supplies, through the mud of northern France.

For Lenin, the news from Russia was alarming. A French newspaper, *Le Petit Parisien*, had reported that Milyukov had threatened to prosecute, on charges of high treason, anyone who travelled through Germany. From St Petersburg, the party leaders could not contact Lenin and discovered to their alarm that their cables were being stopped on orders of the new revolutionary government.

A courier, Maria Stetskevich, was sent to Sweden to communicate with Switzerland. On 2 April (20 March), she was back in the capital with letters from Lenin and Jacob Furstenberg, so the Central Committee knew about the sealed train.She was sent back to Sweden, again with letters. This time, at Tornio, the Finnish border town, she was searched and stripped naked. The letters were taken but she was allowed to proceed to Sweden. It was another ominous sign of what lay ahead for Lenin and his party. For they, too, would have to pass through Tornio on their way to Russia.

The Central Committee were worried by the problem of the train but, like Lenin, accepted the risk. Despite Maria's experience, they got a message to Furstenberg in Copenhagen: 'Ulyanov must come immediately.' Lenin's sisters wired: 'Do not force Vladimir to come. Avoid all risk.'

Romberg, who understood Lenin's predicament, tried to persuade the Socialist Revolutionaries to join the party on the train, but – like Martov and his Mensheviks – they refused. Not without permission from Russia.

On 9 April, only a few hours after the Allies had launched their new offensive on the German line at Arras, Lenin's party gathered – some thirty-two of them including two children – at the Volkshaus in Berne.[12] They were a determined group though uneasy, since they faced danger both at home and within Germany. Despite the guarantee of safe transit, could the Kaiser be trusted?

They boarded a train to Zurich where they had lunch with Swiss friends. Lenin made a speech which was to be historically important.

'Russia is a peasant country,' he declared. 'Socialism cannot triumph there immediately.' Note the last words, conforming with Marx's theory, believed by all Social Democrats, that revolution in Russia would go through two stages: first, a capitalist Western-style government before progressing ultimately to socialism.

Then they went to Zurich station where an angry crowd was waiting on the platform. To cries and catcalls of 'Provocateurs! Spies! Pigs! Traitors!' the party boarded the train that would take them to the frontier. At 3.10 p.m. it pulled out, with the objectors striking the sides of the carriage with sticks, and one of the travellers defiantly streaming a red scarf from an open window.[13]

The train to be sealed was waiting for them at Gottmadingen, a tiny station in the hills on the German side of the Swiss border and, as they approached, the travellers could see ahead the tall hill, topped by a wood, that dominated the little town. The train slowed and they passed the old Bahnhof Hotel, with its curving roof and faded cracked plaster, and came to a steaming halt at the single platform, which was empty except for two German officers in high boots and green-grey uniforms who awaited them.

The sight of the officers caused acute anxiety among the revolutionaries peering through the windows. Nearly all of them had been in jail or in illegal situations. Suspicion of men in uniform was rooted in them.

Uneasily, the travellers clambered down from the train and were ushered into a third class waiting room. The atmosphere was tense. There was a suspicion they might have walked into a trap. When they were separated into two groups – men and women – their unease grew. The officers completed the formalities, collected the fares that Lenin had insisted on, and invited them to board the train that would take them across Germany to Sassnitz on the Baltic.

It was not much of a train – just a green carriage with eight compartments, three second class and five third class, and a baggage waggon. Two escort officers were to travel with them, occupying the end third class compartment, 'sealing' being indicated by a white chalk line on the corridor floor. No one was allowed to cross this line except for the Swiss Fritz Platten. There were toilets at each end of the carriage, so the Germans did not need to enter 'Russian territory', and Platten was the only person permitted to speak to them.

The single men in the party accepted the hard wooden benches of the third class compartments, ceding the brown padded upholstery of second class to wives, husbands and children. By common consent, Lenin and Nadya had the end second class compartment to themselves, so he could work.

The external doors of the carriage were locked, except for one at the officers' 'German' end of the carriage. As soon as the train moved off from Gottmadingen station, the anxious gloom of the travellers lifted. Spirits soared. There was laughter and joking. Some of the younger ones in the third class compartment began to sing the *Marseillaise*. It was taken up in other compartments and the sound of elated voices echoed through the woods beside the track as the train clattered north into Germany.

The journey to Sassnitz was to take three days but Lenin was not allowed to enjoy the peace they had all granted him. Several times he had to act to quell the noise in the next-door compartment. This was occupied by Olga Ravich, the Safarovs and – according to Ravich – Inessa, but they were joined by Karl Radek and some of the young men from third class, all of whom indulged in rowdy high spirits. Eventually Olga's screaming laughter was too much for Lenin. He walked in, took her firmly by the hand, and without speaking led her into another compartment.

Since Anna was on the train with her lover, Abram Skovno, it is odd that Inessa was not with them, but Radek, too, confirmed she was with Olga Ravich and himself. Strangely, the accounts of the journey written by Olga, Safarov, the two Zinovievs and Karl Radek barely mention her: especially odd is Safarov's omission since they had long been close.

But then Zina Zinovieva wrote later of Longjumeau without referring to her, even though she had organised and lectured at the school. This was doubtless because, as time went on – and these were, of course, recollections written years later – Inessa's position became uncertain. She was dangerous to write about.

The fact that she was not with Lenin and Nadya was itself significant but then, for months, she had been showing a different personality, resistant to much of what Lenin wanted. She was a woman of conflicting moods, as displayed by her ability to cope with prison life, and the warm sympathy and easy personality described by such people as Elena Vlasova, Saul Zubrovich from Mezen, and even Nadya.

It is intriguing that she seemed to display no excitement about the March Rising though it seemed like the start of world revolution to which she had devoted much of her life, and would mean her return to her children as a free citizen. Lenin had almost had to beg her to join them on the train. Nor has she written much about the journey. The impression that remains is of her sitting rather quietly, almost an outsider among her elated companions and the giggling Olga, though Olga does report her laughing, too, at Radek.

Inessa did, of course, have much to think about. Lenin was a long way from achieving the revolution he envisaged. The Bolsheviks were a tiny party whom no one in the high levels of the Duma or the Soviet took too seriously. They knew he would be a source of trouble in very unstable conditions, a strident and extreme political voice, which is why they had tried to keep him out. Russia was in enough chaos as it was as the politicians struggled to establish some sort of order, now that the Tsarist regime and its long-established system had disintegrated. In fact, Inessa must have reasoned, there was now a clear danger that they might be arrested on arrival – and there was no doubt at all that the journey through Germany would have provoked anger amongst their many enemies.

So was not the excitement a little premature?

And what would her role be in Lenin's new life, this man who had for years written so many letters to her? That was assuming he, himself, was not put on trial for treason.

The train ran on to Tuttlingen where it stopped to change the engine, then diverted to Stuttgart on its way to Karlsruhe, approaching from the east to avoid the main railway line to the front, which was reserved for military traffic, rushing up troops and supplies to check the new Allied offensive. They went on through Mannheim to Frankfurt, arriving too late for their scheduled connection for Berlin.

The next day, after spending a night in the sidings, they were given priority, the private train of the German Crown Prince being held up for two hours to allow them to pass, as they headed for Berlin. To Zinoviev, the city, as they ran through the suburbs, seemed 'like a cemetery' and the usually buoyant Olga Ravich found it 'deathly still'.

Once they came to a halt within the city, security was strict. No one, not even Fritz Platten was allowed to leave the train. Under the original plan, they should have been at Sassnitz by the evening of that day, the Baltic port where they had intended to stay the night and the next morning board a ship for Sweden.

The plan was changed and they stayed in Berlin for nearly twenty-four unscheduled hours. They were, of course, within easy distance of the Wilhelmstrasse, though there is no evidence of any kind of meeting with Foreign Office officials, except for a courtesy call by a junior officer in civilian clothes, who only spoke to Platten. Yet Lenin was important enough for the Germans to invest 40 million gold marks in the Bolsheviks – billions of pounds sterling in modern money – that is, according to two letters from the Secretary of State to the Kaiser.[14] It was never acknowledged by the Bolsheviks, but German support, plus funding from other sources, is now accepted by most modern historians.

Lenin changed his whole plan of campaign on the journey to Russia, reversing the view of revolutionary development that he had described in the Zahringerhof in Zurich before boarding the train for Gottmadingen. No longer would he believe that revolution would require two stages. They could go straight to socialism via revolution – which was exactly what Arthur Zimmermann and the Germans wanted them to attempt.

Why did Lenin change his mind on so fundamental an issue? Because, in this author's view, he knew by the end of the journey, that the party, which had previously had only limited funds, was now to be given resources that would finance a huge Bolshevik propaganda campaign and put the masses behind them. This did not mean that Lenin was a German agent. He was a Lenin agent. He would have done a deal with the devil if it served his aims – but for this kind of policy he needed a long spoon, and many, including Inessa, were to think in time that the one he was supping with was not long enough.

The next day, 12 April, they reached Sassnitz, boarding the Swedish ferry, *Queen Victoria*, and, after reaching Sweden, travelled by night train to Stockholm, arriving there twenty-four hours later. Inessa rushed off a telegram to the children in Pushkino, which suggested that at last she had shrugged off the gloom of the mountains: 'Soon I shall be with you … I am endlessly happy. I am already on the way from Stockholm to Peter … will be delayed for a week in Peter. As soon as I arrive I will write to you from there. I kiss and hug you firmly my dears.'[15] No word, even of regards, to their father.

At 6.30 p.m. on Good Friday, they boarded yet another train, which would take them the 600 miles to the Finnish border. On the way, Lenin addressed them all in the corridor about what they should do if they were arrested at the border. On no account should they offer any defence for travelling through Germany. Instead, they should attack the government for not helping their return from exile.

Tornio, the Finnish border town, lay across the frozen mouth of the Tornio River. To reach the town they had to travel over the ice in horse-drawn sledges. There, at the frontier, they were searched and stripped, like Maria, the courier. All the women were even forced 'to take off our stockings,' as Zinaida recorded. 'All the documents and even the books and toys my son had brought with him were taken.'

It was ominous, suggesting that serious opposition awaited them in Russia. Neither was Lenin cheered by what he read in a copy of *Pravda*, obtained in the town. The Okhrana files had been opened. There was no longer any doubt that Malinovsky had been a police spy.

'Several times,' recorded Zinoviev, 'Ilyich, staring eyeball to eyeball, returned to this theme. He looked straight in my face. "What a scoundrel! He tricked the lot of us. Traitor."'[16] He had been Lenin's protégé, cleared for lack of evidence by the Commission of Enquiry that Lenin had set up under his own chairmanship. Malinovsky was now, in 1917, outside Russia, a prisoner of war in Germany. And, given Lenin's record of breaking all the rules, a link between him and the Okhrana – as police sometimes have with the underworld – was not out of the question. This was, after all, the man who had raised funds from the robbery of banks. It could be another mark against him at a time when he was highly vulnerable.

Lenin learned that a military guard had been sent up to accompany the train and he queried wryly to Zinoviev: 'To take us to jail?' What awaited them, in fact, was the huge, famous welcome in the Finland Station – out of all proportion to the tiny size of the Bolshevik Party. Even in June, two months later after much campaigning, the party only had 105 out of 822 delegates to the Congress of Soviets.

But the mood of the city, still ecstatic in the new climate of revolution and freedom, where comrade waiters were insulted to be offered a tip, was such that it did not need much to get people out onto the streets – especially on Easter Monday when all the factories were closed. And Nicholas Podvoisky and Vladimir Nevsky, the party's Bolshevik military commanders, were brilliant at assembling militant crowds – so brilliant that they were almost to destroy the party in July when their enthusiasm robbed Lenin of control.

That Monday, though, was incredible. It had become the custom to greet returning revolutionary notables with a parade. Only days before, Plekhanov had been welcomed by a large crowd. But this welcome was on a different scale. 'The throng in front of the Finland Station blocked the whole square,' reported Nikolai Sukhanov. 'Troops with bands were drawn up under red flags. There was a throbbing of many motor cars. Awe-inspiring outlines of armoured cars thrust up from the crowd. And from one of the side streets, startling the mob, cutting through it, a strange monster – a mounted searchlight ...

'Within the station, triumphal arches in red and gold stretched the length of the platform above the heads of the mass of waiting people. Banners hung above several divisions of guards of honour – soldiers, sailors and armed Bolshevik Red Guards.'

At the end of the platform was a small group of Bolsheviks, including Alexandra Kollontai, holding a bouquet of flowers.[17] Alexandra, who was to become both a partner and rival of Inessa, thrust her flowers into Lenin's hands. The waiting officers rapped out their commands, the guard of honour presented arms. 'That very instant,' reported Vladimir Bonch-Bruevich, 'the hubbub died down. All that could be heard was the blare of trumpets … Then suddenly, there thundered forth such a powerful, stirring and hearty "Hurrah" as I have never heard in my life.'

Lenin was greeted by two representatives of the Petersburg Soviet – including the Chairman, Nikolai Chkheidze, who was an old adversary – and made repeated speeches as he moved through the crowd, eventually being driven off in an armoured car, stopping though for brief addresses at fifteen street corners. At last he reached the Kshesinskya Mansion, once the home of Kshesinskaya, the Tsar's mistress, which the Bolsheviks had taken over as their headquarters.

There, over supper, after Kamenev had made a speech of welcome, Lenin told them of his new concept – 'All power to the Soviets' and, instead of Marx's two stages, a one-stage aim for revolution *now* – which had them reeling. It was, of course, the exact opposite of what he had said in Zurich on their day of departure.

His other idea, 'Power to the Soviet' seemed equally absurd. The Soviet was a loose federation of strike committees. How could its 2-3000 members, torn by political differences, ever rule a nation?

That night, he and Nadya went to bed in the home of his sister Anna and her husband, Mark Elizarov, shared of course with Maria, on the sixth floor of 52 Shirokaya Street. The building, in the middle of Petersburg Island, had been constructed on a very sharp street corner. As a result the apartment was triangular in shape and the living room, since it was in the apex, gave an impression of the saloon of a ship. Lenin, when peering out of the windows, must at times, in the months ahead, have felt like a sea captain, and there was certainly rough weather ahead.

ELEVEN
St Petersburg 1917

The next morning, after a meeting with party leaders, Lenin travelled to the Tauride Palace, which housed the Duma, the Soviet and some government offices. His arrival had coincided with a conference of Bolsheviks from all over Russia, providing him with a chance to address delegates of much of the party.

As the group crossed the Neva, it passed through the St Petersburg they all knew so well – the Winter Palace, the setting of 'Bloody Sunday'; the Admiralty with its pillared tower; the Field of Mars – the symbolic gardens where a month before, the hundreds of dead had been lowered into the ground, each coffin being marked by a boom from a cannon.

They travelled along the Nevsky Prospekt which, straight and wide, with its luxury shops and lavish apartments, reached through the centre of the city. It bore little sign of revolution – the same expensive shops, their elegant customers thronging the pavements; the congestion of carriages and automobiles; the commissionaires outside the big hotels, wearing sashes of green, gold, or scarlet. Bourgeois babies were still being pushed in big prams by nurse-maids dressed in blue if the children were boys, pink if they were girls.

However, even if the revolution was not too evident on that cloudy April day, there had in fact been enormous changes. St Petersburg, like much of Russia, faced social collapse. The entire nation had, as Alexander Kerensky put it, been swept by 'a sense of unlimited freedom, a liberation from the most elementary restraints essential to every human society.' Crime had soared. In the factories, people had stopped working. Discipline had vanished in the army and the navy. In the streets soldiers forcibly relieved officers of their swords.

The one factor that prevented a complete breakdown was the Soviet. The government ruled in name, but the Soviet made it possible. Autocracy and feudalism had been overthrown; but, because true chaos was so close, the early extremism, with its undertones of the French Revolution, had now been replaced by a belief among the Soviet that order must be preserved. Clearly, some party aims would have to be shelved for the time being. Certainly, the leading Bolsheviks subscribed to this view, which conformed with Marxist theory. It was seen as that first stage of revolution that Lenin had now decided they did not need.

The ordinary workers and soldiers felt a keen sense of personal achievement. Everyone was 'Comrade'. Everywhere, there were red flags, and imperial insignia had been ripped from buildings throughout the capital. The mood of the city, indeed of the whole vast nation, was one of intense pride – a mood coloured by a degree of complacency that Lenin planned that day to shatter.

After a diversion to visit the grave of his mother, he arrived at the Tauride Palace. There, in the gallery, he addressed an audience of Bolsheviks, who had also been joined by Mensheviks, for a move towards unity was once more afoot in this heady air. Inessa, as Alexandra Kollontai noted, sat with Nadya in the front row.

In ten clear points, to be known as the *April Theses*, Lenin spelled out his new programme intended to catapult a hundred and sixty million Russians towards socialism. They included an end to the war, control by the soviets of all production and sale of goods, confiscation of all private land, destruction of the bourgeois establishment (army, police, bureaucrats) to be replaced by soviet organs with officials elected by the people – rule from below, as he was to repeat so often, not from above – a cry that in time was to have hollow and macabre echoes.

The murmuring began early. Then Lenin spoke of the Paris Commune of 1871 – fictionalised by Victor Hugo in *Les Miserables* – as a prototype and the murmuring became a roar. 'This is the raving of a madman,' yelled the Menshevik Bogdanov.[1]

'Sheer anarchy,' asserted a Bolshevik from *Iskra* days. Nikolai Chkheidze, Chairman of the Soviet who had welcomed Lenin on the Finland Station, declared he was 'a man completely played out'.

Lenin's whole programme seemed wildly impractical but his mention of the Paris Commune touched a nerve. The people of Paris had set up the commune by elections in defiance of the government. It was an experiment in crude socialism. Even the officers of the National Guard, a people's militia, had been elected. The French government, nervous that these ideas might spread, had withdrawn the army from the capital, only to return to smash the experiment in a two-day massacre of some 30,000 citizens.

Lenin's dramatic comparison seemed insane and even dangerous in that climate. In the evening of this raucous day, the British Ambassador happily reported to London: 'All Lenin's proposals have been rejected.' From the enemy HQ, Arthur Zimmermann's liaison officer was happy, too: 'Lenin is working exactly as we would wish.'

Inessa went home to her children at Pushkino for the first time for four years – to Andre, now thirteen, and Varya, sixteen. The two older boys were both away in the army. Inna was at university but doubtless took a train back to greet her mother. And, presumably, Alexander, still her husband, was also there to welcome her.

There is no record of Inessa bidding Lenin goodbye before she left, but she must have done, if only in a note. She agreed with everything he'd said. She was more of an internationalist – i.e. believing revolution would spread like fire throughout the world – even than he was. Later, in 1918, when he was being politically practical, she was to oppose him fiercely from the left of the party.

Certainly, she would have embraced Nadya before her departure. They had both stayed on to hear Alexandra Kollontai, who reported that their encouraging smiles had helped to give her confidence with what, after Lenin's shocks, must have been a very edgy audience.

Inessa knew Moscow better than St Petersburg. It was her home city, far bigger, of course, than the capital. She had worked there for the party in the underground movement, was well acquainted with its prisons, and had contacts throughout the new hierarchy of the city soviet.

Once there, she didn't waste any time. She moved into an Armand apartment at 14 Denezhnyi Lane in the Arbat and, on 19 April, barely two days after her arrival at the Finland Station, she attended a Moscow regional conference of Social Democrats. She took the platform to explain Lenin's *April Theses* since, as Polina Vinogradskaya put it later, with careful understatement, 'not everyone understood the worldwide historical significance of Lenin's prognosis and conclusions.'

Polina found her irresistibly appealing. 'She was so beautiful and the features of her face seemed carved ... Her eyes were green, expressive and magnetic. Her hair was fair, voluminous, worn up at the back with a side parting. She looked disciplined. It seemed that nature had given her something extraordinary.'[2]

Inessa urged the election by soldiers of officers in the army and the fraternisation of the troops in the trenches with the enemy. 'The speech was very important in balancing opinion in Lenin's favour,' Polina concluded.

It was clearly effective at one level, since Inessa was appointed as one of Moscow's delegates to the Seventh All-Party Social Democrat Conference, due to meet three days later in St Petersburg.

By contrast, Nadya, who had expected to continue as Lenin's personal secretary, as she had been for years, soon found herself side-lined in the mansion HQ. The party structures were already established, with a secretariat run first by Elena Stasova, and then by Yakov Sverdlov. And clearly Lenin thought it unwise to rock the boat by insisting that a place should be found for Nadya. Maria, Lenin's sister, who had often mocked Nadya, was now Editorial Secretary of *Pravda* and that made it no easier for her. After a while, Nadya gave up the struggle for a role in Lenin's new life and moved to the Vyborg factory district, where she worked for the party as an organiser and educator.

Meanwhile, Lenin's position was precarious in the extreme. His own party leaders, ranged round Kamenev, were violently opposed to his new plan. The revelation of the Sealed Train, unknown to the thousands who had welcomed him at the Finland Station, produced so violent a reaction that his life was in danger.

His new ideas were a propaganda gift to the right wing – in particular to Paul Milyukov, the Foreign Minister and head of the big Kadet Party, with a powerful newspaper *Rech* and the solid support of the middle classes.

Milyukov was liberal but far from revolutionary and Lenin had given him scope to promote the idea that all pacifists and many soviet members were in league with the Germans. The Sealed Train offered undisputed proof that Lenin had accepted help from the enemy.

Together with the right-wing General Lavr Kornilov, commander of the city's garrison of a quarter of a million troops, Milyukov made a secret plan using well-worn Tsarist tactics. Milyukov's Kadets, including many students, would create disorder on the streets; Lenin and the Bolsheviks would be blamed. And the troops, if their resentment of Lenin's German links could be fanned, would agree to repress the troublemakers. The Soviet itself would then be vulnerable.

Lenin did his best to deflect the danger by appearing with Zinoviev before the Soviet Executive Committee, emphasising the role of the Swiss Fritz Platten and explaining the 'sealed' concept, ensuring that no Russians had spoken to any Germans at all.

The Soviet, though non-committal, published his statement in *Izvestia*, but it made little impact. The bourgeois press attacked Lenin. Mobs paraded through the streets, demanding his arrest. Large hooting crowds gathered outside the Kshesinskaya Mansion yelling, 'Down with Lenin – Back to Germany.' Whenever he left the mansion, he had to be protected by bodyguards.

In several regiments, motions demanding his arrest were carried by large votes. Even the sailors, the most revolutionary element in Russia, turned angrily against him. The naval guard of honour that had presented arms on the platform of the Finland Station issued a public statement, regretting 'our participation in his triumphal welcome to St Petersburg.'

'Not a single Bolshevik,' recorded Nikolai Podvoisky, the military chief in the mansion, 'was able to enter the barracks without risking arrest or even death.'

This was the city to which Inessa returned on 21 April to take her place in the Social Democrat Party Conference. She must have been shocked by the scenes on the streets, and the placards branding Lenin as a German traitor. She is certain to have gone to the Kshesinskaya Mansion and witnessed the alarm. Whether she saw Lenin there is uncertain, for he was fighting for his life with little time even for her or the other comrades of his exile years.

Lenin defended himself as well as he could in *Pravda*, but on the day after his speech in the Tauride Palace, Kamenev had denounced his proposals in the Bolshevik Central Committee and won unanimous support. Kamenev, too, went public in *Pravda*. 'If we want to remain the party of the masses,' he stated, 'then Lenin's base assumption about Marx's first stage was unacceptable.' Stalin supported Kamenev.

The mood in the *Pravda* office was tense. 'It was enough for one of them to read a scrap from an article he had just written,' recorded Bonch-Bruevich, 'for a violent quarrel to break out.' But Lenin, in argument, was on familiar ground. In the columns of the paper he attacked Kamenev point by point. He was under great strain but standing up to it well.

There is no doubt Inessa talked to him in his sister's apartment, for he referred to her visit in a letter in May. 'With us, life is unchanged from what you saw yourself here. There is no end to the exhaustion and I am starting to give way and sleep three times more than other people.'[3]

He was wary even of his own party. His instructions to Inessa about how she should write to him were very precise and repeated in more than one letter. Some weeks before, in April, he had written that 'Everything is boiling, although the persecution is getting less,' but advised her to send all communications to him at the *Pravda* office, addressed to his sister Maria, and to mark all letters 'For V.I.'[4] He spoke in another letter of the emissaries they would use and told her that Sokolnikov, a trusted comrade, would act as his own in the early future.[5]

With Inessa living in Moscow, some 400 miles away, it was clearly hard for contact between them to be retained to anything like the extent it had been when they were in exile. It was to be easier when Lenin himself moved to Moscow in March of the following year but it was not until September, 1918 — when he was badly wounded in an attempt on his life — that their relationship again became as close as it had once been. Sometimes, though, long before then, signs of his influence were to be seen, in duties assigned to her by the Central Committee and in her ease of access to him at a time when he was under great pressure.

Meanwhile, in the spring of 1917, despite internal opposition to him and the hate campaign in the streets, he was not as isolated as he seemed. Many of the ordinary party workers were as extreme as he was. In the Vyborg factories were Bolsheviks as rabid as any sans-culottes of the French Revolution, as some had demonstrated in March. The party membership in St Petersburg, too, had been soaring, now topping 70,000 card-carrying Bolsheviks.

Few of these new party members understood the ideological conflicts – or cared about the 'stages of revolution' – that engrossed their leaders, but they were radicals to whom Lenin had offered a rallying point, as swiftly became evident. A full conference of the city party's members gave Lenin's new policy almost blanket endorsement.

Also, Lenin had strong support in the mansion from two important men: Nikolai Podvoisky and Vladimir Nevsky, who ran the newly created Bolshevik Military Organisation. They were in charge of party contacts within the regiments, the agitators and the Red Guards – those leather jacketed units of armed workers which had been set up in March with rifles they had got from the soldiers.

Podvoisky, at thirty-seven, was tall, bearded and fine looking, but unsmiling. Nevsky had an easier personality and was a brilliant orator, and skilled agitator. Podvoisky was the organisation man, sending out orders on little pink slips or calling the field leaders by phone. Nevsky was the spellbinder who, whenever there was trouble, would speed there by car to deploy his persuasive powers as a speaker.

They were militant, romantic revolutionaries. By mid-April, when Lenin arrived, they commanded only a few hundred agitators. The Red Guards were still being formed and trained.

The two men were at the sharp end of city hostility. Lenin sent for Podvoisky and told him that the daily Kadet processions must be answered. 'It's vital,' he said, as Podvoisky reported in *The Year 1917*, 'that you bring onto the streets some troops marching under Bolshevik slogans – even if it's only one company.'

In the current mood of the city, this would be difficult, but the First Machine Gun Regiment had been prominent in the February revolution and were close to the party. They responded, with only a few companies, backed up by some workers. But they marched under Bolshevik banners.

Also, Lenin was surprisingly willing, given his past caution, to take personal risks. When Nevsky flashed an alarm call to the *Pravda* office that the Ismailovskys – one of the regiments which had wreaked havoc in Moscow in 1905 – were in a dangerously angry mood on their parade ground, Lenin at once went to them.

'They'll tear you to pieces,' someone said as he left. But they didn't. Although at first he faced hostile shouts about Germany, he won them over. When he'd finished speaking – 'explaining', as he'd put it – he was carried triumphantly round the parade ground on the shoulders of two soldiers, as was to happen elsewhere at tense moments.

On 21 April, two weeks after Lenin's arrival, the Kadet campaign climaxed with a vivid and macabre march by thousands of the wounded from the city hospitals. Legless men hopping on crutches, men with stubs for arms, men in bandages with disfigured faces. They crawled along the Nevsky and the Liteiny toward the Tauride Palace, under the slogan 'War to the end. Our wounds demand victory!'

The Soviet was deeply concerned. *Izvestia* attacked 'the dark forces' that were exploiting Lenin. The day after the parade of the wounded, Milyukov publicly assured the Allied ambassadors that Russia had not been weakened by revolution. She was determined to fight on with her allies and he indicated that it would still be a full imperialist war, not the defensive war the Soviet had agreed to back.

Lenin, who had been linking the war to the bankers, was delighted. 'Fight,' he declared in *Pravda*, 'because we want the spoils. Die, tens of thousands of you, every day, because "we" … have not yet received our share of the loot!'

The masses rose, as Milyukov had planned, for now the Bolsheviks really could be blamed. But the Soviet leaders met the long processions as they streamed into the city centre and urged them to return home. The Soviet, they promised, would force the government to amend its policy. And the crowds did what was asked, but they were aching for action.

Late that night, however, the right-wing press published an outburst of abuse. Blaming the Bolsheviks for threatening civil war, they called onto the streets 'all who stand for Russia and her freedom' to support the government.

It was a challenge Lenin had to accept, though he knew its dangers. By the next night the Cossacks could well be charging. But, in the face of a huge Kadet parade under this slogan, following the workers' retreat of the previous day, he had no option. The party called out the crowds for an 'organised' demonstration.

Leaning on his military studies after 1905, Lenin ordered strict tactics. The Nevsky would be the focus. As one worker column marched down the Prospekt, others should be moving simultaneously along parallel streets on either side, forming a 'three pronged claw'. By this technique, they could block off attempts to attack those in the Nevsky from the cross streets.

Only workers were marching – there were no troops, for the Soviet had ordered them to remain in barracks, no matter who called them out. Indeed, when General Kornilov ordered guns into Mariinsky Square, the artillery men refused to comply.

The clashes were serious and many people were hurt. There was shooting on Sadovaya, but it was a civilian affair. Late that afternoon, the Soviet firmly stopped the crisis. The marchers were to return home. There were to be no street meetings for two days. And the Bolsheviks backed the call.

The Kadets claimed victory, but Milyukov and Kornilov had shot their bolt. Within two weeks both men had been forced to resign. The government was re-organised to include six members of the Soviet as ministers. Alexander Kerensky, appointed Minister for War, was the new rising star, which was interesting because, out of all the Russias, the two men who would be principal rivals in this ever-changing situation came from the same Volga River town of Simbirsk. Kerensky's teacher father had taught Lenin and was answerable to Lenin's father, who was the local Inspector of Schools.

Kerensky, a melodramatic but mesmeric lawyer who had won much support by his defence of strikers in 1912, headed a small party that worked with the Socialist Revolutionaries, but he was a patriot who wanted to win the war. And, brilliant speaker that he was, he set out now to mount an offensive that would smash its way through the German lines and tap the basic public affection for 'Mother Russia'.

Lenin – commanding a party that was noisy but still very small – built an army of agitators throughout the nation. 'Keep it simple,' he ordered. 'Speak only of bread, land and peace.' At the Kshesinskaya Mansion, orators spoke from the walls all day to crowds who gathered to listen to them. Even Lenin himself took his turn.

Meanwhile, deploying their new funds, the Bolsheviks launched forty-one newspapers and journals throughout the nation, twelve in local languages, including *Soldatskaya Pravda*, which urged the troops at the front to mutiny.

In Moscow, during these chaotic weeks, Inessa was active. As a representative of the Moscow Soviet she attended an All-Russian Women's conference – and staged a walk-out because, she insisted, working women could have nothing in common with bourgeois women.

She was elected to the Moscow Duma, with the help of women who now had the vote for the first time. She took an instructing role in a school for agitators, with its echoes of Longjumeau, as she had done in the underground movement in the city, way back in 1905. And in late June she was elected to the seven-person Executive Committee of the Moscow Soviet.

She wrote articles for *Zhizn' Rabotnitsy*, Moscow's sister paper to *Rabotnitsa*, which had been revived in St Petersburg, and, in one important piece, defended Lenin against the attacks portraying him as a German agent, which were soon to reach a new peak, less public but more serious.

The French Secret Service had produced what they claimed was proof of the German funding and there was other evidence of large sums of money being channelled through Alexander Helphand's company. In fact, Jacob Furstenberg, Lenin's friend, who managed it, was reported to be on his way to Russia. Kerensky ordered action to be delayed until Furstenberg could be held at the frontier.

Back in the capital, a new Congress of Soviets, from throughout Russia, was in progress, to take over the national central role, occupied until now on a temporary basis by the St Petersburg Soviet. Irakli Tseretelli, a leading Menshevik, was appealing for unity of all factions. 'Today,' he declared, 'Russia has no political party which would say: "Give us power." Go ... and we will take your place.'

A voice rang out from the back of the hall. 'There *is* such a party!' Lenin had stood up. 'It is the Bolshevik Party!'

The shocked silence was broken by a wave of laughter. To men from outside St Petersburg, the idea that the Bolsheviks – with only 105 voting delegates out of over 800 – could govern seemed absurd. Kerensky had answered him in a reasoned speech. Lenin walked out in the middle of it and the Soviet rejected all the important Bolshevik resolutions.

The city was seething and Podvoisky and Nevsky saw the picture in optimistic but starker terms. In a meeting at the mansion two days after Lenin's clash with Kerensky, they warned that they were under heavy pressure from many regiments in the garrison, now in danger of transfer to the front, to mount a demonstration against Kerensky's planned offensive. Two weeks earlier, Lenin had vetoed this since it was far too soon. Now, Podvoisky asked him to reconsider because some regiments were threatening to act on their own.

Lenin bought time, helped by the diversion of twenty-eight factories suddenly staged a strike, since this had to be subject to discussion. But eventually the Central Committee reluctantly authorised a 'peaceful' demonstration – to start on 18 June at 2 p.m. But his military commanders, certain he was wrong, were actually planning violence.

Only hours before the demonstration, the Congress of Soviets ordered the Bolsheviks to cancel it. How could Lenin refuse? 'Power to the Soviet' was his slogan. After much heated debate they did what the Soviet ordered, but would the troops and the masses obey the party? The result was impotent fury in the barracks and the factories. Nervously, the Soviet leaders decided to help by organising a demonstration of their own, open to all parties, to show the unity of 'Revolutionary Democracy'. Lenin and his leaders, but not his militants, heaved a sigh of relief. He could now mount his cancelled parade under the cover of official Soviet respectability.

18 June was a great day, with a clear blue sky and the sun glistening from the golden cupolas and spires of the city. Marchers from regiment after regiment, factory after factory, paraded past the saluting base at the Tomb of the Martyrs in the Field of Mars under red and gold Bolshevik banners,: 'All power to the Soviets! Down with the Ten Capitalist Ministers! Down with the War!' And as each contingent passed the tomb, they lowered their banners in tribute to the dead.

'Soldiers in drab and olive,' recorded an eyewitness, 'horsemen in blue and gold, white bloused sailors, black bloused workers, girls in varicoloured waists surging through the main arteries of the city. On each marcher a streamer, a flower, a ribbon of red, scarlet kerchiefs around the women's heads, red *rubashkas* on the men ...

'As this human river flowed, it sang ... the spontaneous outpouring of a people's soul. Someone would strike up a revolutionary hymn; the deep resonant voices of the soldiers would lift the refrain, joined by the plaintive voices of the working women; the hymn would rise, and fall and die away; then down the line it would burst forth again – the whole street singing in harmony.'[6]

That night, in the dining room of the Elizarov apartment on Shirokaya Street, the Central Committee and the two military commanders sat round a table. The day had been a great success but Podvoisky was grim. 'After this,' he said, 'the workers and soldiers will want to stage an uprising.'

Lenin feared he was right and insisted that Podvoisky curb them. 'At this stage, a rebellion would be doomed to defeat because there would be no support from the armies at the front or from the people in the provinces ... This must be explained ... Forces must be alerted for a decisive assault but the party will indicate the time ... '

That morning, Kerensky's offensive, which he was relying on to rally Russia and check the Bolshevik threat, had been launched. At first it had been successful, but then it began to falter. Although the news of the early advances had been greeted with rapture with Kadet parades, the Bolshevik leadership had not ordered any demonstrations in response. The attack had alarmed those troops still in the capital, who might well be ordered to the front at any time. They could not understand the need for delay in the Bolshevik takeover of power. Nor could the agitators from all over Russia who had been called to a meeting in the mansion. Nor could Podvoisky and Nevsky, their commanders. Lenin addressed them with the same old arguments. 'If we seize power,' he insisted, 'it is naive to think we would be able to hold it ... Events should not be anticipated. Time is on our side.'

They didn't believe him. The agitators said they were being used as 'fire hoses', damping down the embers of the enthusiasm for the party which they had ignited on previous orders. For once, Kamenev joined Lenin in urging patience but *Soldatskaya Pravda*, the party's own paper, came out in open challenge: 'Wake up, whoever is asleep!'

The mansion was burning with rebellion. Yet, rather oddly, Lenin chose this moment to leave St Petersburg for a holiday. On 29 June he arrived at the Bonch-Bruevichs' villa in Neyvola, on Finland's Karelian Isthmus. Four days later, he was called back. A revolution had started.

In fact, it had started on 1 July, when the First Machine Gunners had refused to obey orders to leave for the front. It was a spark which ignited a city that was waiting to explode. The troops and the workers took to the streets. The Central Committee tried to distance themselves from an uprising they hadn't ordered. Then they decided to take control, glad that Lenin was out of the city, which would make more credible their pleas of innocence. The only people in the higher levels in the mansion that were happy were Podvoisky and Nevsky who wanted the uprising, believing, despite Lenin's warning, that now was the time.

On his return, on 3 July Lenin watched glumly from his cab the marching troops and workers on all the roads they passed along. There was shooting on the streets, Cossack charges, and finally the

Izmailovsky Regiment marching to protect the Soviet when the whole event ran out of steam.

The next day, government forces surrounded the mansion and broke into the *Pravda* offices. Kerensky telegraphed orders from the front for the Bolshevik leaders to be arrested, planning to put Lenin on trial with the evidence they had collected, even though Furstenberg, sensing trouble, had turned back before he reached the frontier.

Lenin and Zinoviev escaped from the city in disguise, catching a train, with the help of a Bolshevik railway man, to a small station near Belo-ostrov, a border town, and hiding in a shack in the nearby woods. Then Lenin crossed the frontier, dressed as a stoker, riding in the engine driver's cab, while the genuine stoker moved into a carriage as a passenger. For a few days he stayed in a village called Jalkala, but then he headed for Helsinki to the home of a friend who just happened to be the city's police chief; then, knowing from experience it was always unwise to remain in one place, he moved on to other addresses. Meanwhile, Zinoviev returned to the capital where he stayed in hiding.

In Moscow, Inessa had been active. On 22 June, four days after the big Saturday parade in the capital, she urged, in the name of the Soviet Executive Commission, that mass demonstrations supporting 'All power to the Soviets' should be held in Moscow.[7] But times were changing. By mid-July all the party leaders had been arrested, except for Lenin and those in hiding.

There were no arrest orders out for Inessa, and she attended an illegal party conference in St Petersburg on 26 July, but made no speeches and had to witness the appointment of Alexandra Kollontai as the first woman to join the party's Central Committee, even though Alexandra herself was not present.

Inessa had never displayed great jealousy, even seeing Nadya, whom some women in her position might have resented, as a friend. However, she cannot have been pleased, given her own close contact with Lenin, to see this elevation of Kollontai. She hardly knew her, but she knew much about her, knew doubtless that she had exchanged a lot of letters with Lenin, especially after the war started;

she was in Norway, and had been the mistress of Alexander Shlyapnikov, a close ally of Lenin and the Central Committee member in charge of foreign communications.

Also, Kollontai had great style and a fine reputation as a speaker and writer, whereas not many people outside Lenin's immediate circle had ever heard of Inessa. The two women, different as they were in personality, were doomed to be rivals in post-revolutionary Russia but, in time, Inessa's moment would come.

For now Inessa returned south and retreated discreetly to Pushkino, where Andre was ill again with suspected TB.

By now Kerensky's offensive had clearly failed. On 19 July the Germans had counter-attacked and checked the Russian Army's advance.

In St Petersburg the Bolshevik press had been banned, its HQ taken over and its leaders indicted. And Kerensky was now also having trouble with the right. General Kornilov, whom Kerensky had appointed Commander-in-Chief of the Russian Army, became the central figure of a military coup, supported by all Lenin's old enemies, the officer hierarchy, Milyukov and his Kadets and, probably, the Allied governments.

They planned a dictatorship to liquidate the soviets, restore order to the country and discipline to the army. Almost certainly Kornilov allowed Riga to fall to the Germans to create the crisis climate for his coup. Then he telegraphed Kerensky demanding the transfer of all power to himself – and ordered his troops to advance on the capital.

Kerensky had no choice but to ask the Soviet for help and the Soviet had no choice but to turn to the Bolsheviks, the only party with a military organisation, frayed though this was by the events of July.

The Bolsheviks summoned the people of St Petersburg to defend their city. Once more, the Red Guards were issued with rifles. Once more, Podvoiksy and Nevsky moved onto centre stage. The railway men took up the tracks which stopped the advancing troop trains. Kornilov's communications were broken by the telegraph operators. Bolshevik agitators, now acting for the Soviet, were despatched to his troops to explain how they were being used by the counter-revolution. On 1 September Kornilov was arrested.

The army reacted violently against the entire officer corps. Throughout Russia many were murdered. Kornilov's coup gave a new dynamic to a gigantic movement that was already swinging back to the Bolsheviks. Within a week the party had gained voting control of the Petersburg Soviet and Trotsky had replaced Chkheidze as its President.

To Lenin, in Helsinki, conditions seemed now ideal for the party to stage an uprising, but the pendulum could swing again to reaction, so he saw speed as essential. But the party leaders were more cautious than they had ever been before. Even the left-wingers were not demanding militancy after their savaging in July. Compromise with other parties was once more the mood of the day.

Lenin flew into one his old 'rages'. 'You will be traitors and scoundrels,' he wrote to the Central Committee. If they did not take immediate militant action and 'arrest all the scum', meaning Kerensky and the ministers, they would 'face dire punishment'.

The leaders were tolerant. Lenin had become temporarily unstable. The embarrassing letter was formally burned. When Lenin informed them he was returning, they ordered him not to. So he organised it himself with his old friend the Helsinki police chief and Hugo Yalava, the engine driver who had brought him into exile during July.

On 10 October, in an apartment overlooking the Karpovka River in Old Petersburg, Lenin called a meeting of the twelve members of the Central Committee, demanding an uprising before another All-Russian Congress of Soviets that had been called for two weeks later. It took him ten hours, and even then the old 'Troika' comrades of his exile, Kamenev and Zinoviev, opposed him, even pleading their case in print in their certainty that success could now be gained by constitutional methods.

But Lenin had won the issue by a big majority. Trotsky organised the rising, with the aid of the two military commanders who had brought disaster in July. They did not make the deadline, though the Congress of Soviets was still sitting. Kerensky was already taking defensive measures. The bridges over the Neva were raised and government relief forces were on their way into the city when at 2 a.m. on 24 October, Trotsky launched his operation.

Units of soldiers and workers, under MRC (Military Revolutionary Committee, run by Podvoisky and Nevsky) commissars, took control of the railway stations, the electricity plants, the waterworks, the state bank and the food warehouses. Already they had control of the telephone exchange and the telegraph office. The phones of the Winter Palace had been disconnected.

One by one, the bridges were captured with little fighting. The defending troops just surrendered. The cruiser *Aurora* moved up the river within gunshot of the Winter Palace where Kerensky and his ministers were meeting. He tried to organise a counter-attack, but even the Cossacks played for time. 'We are saddling our horses.'

Soon after daylight on 25 October, Kerensky drove out of the city to Pskov to meet the troops and Cossacks called back from the front.

But his ministers remained. The attack on the Winter Palace, under the command of Podvoisky, having been delayed for twenty-four hours, was met with little resistance.

In the Congress of Soviets there was much argument, especially from the Mensheviks and the SRs. The Bolsheviks were labelled 'political hypocrites'. Julius Martov, Lenin's partner of his youth, declared that 'Civil war is beginning ... The question of power is being settled by means of a military plot ... Comrades, we must put a stop to bloodshed.' And Trotsky ordered him, in his famous phrase, to 'Go where you belong from now on – the dustbin of history.'

At 8.30 p.m. Lenin rose and went to the podium, 'gripping the edge of the reading stand,' as John Reed reported in *Ten Days That Shook The World*, 'letting his little winking eyes travel over the crowd as he stood there waiting, apparently oblivious to the long-rolling ovation.' Then, when he could make himself heard, he declared: 'We shall now proceed to construct the socialist order.'

After he had spelled out his vision of revolution spreading through the workers of Europe, Kamenev, in the chair, stood up and asked all in favour of the proclamation to hold up their cards.

'Suddenly,' Reed recorded, 'we found ourselves on our feet,

mumbling together into the smooth lifting unison of the *Internationale* … The immense sound rolled through the hall, burst windows and doors and soared into the quiet sky … '

TWELVE

Moscow 1917

In Moscow, the coup was not so easily accomplished. 'The shooting began last night at midnight ... ,' Yury Gautier, who had known Inessa in her Pushkino days, wrote in his diary. 'They [Kerensky's troops] took the Kremlin this morning. Right now they are fighting in the centre of the city north west of the Kremlin and on the outskirts of town ... The impressions are strongly reminiscent of 1905.'[1]

Gautier was a professor and bitterly opposed to Lenin. 'We spent our time on the telephone,' he wrote of it the next day. 'Occasional shots could be heard on Prechistenka and in the side streets. There are all kinds of contradictory rumours. The telephone is our only contact with the world.

'There was an inspection of the attics in our building. Among the officer-volunteers were Fedor and Andryusha Armand [a cousin]; Fedor is making amends for his Bolshevik mama. We treated them to lunch.'[2] Fedor was in the army and had absorbed cadet school politics, at sharp variance to those of Inessa. Right-leaning views were not too healthy to have in the new order – as he was to discover.

Three days later Gautier recorded: 'The situation is getting worse. Regular firing on the centre from the outskirts has begun ... The Bolsheviks have artillery and people who know how to shoot ... '

The fighting went on for some ten days. A grenade dropped into the courtyard of Gautier's home exploded and broke the windows. It wounded a cook, and a tenant in the block. 'There is no news from the outside world ... The new regime is publishing decrees ... Apparently the victors are routing the Kadets, locking them up in prison [with] taunts from the barbarised soldiers ... The situation in Moscow is reminiscent of Rome under Marius or Sulla ... Rumours proliferate … Minsk, Dvinsk and Reval have been taken … [Generals] Kornilov and Kaledin are surrounding Moscow. Where is the truth? It seems that we are approaching the final catastrophe. The banks are closed … apparently everyone who can is quitting Moscow … '³

The resistance ended finally, which would have relieved an anxious Inessa in her apartment in the Arbat. At last it had been justified, all that planning and dividing that she had helped Lenin develop in exile as he rigidly carved out his tight, disciplined Bolshevik party; all the intense, studied opposition he'd maintained to those who had disagreed with him.

It was a glimpse of a dream that had materialised. Possibly. She knew that for all the triumph at the Congress of Soviets or the peace now established in Moscow, the Bolshevik success was fragile. Danger came from several directions – ranging from the Socialist Revolutionaries, because they were so big and deeply rooted, but also from the Mensheviks and other Social Democrats who wanted elected multi-party government; from Kerensky and the generals; from the German armies; and ultimately from the civil war that would soon break out around the disaffected officers, supported by many Cossacks and other dissidents, including peasant forces; and, in time, from the Allies. Even the right-wing Bolsheviks who gathered round Kamenev were opposing what they realised was Lenin's plan for dictatorship.

And overriding everything, now with the winter upon them, was the spectre of famine, aggravated by the transport chaos, which made Lenin suspect the kulaks, the more prominent peasants, of hoarding grain. But there was nothing new about food shortages and the kulaks had no control of the railway lines. Lenin needed no reminding that the spark which had started the February revolution had come from the queues for bread – which was why it had been one of the three promises, along with peace and land, offered by his agitators.

But Inessa was confident that the revolution she had worked for from her earliest days with Volodya Armand, even if its practical form had always been rather misty, was now on course.

Much of what we know about Inessa at this time was subject to later party control, and she presented a difficulty for them. The fact that Lenin had a warm friendship with a woman, that was not entirely appropriate and subject to rumour, did not sit easily with the image of the nation's leader. Yet Lenin's group of exiles, of which she was so prominent a member, were seen as almost heroic, which gave her a high ranking in the party mythology. So, while in time Lenin was given iconic status, any written treatment of Inessa required a dangerous delicacy.

Within two weeks of the takeover of power, she was back in St Petersburg with an unusual target – the peasants, who formed so large a proportion of the Russian population.

She was there primarily, on behalf of the Moscow Soviet, to attend the Congress of Peasant Deputies. The Congress was dominated by the SRs, being the party of the peasants, as the Bolsheviks were the party of the workers. Inessa made one of her dramatic walk-outs with most of the Bolsheviks, which always caused a stir, even made a point, but had little impact on the voting pattern.[4]

Far more significant was her assignment by the Bolshevik Central Committee to work on peasant matters for two months, with a pass, issued on Lenin's orders, to attend meetings of the Council of People's Commissars, Lenin's inner cabinet.[5] She was clearly chosen by Lenin, supported probably by those commissars she had known in exile. It underlines his high opinion of her but also indicates how important the peasants were now seen to be.

As has been seen, Lenin – like Marx – had expected revolution to break out through the workers in industrially advanced countries. But Russia had a huge number of peasants. The fact that Russia had become the starting point of the new social order had not exactly caught the Bolsheviks on the wrong foot, but it did not conform with the party's philosophy nor its long-term planning.

The SR Party, with whom the Bolsheviks had often co-operated, had now become a major rival. It was well entrenched with some seventy per cent of the nation behind it. What's more, its romantic, if violent background, and its inheritance of the image of the old terrorist martyrs, gave it a defining cachet.

This all came to a climax when the Constituent Assembly, an

elected All-Russian Parliament planned in mid-1917 by Kerensky, met for the first time in January 1918. Thirty-eight per cent of the delegates elected were SRs while only twenty-four per cent were Bolsheviks. Lenin decided he could manage without such a body and closed it down, to cries of alarm, even from within his own party, since the assembly could have been a truly democratic base. Lenin shrugged off the protests. The power would now rest within his party, which is where he wanted it.

Meanwhile the peasants remained a great issue, being crucial to the whole question of land, another of the three Bolshevik rallying cries. Inessa was a curious choice to help handle it, for what could she know about the intricacies of peasant lives, apart from what she'd learned as the young wife of a rich landlord? Perhaps not that much, though even as a young wife she had been shocked by the conditions in which they lived. More important was that she was a person on whom Lenin could rely.

These were crucial days. Lenin was using a broad sword – and using it wildly – making laws by a series of decrees, 'meaningless decrees,' as Maxim Gorky, the people's writer and Lenin's friend, was to observe, 'written with a fork on water.'[6]

One of the first decrees was about land, the ownership of which was to be abolished, though how was rather vague. 'The peasantry,' wrote Robert Service, 'was invoked to take collective action to seize … all land not currently owned by peasants.' It was a war on the wealthy and the bourgeois, whom Lenin had hated ever since the hanging of his brother Alexander had made pariahs of his family in Simbirsk.

What was not vague was the absorption of the MRO (Military Revolutionary Organisation), the Bolsheviks' military force, still directed by Podvoisky, into a new secret police, the Cheka, which was to become far more ruthless, indiscriminate and all-embracing than the Okhrana had ever been.

The nature of the new society soon became horrifyingly plain. The people were urged to destroy and even to kill the wealthy and the middle class, to strip them of their possessions – the 'looting of the looters', wealth being seen as theft – justified by Lenin as a natural need for revenge. The management of companies, like those owned by the Armands, was to be controlled by workers' committees. The holding of shares and bonds was forbidden. Banks were nationalised and 1,000 roubles was the maximum withdrawal permitted, soon to be made worthless by soaring inflation. Jewellery, foreign currency, and valuables were confiscated.[7]

The local soviets started to impose their own taxes on bourgeois families at levels they could not possibly afford, and then they would take a son or a father as 'hostage' under the threat of death or a labour camp, sometimes for the entire family, if the levy was not paid. The sharing of living space in bourgeois homes was introduced and controlled by vigilant 'housing committees' who sometimes urged servants and their friends to take over the best rooms, leaving their old quarters to their one-time employers.

Black marketeers were to be shot on the spot. But who exactly did this order cover? The black market was a fact of of almost everyone's life. Lynch mobs were encouraged and in time were institutionalised with people's courts and revolutionary tribunals, rich in echoes of the French Revolution. The judges, usually with no legal background, were elected by local people. Many old scores were settled. Hundreds of thousands, perhaps millions, of innocent people were condemned to labour camps and often to death.

In the army, officers were subject to election by their soldiers. Officers suspected of Tsarist loyalties, it was ordered, should be arrested, with their wives and families, until local authorities were satisfied that each was a 'compliant hero'. Should any Army Commissar report adversely they would be returned to prison or hard labour.

Armed gangs roamed the country under the pretence of this political cover and fought for their spoils with other armed gangs. It was mayhem and Lenin delighted in it. He saw it as 'cleansing'. What emerged would be strong, a Darwinian survival of the fittest.

Maxim Gorky continued to condemn it. 'Lenin and Trotsky,' he wrote, 'are forcing the working class to organise bloody butcheries, pogroms, arrests of people who are not guilty of anything.' By destroying press freedom 'they are legalising their own suppression.'

179

Later he was to despair that 'we are breeding a new crop of brutal and corrupt bureaucrats and a terrible new generation of youth who are learning to laugh at daily bloody scenes of beatings, shootings, cripplings, lynchings.'

Lenin had closed down the opposition press in October but he allowed *Novaya Zhizn*, Gorky's newspaper, to continue publishing for a while and the writer did not let up. He described people dropping dead from starvation in the street and went to the zoo, where the animals were dying from hunger. No one had even thought to shoot them.

By August 1918, Lenin was stepping up the terror. Responding to insurrection in five kulak districts he demanded: 'Hang, in full view of the people, no fewer than one hundred kulaks, rich men, bloodsuckers. Do it in such a fashion that … people might see, tremble, know, shout: they are strangling and will strangle to death the bloodsucking kulaks … Telegraph implementation. Find some truly hard people [to do it].'[8]

'In every grain growing district,' he ruled later, convinced that prosperous peasants were hoarding, 'twenty-five to thirty rich hostages should be taken who will answer with their lives for the collection and loading of all surpluses.'

It was a holy war, waged with terror but little logic beyond the destruction of the bourgeoisie, which in fact ran the country. The heads of the civil service had been arrested early, their places being taken by ambitious, and often unscrupulous, juniors. Lenin conceded that middle class 'specialists' might be needed until ordinary 'workers' could be trained to take their place, but within months he was forced by practicalities to change his mind – to the despair of the visionary left of the party, including Inessa.

Lenin's object, written during one of his breaks at Halila in Finland just after taking power, was clear and admirable: namely 'that everyone should have bread, sturdy footwear, decent clothing, a warm dwelling – and should work conscientiously.' It was his method that was so chillingly dubious.[9]

Against so large and multi-faceted a canvas, Lenin's complex relationship with Inessa must be put into perspective. She was still in love with him, and always would be, as she was to confirm in writing only days before she died. That he still loved her too, in his way, was also in time to be vividly demonstrated.

The two of them were also bound by a faith in a personal vision of a common cause, shared for years, which was coming to fruition – though whether Inessa had realised in those exile days quite what Lenin would unleash in terms of barbarity, terror, massacre, injustice, total restriction on freedom, in a nation with now no real rule of law, is uncertain.

But when it happened, Inessa seemed to accept without question that everything Lenin ordered was necessary. As she wrote with bated breath to Inna, who was in Astrakhan with the Red Army in September 1918, 'The masses understand how dear he [Lenin] is to us and how indispensable he is to the revolution. More than ever,' she emphasised, 'we understand how important he is for our cause.'[10] And this was just after the savagely crude murder of the Tsar, his wife, daughters, invalid son, his servants and his doctor – as well as six other royal relations who were held elsewhere.

Izvestia announced only the death of the Tsar, but the whole truth would have been known in the upper echelons of the party and had probably reached Inessa. Interestingly, her old friend Georgi Safarov had been one of the three signatories to the order, though it had been initiated at the highest level. Still, perhaps she considered that this had been necessary for the greater good. Certainly, any of the Romanovs, if left alive, would have been a rallying point; and enemy forces had actually been at the gates of the Ekaterinburg, where the royal family was held.

There is, of course, a history of women loving men who do terrible things, though Lenin was operating on a massive scale. Even so, he had found Inessa positioned against him, with many others, on an issue that was an immense threat in the months following October, 1917: how to deal with the German army that was breathing down his neck.

For the Germans, their policy of 'revolutionising', of funding Lenin, had worked quite brilliantly. The collapse of the Russian Army was almost complete, in part because of Bolshevik-provoked mutiny, but now because the land decree had sent many more dashing for home to claim their share.

Nothing stood in the way of the Germans' easy conquest. They could write their own peace terms, and they did, shocking the Russians at the peace conference held in January, 1918 at the frontier town of Brest-Litovsk, for these called for the handover of a huge amount of territory containing one third of the Russian population, one third of its cultivated land and one half of its industry. They also demanded a payment of 120 million gold roubles, far more in value than the funds they had contributed to the Bolshevik cause.

Lenin was aghast but urged acceptance, only to be fiercely opposed by Bukharin, one of the most revered of the leaders, who was convinced the revolution would quickly spread into Germany making agreement unnecessary. He had a big majority of the committee behind him, supporting what was truly a fantasy.

The Germans, though, with their eyes on the Americans, were in no mood for delay. On 9 February, 1918, the Kaiser ordered a new attack and in five days the Germans gained more territory than they had won in three years of war. Now their army was advancing on St Petersburg.

Lenin called a large meeting of party leaders and begged them to agree the German terms, arguing that if the revolution did travel as they all hoped, they could rewrite the treaty later. Meanwhile, to not sign was like a pet 'lying down with a tiger'.[11] For him, the danger of military defeat by the Germans was enormous. It would doom his revolution and rob him of the tenuous power he had won. A peace treaty, even as humiliating as this, could save him.

Bukharin was adamant in his opposition. However, he lost and Lenin gained a very slender majority of one in the Central Committee, with four members abstaining, so the Russians signed the humiliating treaty. But the response of the horrified soviets throughout the nation was violent, especially from the left wing of the SRs, who had moved closer to Inessa and the leftist Bolsheviks on this issue.

Inessa was on the executive of the Moscow Soviet – which was important, being the old capital with a vast population – and insisted vehemently that they should *not* ratify the treaty.[12] Like others, she just could not believe that Europe would not grasp at the chance of glorious revolution.

Crisis came much later in July when an SR zealot, with much support in the party, murdered the German ambassador, Wilhelm von Mirbach, in the hope that this would incite the Germans to attack again. An anxious, angry Lenin ordered the arrest of the leftist SR leaders and apologised to the Germans in person. The issue was soon to become academic. Germany lost the war in the West and Lenin annulled the treaty. Meanwhile, the arrested SRs were sent to labour camps and one was executed.

Since Inessa had placed herself firmly with the left over the signing of the peace treaty, it is tempting to wonder if she'd sailed a bit too close to the wind. But, with Lenin, she knew precisely how far she could go and she took what might seem a wise precaution: she would never, she said at the time, support a split in the Bolshevik Party. She was, of course, highly familiar with party splits.

In March, 1918, Lenin had moved the government to Moscow, mainly because of the German threat to St Petersburg. The National Hotel was taken over to house government functionaries and Inessa moved there too. Quite why she left the apartment in Denezhnyi Lane is not certain. Perhaps, with Lenin now in Moscow, she wanted to be closer to the action.

Meanwhile, the Armands, once liberal employers, did not escape what their children and the people they'd married had helped to bring about. Gangs roamed through the territory. In one of the Armand homes, probably Alyoshino not far from Eldigino, Alexander was present when looters swept through the property. He saw one man readying to smash a beautiful old mirror and said: 'For God's sake if you want it, take it. But don't break it.'[13]

An elderly couple, probably Emil, Alexander's uncle, and his wife went to register the family property, as required, with the Moscow Regional Party Committee. In the city this consisted of four houses and a factory. On their return to Trubnikovsky Lane, where they had a city home, they found the locks had been changed. They were not allowed access even to their clothes or personal possessions.[14]

Inessa still saw something of Alexander. In fact, he stayed in Denezhnyi Lane when he was in Moscow. She had persuaded the Bolshevik Party to accept him as a member, which was an honour in itself, but would also give him what was now much-needed protection. He was a dubious choice for them, being both bourgeois and wealthy, but she argued that he was a 'natural' communist and she did, of course, have influence.

But Alexander declined the offer. He believed he would be conspicuous in party circles, which would render him more vulnerable, not less so. He was also, possibly again with Inessa's influence, invited to continue running the Armand factories in Pushkino, but he turned this down, for much the same reason. To him, a low profile seemed highly advisable.[15]

Inessa had a more receptive response from Inna, who was doing political work with the Red Army in Astrakhan. 'Your absence weighs heavily on me,' Inessa wrote to her in September, 1918, 'but I rejoice at your enthusiasm for the cause. I have been wanting to tell you this for a long time.' Inessa was missing her daughter badly. 'I not only think about you every day, my darling, but several times a day. I long for you. For me, you are not only my daughter, but also a very dear friend,'[16] as well as being now a fellow revolutionary.

The older Armands continued to live in the main complex at Pushkino for a while. Yury Gautier visited Pushkino a few months later. 'God, what horror in Pushkino,' he recorded. 'In the garden they are cutting down the trees for firewood and calves are grazing in the flower beds. The old folks are immobilised in anticipation of death, which has already overtaken half of them.'[17]

Inessa, according to family lore, used to escape sometimes from Moscow to Eldigino, her bridal home, to work. It was while she was there, so one story has it, that David Armand, Emil's grandson, then aged twelve, went to see her with a letter from his mother. Family 'hostages' had been taken, believed to be relatives of his mother, Lidiya Maryanovna. Could Inessa help with their release?

David is said to have reported that she took the letter but dismissed him abruptly and the hostages were not released. This seems out of character for Inessa and could reflect the resentment towards her from some members of what was a very large family. Certainly it is not mentioned in David's own unpublished autobiography, written as an adult – but also written under a Communist government and requiring caution.

No one was sure about the changing attitudes to Inessa, even long after she was dead. One Armand family, who interestingly still had servants, maintained a rule that she was never to be mentioned in front of them except in French. This was not a totally new experience. Even before the revolution – when Inessa was wanted by the Tsar's Okhrana – the children were told not to talk about her in front of the staff.

Eldigino followed Pushkino into state ownership in due course. But Alyoshino, the family's third home, about ten miles from Pushkino, was to remain in Armand hands throughout the whole period of Communist rule and after it – a result, so some of the family have suggested, of Nadya's intervention, which effectively, of course, meant Lenin's. At the end of 1918, as Inessa reported to Inna, Alexander had given up the Moscow flat and was working to repair an old mill near Alyoshino. He understood machinery, having run the family factories.

In time, he was to become a brilliant jobbing mechanic, working on what had previously been Armand lands, with the agreement, necessary under the collective system, of his former workers. Given the way so many employees in Russia at that time were motivated by hatred and revenge, this said much for the family.

Inevitably, Inessa had become distanced from the Armands. 'Grandmama and Grandpapa are well,' she wrote to Inna, 'but I haven't seen them for a long time. You know why. It saddens me because I am very fond of them, but there is nothing I can do. It's the way things are. I haven't seen Renee or your other grandmother for a long time either'[18]

Those words, which tell a bleak story, were written in December, 1918, when civil war was raging. This truly concerned her, it seems, though there was a note of resignation. It is unclear whether this parting was the wish of the older Armands, whose life had been devastated by Lenin, or of Inessa herself, embarrassed by her bourgeois background in a proletarian revolution. Most of her prominent comrades were also middle class and many of them tried to conceal this. It is doubtful if Inessa would have done this, even without her close connection with a bourgeois head of state, though the party propagandists tended to represent even his background in more acceptable form.

The extreme distress of the Armands cannot have been eased by Anna, their eldest child, who had also followed Lenin and was still close to Inessa, or by several of their other children who had sympathised with the revolution – though the question remains: Did they realise what they were supporting until it was too late? Had they been absorbed by the drama and the hope on the horizon that so gripped Inessa?

During the autumn and early winter of 1918, Inessa wrote several letters to Inna in Astrakhan, reflecting the immense changes in society. Varya had got into an arts and crafts school, where the pupils chose their teachers. Andre was about to go to a new model school – strangely, a boarding school of which his mother disapproved – where, again, the pupils selected their teachers.

Fedor was serving on a war committee, though he would soon join the Red Army as a pilot-observer, presumably having concealed his political views, though these were soon to put him in danger of a firing squad. Her son Sasha, despite being in the Red Army, was leaving for Mogilev Province to do enlightenment work in schools.[19]

Inessa was still living in the National Hotel. In one letter to Inna, beginning 'Sweet Inochka, sweet little girl, sweet little sister,' she explains that 'Varya and I are sharing the same room … It is a bit of squash but we are not too bothered. Varya sleeps curled up on the divan. Every day she works [as an artist], favouring landscapes, drawing with chalk and sculpture. She has done a head I like, but Varya [herself] doesn't.

'[In Varya's school] they enjoy the greatest freedom … At present, they only do drawing, but soon they will have "conferences" [in lieu of lessons?]. There is a workshop without staff. In fact, they do not have a teacher at the moment because they cannot choose one (Varya says that is slander!).

'There is another event. I hesitate to admit it, but Varya says: Go on, go on. I confess. I've had my hair cut. It is Varya who, with her own hands, has committed this crime, assuring me she got a sense of achievement in her heroic act. What a cheeky girl, don't you think? Fidya asks if I have gone mad.'[20]

At this time, Inessa was under heavy pressure. One of her many assignments was helping to organise an All-Russian Workers Congress. 'Oh, make sure *you* get sent here [presumably as a delegate],' she pleads with Inna. 'It will allow us to spend a little while together.'

She was soon back writing of 'internationalist' politics. In Germany the revolution was 'striding along'. Mutiny had broken out in the German and Austrian armies. They were killing their officers and declaring themselves Bolsheviks. At Kharkov, 40,000 German troops had entered the town carrying red flags, shouting 'Down with Wilhelm and the War.'

'You have probably read Lenin's [public] letter of 3 October and the Resolution of the Central Committee. I think these events are extremely important. Soviet Russia will become the cradle of the proletariat of the entire world. ... '[21]

This was true Inessa. Lenin's public letter declared that Germany was in the throes of a political crisis. 'It will inevitably lead to the transfer of power to the German people who are struggling for their liberation.' He saw it as an opportunity to create the 'proletarian Red Army' – i.e. a European or even a global class army in a new world where 'the worker has no fatherland.'

He was wrong. The main German socialist parties, horrified by what was going on in Russia, favoured the more democratic Menshevik-style philosophies, and failed to support the famous Spartacist uprising. This was put down sharply in 1919, the leaders Rosa Luxemburg and Karl Liebknecht being brutally killed as they were led to jail. Attempted risings in Austria and Hungary were also put down.

It was an end to hazy, romantic ideas about a proletarian army. Germany would swing to fascism and yet another world war. And, though the concept was not yet spoken of, 'socialism in one country' was what lay ahead for Russia. By then, the party would have changed its name becoming, in only a few months, the Communist Party.

In another letter, Inessa was back to domestic news. 'Papa ... has moved to Alyoshino once and for all. He is looking for an engine for his mill and I think he has found it.

'We no longer have the apartment at Denezhnyi Lane. Now Aunt Anna, Abram, Elena and Katya live there. [So it is still clearly in Armand hands.] The four of them live where all eleven used to live. In fact, Papa has reserved a room there for himself for when he stays in Moscow.' Presumably they escaped the Buildings Committee. Andre was also sleeping in the flat, his model school having not yet opened.

There was a PS from Varya in her own hand: 'I will also write to you a lot of stupidities, but not in such a pretty style as Mama's.'[22]

By December Inessa was writing to Inna about Varya's 'passion for you know whom. I don't think he is suitable for her. I can always talk about it to Varya, but I must do it calmly and not rush it.'[23] What had happened, it has to be wondered, to the independence she urged on Inna from exile when she, too, had been anxious about falling for a man her mother might not like?

By then Inessa's relations with Lenin had changed again, this time dramatically and, so far as she was concerned, very much for the better.

THIRTEEN
Moscow 1918

On Saturday, 30 August, Lenin addressed a crowd of workers at the Michelson plant on the far side of the Moscow River.[1] That day, news had come in that Mikhail Uritsky, head of the St Petersburg Cheka, had been killed by a Social Revolutionary assassin. Maria, Lenin's sister, and the family had pleaded with Lenin to call off his visit, but he had refused.

He ended his speech by declaring: 'For us there is one alternative – victory or death.' He was leaving the building as two SRs approached through the crowd – a man named Novikov and a girl, Fannie Kaplan. As they got near to him, Novikov pushed several workers aside to clear Kaplan's view of Lenin. She drew a revolver and fired three shots at him. Lenin fell to the ground. Only two bullets hit him, both in the left shoulder, but one had penetrated his chest cavity and damaged his lung, causing haemorrhaging into the pleura.

Lenin was rushed to his car. Stepan Gill, his chauffeur, drove him at top speed to the Kremlin, guessing this would be safer than a hospital, where other assassins could be waiting. On arrival, Lenin refused help, put on his jacket and climbed the stairs to the third floor. Maria opened the door and Lenin said, 'I've been slightly wounded, just in the arm.' His personal physician dressed his wounds. By that night, several specialists had examined him and decided that his heart function had returned to normal.

By then, Fannie Kaplan had been interrogated in the Cheka HQ in Lubianka Square. She had a background as an anarchist and had been sentenced under the Tsar to 'eternal hard labour', spending years in hard-labour prison camps. She insisted that, although she was a member of the SR Party, she had been acting on her own behalf. 'I regard him [Lenin] as a traitor. The longer he lives, the further he'll push back the idea of socialism. For dozens of years.'

There were rumours of a conspiracy, suggestions that Fannie Kaplan herself had not fired the shot but had merely agreed to take the blame. Stepan Gill, the chauffeur, said he had only seen the revolver – not the killer – but in a woman's hand, attracting theories that another woman did the shooting, and there were suggestions that Kaplan's sight was so bad she was almost blind. The revolver that was eventually handed in did not match the bullet cases on the ground – of which there were four although only three shots had been heard.

In the climate of the times, justice was carried out swiftly, in secrecy. The Kremlin Commandant, Paul Malkov, was ordered by Sverdlov to shoot Kaplan himself, in a garage with a car engine running to muffle the noise, the body to be destroyed without trace.[2]

Lenin was confined to bed for a couple of weeks but, according to his doctors, he would have been dead if the bullet had been a millimetre off its route through his neck to his shoulder, which, perhaps, caused him to contemplate his life.

Among the first people he sent for was Inessa, who visited him at once with her daughter, Varya. Nadya took the girl off to look at some old family photographs, leaving her mother alone with the man who had become such a major figure in her life.[3]

Both Lenin and Inessa found the visit rewarding. 'We have been very shaken by the attempt on Lenin's life,' Inessa wrote to Inna. 'This event has re-united us and brought us even closer. It has had much influence on the masses ... The meetings are better attended ... especially in Peter, which is always the first [area] to react.

'I await your letter. I am writing to you from my bed in the middle of the night.'[4]

For Inessa the renewed closeness led to advantages, too. A request from Lenin to Paul Malkov, who had despatched Fannie Kaplan, got her an apartment near the Kremlin in Neglinnaya Street (now Manege Street). When a new closed-circuit telephone system was set up in Moscow so that the party leaders and officials could communicate directly with the Kremlin without using an operator, Inessa's new apartment was one of those connected up to the system.[5]

When Inna returned to Moscow from Afghanistan, she called at the Kremlin with some young friends and asked boldly to see Lenin. The guard on the gate turned her away, so she went home and phoned him on her mother's private line. On being asked who was calling she had replied: 'Inessa Armand' and was quickly connected. Lenin took the call, but knew at once that it was not Inessa's voice. 'Who is this?' he asked. 'Inessa Little,' she answered using a nickname he had given her in exile. He'd laughed. 'Little but shrewd.' But he didn't have time to receive her and her friends.

Following the assassination attempt, Nadya began to behave strangely.[6] She had tolerated the Inessa relationship since Lenin had asked Nadya to stay with him as his wife. She appeared to like Inessa, praising her in her *Memories Of Lenin* and, after her death, editing a volume of favourable reminiscences by other people. Also, they had much ground in common – the party they had both helped to shape, and a campaigning feminism.

Inessa liked Nadya too, as she had spelt out in the long letter she had written to Lenin from Paris in January, 1914, after their first big parting. Inessa could be suspect because she seemed to be urging a *ménage à trois*, but never in her letters to anyone is there any hint of the spite that mistresses sometimes show towards wives.

Lenin was urged by his doctors to convalesce and he chose a mansion in the village of Gorki, twenty-two miles south of Moscow, from which he continued to control the running of the country. But Nadya did not go with him. When he eventually returned to the Kremlin, she left almost immediately for Sokolniki Park in the north east of Moscow, choosing to stay at a school, where she was given a small room on the first floor. Still suffering from Graves' disease, Nadya needed regular visits from the doctors, who could so much more easily have attended her in the Kremlin. She had distanced herself from her husband at a time when a wife would normally stay at her husband's side. It seemed to be a silent protest.

She had been sidelined ever since she had arrived in Russia. Before the October coup, she had been made to feel uncomfortable in the

Kshesinskya Mansion. After the October revolution, she had been appointed Deputy Commissar of Enlightenment, which hardly ranked prominently in the new hierarchy.

Until the attempt on Lenin's life, Inessa may not have seemed to be a continuing threat. Her relationship with Lenin appeared to have stabilised on a platonic level and, though they were fond of one another, they had even grown distant under the pressures of his position.

But suddenly, when he had so nearly died, there was Inessa back at his bedside – and clearly, since no one could get access to him without his orders, it was at his own instigation. Inessa's large new apartment, though it was not to be available for several weeks, was just outside the Kremlin walls – leading to rumours that she was living in the Kremlin itself – and this could have done nothing to alleviate the fears of a wife. Maybe it was the last straw for Nadya. Resentment was certainly understandable.

Lenin, however, seems to have ignored it. He travelled out to Sokolniki Park often to see Nadya – usually in the evening after he had finished work. Legend has it in certain Armand circles that once again Nadya had offered to leave him and once again he had refused. It sounds possible but is unlikely and unconfirmed.

By now, even without Lenin's direct assistance, Inessa had made progress within the party. She held the chair of the important Moscow Economic Council, the most prominent of thirty-eight similar councils throughout Russia. She co-edited a French language journal published in Russia, *La IIIe Internationale*, and was prominent in a feminist group, as well as being on the executive of the Moscow Soviet, of which she was a voting delegate at the All-Russian Congress. 'Truly I am overworked,' she told Inna.

Her position in the political hierarchy is clearly demonstrated in the Moscow diary of Yury Gautier, the academic from the French community, who had met Fedor in October, 1917. Members of the Gautier family had come under unlikely suspicion of involvement with a railway explosion and questions were being asked about both Yury and his brother. The university was hostile to the new regime – especially since a new decree allowed anyone of either sex over sixteen to enrol in it – but blowing up railway tracks was not the way its academics would normally show their disagreement.

'Truly,' he wrote in his diary, 'you don't know what affair blind fate will entangle you in ... In my search for any means [of help] I ran into Fedor Armand yesterday, who proposed that I turn to the famous Comrade Inessa, his mother, and my childhood friend. ... Today I got from her a billet d'introduction to the Commissar of the Military District, Muralov: "Respected Comrade. I beg of you to receive my acquaintance, Yury Vladimirovich Gautier. I will be grateful to you. Inessa Armand."'[7]

Her wish was enough, as she knew it would be. It was an indication of the power she could deploy. Everyone in authority knew her role in the life of Lenin. Gautier does not mention the matter again but he continued writing his diary of life in Moscow for another four years, so the pressure had clearly eased.

Shortly after her help for Gautier, Inessa found herself once more ranged with her comrades of the left against Lenin, despite the new dynamic of their relationship.

Lenin had realised that worker control in factories was not proving successful. He promoted the idea of labour discipline – i.e. production efficiency – and shocked Inessa and Bukharin's Baugy Group. To the left, the idea that workers would not strive their hardest now that they were working for the people was anathema.

Lenin, though, was facing the facts in front of him. Indeed, the first thing many workers' committees had done was to vote themselves huge wage increases. And reluctantly, Lenin did the unthinkable. He ordered the creation of state managers, supported sometimes by managerial boards.

The same was to happen to the army in the civil war that, in addition to the existing chaos, would soon engulf the nation. The election of officers by soldier committees was not working as a system. Primitive operational plans were drawn up, so Leon Trotsky, as Commander of the Red Army, declared, by men who 'could not even read a map.' The result was inevitable defeat.

Trotsky recalled officers of the regular army, making threats to their families if they failed in their duties, re-introduced saluting, dissolved the soldier committees, brought back pay differences and privileges. The result was anger from the troops and another howl of outrage from the left in impassioned attacks in *Pravda*, though Inessa allowed others to do the howling.

After a tough start, however, when the White forces seemed overwhelming, Trotsky's new policy began to win battles. And Lenin, of course, backed Trotsky. Winning in the field was more immediately important than socialist theory.

Inessa was flirting with danger, but she knew Lenin – knew, too, that he was always on her side, and granted her a freedom of thought that he would often deny to others – as their long argument about 'the worker has no fatherland' had showed. And she, though staking out her views, would always, in the end, support him, no matter what he did.

For Lenin, the left was a big problem for its stubborn clinging to utopian theory did not stand up to immediate conditions. Always, Lenin was pragmatic. When, earlier in 1917, he had learned that the right-wing Kamenev had proposed that the death penalty should be abandoned, he had stepped in at once. 'How can we run a revolution,' he'd demanded, 'without the firing squad?'

By the later part of 1918, the Cheka, as a vast organ of terror, with tentacles throughout Russia, was committing ever more ghastly atrocities. Torture techniques varied according to the district, ranging from burning the skin off a victim's hands to fixing a cage of rats to his body, its door open, so they could only escape by eating their way out, or to sliding him into a furnace.[8]

Cheka round-ups of 'hostages' were often random, simply taking the occupants of a street. But this is what terror meant – control of a people who lived in fear of a knocking on the door in the middle of the night. And Lenin, Sverdlov, and even Trotsky always opposed any attempt to weaken this control.

The civil war, which had been gradually developing since the October revolution, became serious in the summer of 1918 and would continue until April, 1920. It was complex, partially because of differences in aims and tactical views. In time, however, there developed, from a range of different forces, two main anti-Bolshevik armies, under General Denikin and Admiral Kolchak. In their ranks were disaffected officers and many Cossacks, and the Allies came in on several fronts to support them.

There were other forces – such as a big Czech unit, which had fought for Russia in the European war, and now supported a right-wing SR attempt to establish an independent provincial government in Samara. There were peasant armies, which sometimes switched sides and could be just as barbarous as the Cheka; and the 'Greens' which were bandit groups made up mainly of deserters who lived in the forests.

At the heart of the chaos was the need for food. Lenin blamed the greed of the rich kulaks for the shortages, though many kulaks were not wealthy and were merely commune leaders. In many areas, there would be one horse in a village that was moved around from family to family. The kulaks were accustomed to storing food for themselves in the winters and selling the surplus to the cities, but currency was useless now with soaring inflation.

With armies on both sides demanding grain as they swept through the country – often flogging or torturing whole villages to force them to reveal their secret storage places – it is not strange that there were nearly 300 peasant revolts between July and August, 1918.

Lenin sent out food brigades with the same purpose as the armies and, closer to the cities, formed new units to police the trains, confiscating from passengers any excess food over the small legal allowance. This, too, was not successful, for the 'bagmen' also acted like bandits and confiscated whatever else might take their fancy.

In the cities, the situation grew desperate. Half-starved children were seen pulling carts that would normally be drawn by horses. More and more people fled to the country, as reflected in Boris Pasternak's *Doctor Zhivago*, to be nearer the food sources.

By early 1919, Lenin's revolution was under serious military threat in four different areas of Russia – including the north where British and French troops had landed at Murmansk and Archangel to support the anti-Bolshevik forces. The south was already under White Russian control. In the east, Soviet power had been overthrown in Siberia, the Urals and the mid-Volga Region. In the north west, yet another general, Nikolai Yudenich, was also planning an attack on St Petersburg.

And Trotsky, the highly able Commander-in-Chief of the Red Army, was racing between the fronts in a special armoured train, complete, it was said, with a gourmet kitchen. Until mid-1919 it seemed the White armies might succeed. Denikin launched a three-pronged pincer attack, aimed at Moscow – Baron Wrangel moving from the Caucasus, advancing up the Volga; General Sidorin marching with a Don army from Tsartsyn; Mai-Maevsky coming from Kharkov, all on the main railway lines. But the front was too wide, making back-up hard. The cavalry leaders resisted orders. There was disagreement among the generals. The Reds began to win.

It was against this setting that Inessa, in addition to all her other areas of activity, had returned to the 'woman problem', especially crucial now as more and more men were called up from the factories and the farmlands to join the Red Army, and women were needed at the front both for support purposes, such as nursing, but also at times for combat.

There were, in fact, women's regiments on both sides – the most famous being Maria Bochkareva's Women's Battalion of Death, who shaved their heads and wore trousers. Bochkareva demanded discipline. In the chaos of Kerensky's failed offensive in July, 1917, Bochkareva had found one of her girls having sex with a soldier in a shell hole – and had run her through with her bayonet.[9]

Inessa's feminist group was built around the editorial board of *Rabotnitsa*, the women's newspaper that Inessa, Nadya and Lenin's sister, Maria, had, with others, conceived in 1914. This had resumed publication in St Petersburg and Inessa had launched a sister paper in Moscow. Neither paper lasted long but they were replaced by women's columns in the main dailies, where they in fact reached a far wider audience.

However, the new interest of Inessa and her friends lay outside the needs of war: they wanted to drag the old-fashioned family – which they saw as a hangover from the past – into the socialist present.

Within the new movement Inessa, with Lenin supporting her,

began to take centre stage alongside Alexandra Kollontai, with Sverdlov behind her. The two women were natural rivals not because of their political aims, which were roughly the same, though Kollontai had a more forward position on sexual freedom, but because of their personalities. They could never have been friends.

Kollontai had organised a delegation to the first women's conference which Inessa had attended in St Petersburg back in 1908 when she'd been on the run from Mezen. Even then, while Inessa was not even a member of the party, Kollontai had had a reputation in revolutionary circles.

She had a fine mind, was an acknowledged theoretician, and she was superb on the platform – something at which Inessa was competent but not outstanding. Alexandra was flamboyant but passionately impulsive and, by contrast to Inessa who now dressed down to the mood of the times, wore challenging, colourful clothes.

Although Kollontai had been appointed as the only woman on the Central Committee after the October coup, she had resigned in horror at the Brest-Litovsk peace treaty, unlike Inessa who had simply voted against it in the Moscow Soviet without making too many waves.

Alexandra had been the lover of Alexander Shlyapnikov, who was prominent among the new leaders. Then, in 1917, she had fallen in love with Paul Dybenko, a huge, fine-looking sailor whom she'd met after Podvoisky had recruited her as a celebrity agitator to tour the fleet.

Dybenko, who had won fame by throwing the visiting Kerensky overboard, was seventeen years younger than the forty-five-year-old Alexandra. After the October coup he was made Commissar for the Navy, insisted on marrying her – in the new civil system – and had opposed Brest-Litovsk in a dangerously hot-blooded way: He had refused to stop fighting, this time deploying his sailors on land, and had checked, temporarily at least, the German advance on St Petersburg.

For this disobedience, he was arrested for treason, which almost caused a naval mutiny. Alexandra was terrified he would be executed and appealed to Lenin. Dybenko was acquitted but expelled from the party. And these activities did nothing to help Alexandra. There was no longer a place for her on the Central Committee. Her talents remained recognised but she did not have the political acumen of Inessa, who had been well-schooled by a master in tactics.

By then, the feminist agenda had already been addressed to some extent. After the revolution in February, 1917, women had been given full political and civil rights – by the new-style civil marriage in particular. Soon after October, all restrictions on divorce had been removed, the demand by one partner being enough. Illegitimate children had been given the same rights as other children, and women had equal pay for equal work –in theory, at least.

In 1917, these laws took Russia way beyond most Western nations, but Russia was still a deeply patriarchal society – and again the fifteen million peasant families resisted the changes. In this population of 160 millions, occupying one sixth of the inhabited surface of the world, peasants represented close to seventy per cent of that whole vast nation. And they were conservative.

In May, 1918 Inessa organised an All-Russian Congress of working women. It did not prove a great attraction, perhaps because Inessa was too pressed to give it the attention it needed. Only 130 delegates arrived in Moscow – because of, Inessa assessed later, the allegiance of most women in factories to the SRs and Mensheviks. But when some of them asked to see Lenin, she waved her magic wand and there he was on the platform, not saying too much of record but impressing them with his welcome.

In June, with Kollontai she was elected to a commission to organise a national congress of working women. They were given an office, staff and a small budget with a brief that included the despatch of women agitators across the nation to round up delegates.

The campaigning was embarrassingly successful. Instead of the 300 delegates expected for the congress, 1,147 red-kerchiefed women arrived in Moscow from all over Russia after long and dangerous journeys across the war zones, creating an acute crisis as to how they, and the children that some had brought with them, were to be accommodated and fed. They had to be satisfied by soup and porridge and somewhere was presumably found for them to sleep.

The next day, they assembled in the House of Unions, where the

Moscow Duma had once sat and, as Elwood writes, the two women 'must have derived a sense of satisfaction and accomplishment when they sat on the podium and looked out over more than a thousand working women.'

What they had to say, however, was not welcomed by everyone. In a major speech, Inessa spoke of women returning home from long hours at work to the 'household slavery of cooking, cleaning and child rearing.' The problem could be solved, she said, by communal dining rooms, laundries, schools and nurseries, thus freeing house-wives for other activities – which provoked cries of 'We won't give up our children.' Certainly, Inessa did not believe that collectives could solve her own problems. She had, after all, strongly resisted the idea of Andre attending a state boarding school.

Kollontai followed Inessa with her optimistic visions of a new kind of relationship which she called 'Great Love' – the title of the novel she was to write. This was a kind of sexual promised land that would be stripped of jealousies and selfishness. She conceded it would take generations to reach this happy state. Meanwhile, however, as people strove to achieve more honesty and equality in their relations, these would not necessarily be monogamous or long-lasting.[10] This was touching on Kollontai's belief in full sexual freedom for women which Lenin, Nadya and Inessa did not agree with.

Lenin, Sverdlov and Bukharin all addressed the meeting, which gave it authority, and the fact that there were more than a hundred peasant women among those in the hall was encouraging. Inessa proposed that back at home they should form local feminist groups to whom the delegates would report and thus spread the ideas they had discussed in Moscow.

The lesson foreshadowed by all the speeches and discussions about the 'woman problem' was that you could change the law but you could not so easily change long-established custom. Nevertheless, it was with this aim that, in December, 1918, the Central Committee appointed Inessa to the chair of a new Central Commission for agita-tion and propaganda among working women – an appointment that cannot have pleased Kollontai too much.

There was little opportunity then for conflict between them. In

March, 1919, Kollontai was despatched to be a propagandist for five months on the Southern Front. By then Inessa had already left on a new assignment, as one of a three-person Red Cross mission to France to make arrangements for the repatriation to Russia of 45,000 Russian troops who had been fighting on the Western Front.

This was potentially dangerous. Four members of another Red Cross delegation to Poland had been taken to a field and shot and a second delegation, also under the Red Cross banner, had been arrested in Hungary.

Relations with France were particularly bad. A hundred French residents in Russia were being held as hostage. French troops were fighting alongside the White armies. And leaders of all the developed Western countries were terrified that the revolution might infect their own workers. George V, who had early offered asylum to the Tsar, had been forced to retract his offer for fear of its effect on British labour.

The French government was not fooled by the Red Cross cover, at least so far as making travel arrangements for the Russian troops went. Presumably, it knew of Inessa's background in France, but it wanted those of its nationals held hostage in Russia to be released and it was keen that the Russian troops should be taken off its hands.

'I nearly left for France,' Inessa reported in December to Inna in Astrakhan, 'to bring back the Russian soldiers who remain there, but I could not go through because of the German events. I think we will be able to pass when the revolution in Germany has further developed. Events take place so quickly! How fast, my dear! Here we joke about not being happy unless each day brings us at least one revolution ... I suffer without you, my little girl. I send you a thousand kisses.'[11]

In fact, the German government would not let the delegation through because diplomatic relations with the Soviet government had been severed, and they had to go by sea. The French had guaranteed their personal immunity but warned that they would be expelled if they used the mission as a cover for propaganda.[12]

Although propaganda was certainly Inessa's intention, the most urgent Soviet reason for the mission was that it could lay the ground for talks about a formal peace with the French government – since the Allies had all declined to recognise the Soviet government, leaving the issue for discussion at the Versailles peace conference.

All three of the mission delegates were experienced Bolsheviks and fluent in French. Headed by D.Z.Manuilsky, with whom Inessa had worked in the St Petersburg underground in 1912, the third member was Jacques Davtyan.[13]

The two men bought formal clothes suitable for a diplomatic mission, recorded Polina Vinogradskaya. Inessa planned to wear the ordinary, rather drab dresses she'd favoured since her return to Russia. The purchase of fashionable frocks, she said, would be a waste of the people's money. Her two companions were worried that the French would think that Soviet men forced their wives to wear rags, while they preened in well-cut suits.

At last, the three delegates left by ship on 4 February, 1919. From St Petersburg Inessa wrote to Inna, enclosing letters to Sasha and Fedor and a third one for Lenin. 'Only you are to know of this last one... Keep [it] yourself for the time being. When we get back I'll tear it up. If something happens to me ... then you must give the letter personally to Vladimir Ilyich ... Go to *Pravda* where Maria Ilyinichna works, give her the letter and say that it's from me and is personal for V.I. Meanwhile hang on to it ... It's sealed in an envelope.' She did not expect 'special danger,' she said, but 'just in case.'[14]

They reached Dunkirk on 21 February. To their angry astonishment, their luggage was searched. More than a million roubles and 49,000 Swiss francs were seized and they were alarmed to be placed under house arrest in Malo-des-Bains with constant surveillance.

They had been forbidden to bring staff such as translators and secretaries as the French would supply any such needs, but they were not permitted to communicate with Moscow by code and the Quai d'Orsay refused to transmit their first messages in plain language. The mission was not even allowed to visit the Russian troops whose travel arrangements to Russia were the ostensible reason for their presence.

However, news of their arrival had permeated socialist circles and after a few days a reporter from *Le Populaire* arrived in Malo, only gaining a few brief words with Inessa.

Their contact with the outside world was Lieutenant-Colonel Wehrlin, whose orders were severely limited. They complained. They tried to wire G.V.Chicherin, Soviet Commissar for Foreign Affairs, asking him to intervene, which again the French refused to send. Surveillance was increased.

They faced stalemate. A Colonel Langlois replaced Wehrlin and his orders gave him more scope: they could communicate with Moscow on repatriation matters. They would be allowed to visit the Russian camps, accompanied by French officials. Manuilsky and Davtyan were prepared to accept this but 'Madame Armand objected.' Langlois concluded that she wanted a 'rupture of negotiations' – which sounds like Inessa.

The Russian Red Cross wired that these conditions were acceptable and Manuilsky and Davtyan agreed. But Madame Armand 'dissented' and this time she wasn't alone. Chicherin signalled the Quai d'Orsay, threatening to re-arrest those French citizens in Russia who had been released. The French countered angrily by demanding unconditional acceptance of its proposals or the mission would be expelled.

Inessa was 'growing increasingly irritable', as Richard K.Debo wrote in his account of the venture. Unlike her two associates, she displayed what Langlois called 'a hateful state of mind', demanding they should be able to get on with the purpose of their visit. She clearly felt that Manuilsky and Davtyan were giving their captors far too easy a time.

She was, Langlois concluded, 'prodigiously sly' and Inessa, experienced as she was in captivity, was clearly in her element. She delighted in tormenting the colonel by such escapades as posing for a photographer for *Le Petit Parisien*, while her guard watched helplessly through a window.

This gave Inessa a taste for mischief. Her next plan was to feign an escape plan, which the French police were horrified to discover. A fast car was to be parked beside the beach along which the mission members were allowed to exercise. Two armed men were to overpower the guard and drive her to Paris where she hoped to make a triumphal appearance on May Day.

It was nonsense, of course. The plan got into the hands of the police, as she must have intended. They believed it and feared that another attempt might be made to rescue her or even the whole mission. An order was issued for the three Communists, as they were now called, to be transported to the *Dumont d'Urville*, the repatriation ship for the next contingent of Russian troops. They were to be held aboard until she sailed.

Manuilsky, who had been unnerved by the fate of the Red Cross mission in Poland, was petrified. 'Was the French guarantee of their immunity effective on board ship as well as on shore?' he asked Langlois anxiously and was assured it was. During the journey he demanded the escort officer's word that they were truly heading for the ship. He was not totally convinced. The unit in Poland had been told they were going to be deported before they were shot.

Three days later, he could at last breathe easily. The ship sailed with a thousand Russian soldiers. The difficulties were not over. She put into Hango in Finland, rather than a Russian port, possibly because of lingering Baltic ice. The Finnish authorities, who were also scared of revolution, refused at first to allow either the soldiers or the mission to disembark, but eventually conceded so they could proceed, presumably by train, to Russia.

It was while Inessa was in Hango that Fedor, serving as a pilot in the 38th Squadron in Minsk, was arrested on suspicion of treason. He had always been a bit cavalier as a military cadet and rather free with his opinions at times when it paid to be careful. Perhaps, he had been emboldened by the fact that his mother had special access to high places where Lenin had greater power than ever. Perhaps, too, his right-wing allegiances in Moscow in the October revolution had been noted.

However, Fedor faced great danger this time and his mother was away and out of touch, on the wrong ship in the wrong port. He had come under suspicion from a new commissar, who doubted the authenticity of documents he produced and, since Fedor was an officer of the old regime, suspected his loyalty. He subjected him and his brother officers to heavy harassment which culminated in Fedor's arrest.

Fedor gained permission to telegraph the Kremlin and Lenin responded fast, as he always did when Inessa was involved. He wired the Commissar of the Armies in the Minsk Region on 3 May that F.A.Armand of the 38th Squadron 'who is personally known to me, is trustworthy even if he is a former officer and non-Communist. I ask the Red Army comrades not to treat him with suspicion.'

Three days later the Commissar of the Armies telegraphed a reply: 'Armand, arrested by the Commissar of the West Division, has been released. The Commissar of the 38th Detachment has been dismissed.'[15]

So that was one commissar who got his come-uppance – as Inessa must have been relieved to discover when she at last got home to Moscow. It was more proof of the power she now had but she was a realist for all her head-in-the clouds idealism, and she used her position with a care and discrimination that was deeply resented by people she had known as children.

'One more remark,' wrote Yury Gautier in his diary during July, 1919 in the midst of 'a beautiful summer'. 'Inessa has refused to vouch for Georges Wilken; such is her memory for hospitality extended to her in her youth. I admit that I didn't expect that even from her.'[16]

Inessa must have had a reason for this. Georges Wilken had been an actor, with Inessa and her sisters, in the amateur production of *A Tale of Summer* put on at Pushkino soon after her marriage. Her reluctance to help him could have been due to a need to distance herself from her bourgeois past, but disloyalty was unusual in her. It is more likely that Georges Wilken had done something unwise that had darkened his record to an extent that was embarrassing.

Despite the bitterness of Yury Gautier's tone and his use of the words 'even from her,' he seems to have forgotten that only months before, Inessa had saved him from almost certain despatch to a prison camp, if not death. It didn't take much to be arrested in those days when the Cheka was flexing its muscles. Even to be suspected of the remotest link to an explosion, despite having nothing to do with it, was enough for one to be shot. Especially for a classic bourgeois like Yury Gautier. Still, from his point of view, she *was* on the other side – and appallingly close to the devil himself.

Inessa had also resisted a request from her old comrade, Ivan Popov, whom she had met in Mezen and partnered at the Brussels conference in 1914. 'Dear Ivan,' she wrote. 'Unfortunately I cannot do anything for Boris Konstantinovich Viktorov.' She suggests a personal visit by a mutual acquaintance to Dzerzhinsky, head of the Cheka and just about the most feared man in Russia. 'I would be happy to see you, dear Ivan,' she ends. 'Come over one evening. We are all often at home.'[17]

A year later, Gautier was again to visit the old Armand home in Pushkino. 'Such horror and neglect there, where life once burgeoned!' he recorded. 'E.E.'s house [Alexander's father] has been turned into a club; everything has been pilfered, is falling down and leaking; A.E.'s house [one of Alexander's two uncles] is serving as a nursery and not a single object has remained in the rooms.

'The two old women have been stuffed into an old people's home and are sadly living out their lives among the ruins of the past. The garden is overgrown and there are tall weeds everywhere, the gazebos have been wrecked. Horror and abomination.'

By then, in 1920, Inessa had been working so hard on the new world she was helping to create that Lenin was worrying about her.

Soon after she had returned from her disastrous mission to France, she had been given a big new job as head of the Women's Section of the Central Committee. This, like the other sections, had the authority of the Committee and could issue edicts in its name, surely enough to make some impact on restrictive paternalism. It was known by its shortened version as Zhenotdel and, in effect, it could make law.[18]

This was another, more serious setback for Alexandra Kollontai, who had been the main promoter of the socialist feminist movement since 1905. But, in contrast to Inessa who had been a Bolshevik for ten years, Kollontai had been a Menshevik until 1915. She was also less dependable than Inessa who could be relied on not to resign in an explosion of emotion. Doubtless, though, Kollontai saw Inessa's closeness to Lenin as a major factor, and maybe it was.

Worse, Kollontai was given a brief that she regarded as demeaning – the organising of peasant women – while Inessa ruled the whole organisation from an apartment head office on Vozdvizhenka, near the Kremlin. According to Polina Vinogradskaya, who worked with them both, they had quarrelled from the start. Possibly, Inessa had chosen this assignment for Kollontai to get her out of the office as much as possible. And was the job so demeaning in its practical purpose? There was a huge army of peasant women, almost certainly larger in number than factory workers, *and* more backward and in need of political education.

Zhenotdel's original brief, like that of the commission that preceded it, was to mobilise Russian women for defence in the civil war, by taking over men's jobs in factories so that they could join the Red Army and could themselves serve at the front, as indeed Inna had. An estimated 70,000 women served with the army. Nearly 2000 were killed.

Inessa's new position also gave her a big chance to help women catch up with the recent liberal laws – such as insisting that all worker committees in factories, normally limited to men, should include at least one woman. And, since many women were not equipped by experience for this, she enforced a system of apprentice delegates who would actually be trained for the role. In short, Inessa, with the force of the Central Committee behind her, had a degree of muscle that many modern feminists would envy.

The new concept of marriage was aided by the war. Crèches were set up in factories as well as communal cooking facilities, free canteens, and dining facilities. In cities this system was more widespread and, by 1921, ninety-three per cent of Moscow residents were eating in public dining halls.

Through the latter part of 1919 the work load for Inessa was immense and staff shortages were made worse by sickness in a city that was suffering from a huge epidemic of Spanish flu. In November, 1919, Kollontai had suffered a heart attack from which she was not to recover until March, 1920. Meanwhile, in February, 1920 Inessa had herself fallen ill.

Polina Vinogradskaya wrote a vivid account of a visit to her in

Neglinnaya Street (Manege Street) on returning from work at the front. 'I had to knock a long time. The bells didn't work. As I started to return down the stairs, I heard a door opening. Inessa appeared in the doorway. She was ill and because no one else was in the apartment she had to get up and answer the door herself.

'When I expressed surprise that she'd been left alone by the family, she became indignant and said, "The children are working and shouldn't stop for such a stupid reason as my illness."

'It was terribly cold in the apartment because there was no heating. Thick layers of dust covered everything. Only the books were tidy in the shelves.

'She had a terrible cold. She was coughing and shivering. She blew on her fingers to warm them. She looked so haggard I hardly recognised her. She was wearing a very old bed jacket.

'She didn't complain, though. She asked me eagerly in her hoarse voice about the front and was pleased about our successes.

'I wanted to make some tea, but couldn't find a single match in the house and I left her still shaking.'[19]

Lenin soon discovered her situation, probably because of Polina. 'Dear Friend,' he wrote, 'I wanted to telephone you when I heard you were ill, but the phone doesn't work. Give me the number and I'll tell them to repair it.'[20]

Two or three days later he wrote again: 'Please say what's wrong with you. These are appalling times: there's typhus, influenza, Spanish flu, cholera. I've just got up and I'm not going out. Nadya has a temperature of 39°C [102.2°F] and wants to see you. What's your temperature? Don't you need some medicine? I beg you to tell me frankly. You must get well.'[21]

He was soon in touch again, having meanwhile given orders for a doctor to attend her. 'Has the doctor been?' he asked. 'You have to do exactly as he says. The phone's out of order again. I told them to repair it. I want your daughters to call me and tell me how you are. You must do everything the doctor tells you. To go out with a temperature of 38°C or 39°C is madness. I beg you earnestly not to go out and to tell your daughters from me that I want them to watch you and not to let you out: 1) until your temperature is back to

207

normal, 2) with the doctor's permission. I want an exact reply on this.'[22]

Presumably her daughters obeyed the orders of the head of state, though it seems she was soon out of the apartment and probably back at work. 'Comrade Inessa,' he wrote again, 'I rang to find out what size of galoshes you take. I hope to get hold of some. Write and tell me how your health is. What's wrong with you? Has the doctor been?'[23]

Again he persisted. 'The doctor says it is pneumonia. You must be extremely careful. Tell your daughters to ring me daily. Tell me truly what are you missing? More firewood? Who tends your fire? Do you have food? Who cooks for you? Who is tending you with cold compresses? You're avoiding answering. This is not good. Answer me, even on this piece of paper, all my points … Your Lenin. PS: Have they mended the telephone?'[24]

What is surprising about this string of letters is Lenin's effort and allocation of time, given the immense range of other things he had to direct. The civil war was in its last days but, only weeks before, St Petersburg had been so threatened, with Whites in possession of the Polkuvo Heights overlooking the city, Lenin had urged its evacuation, a suggestion that shocked Trotsky who could not accept abandonment of the birthplace of the revolution.

Trotsky rallied the residents of the city, men and women. Barricades went up in the streets. Machine guns were posted on high buildings. For three days, although most were armed with little more than rifles, they held off the Whites, who had tanks, until reserves could be rushed up by rail from the south.

The battle had been fierce, with Trotsky at one stage on a horse personally stopping desertions, though he never had to set up the machine guns behind the defenders to deter retreat, as Lenin had urged.

Now Moscow was in the midst of another awful winter. In addition to her articles in the women's page of *Pravda*, also circulated to other Russian papers, Inessa had launched a new monthly, *Kommunistka*, published by Zhenotdel, and was soon involved in planning three conferences, one of them the First International

Conference of Communist Women, for which, according to Vinogradskaya, 'she took on herself all the work of preparing, organising and conducting.' She had been temporarily stripped of two top members of staff which, with others ill, Kollontai still away and the editorial demands on her, meant working fourteen to sixteen hours a day. Often she fled to the reading room of the Rumyantsev Museum, where she had often worked as a fugitive in 1908, to gain respite from the chatter in the office.

The International Conference was not a great success, despite a fervent rendering by the audience of the *Internationale*. The attendance was small, in part because European women had not been invited, possibly because of the Soviet government's uneasy relations with these countries. By the end of it, Nadya recorded, 'Inessa was on her last legs.'[25]

Lenin was still concerned. A few days earlier, he had written to her. 'My dear friend, it was sad to find out that you are overtired and dissatisfied with your work and the colleagues that surround you [re: disagreements with Kollontai, an archivist notes]. Can I help you by arranging a sanatorium for you? With the greatest pleasure I'll do what I can.

'If you go to France, I'm very afraid that you will be arrested and I doubt they will exchange you for someone else ... Would it be better to go to Norway – many people speak English there – or to Poland? Or to Germany, as a Frenchwoman or a Russian?

'I had a wonderful holiday (in the woodland near Pushkino, rather strangely) suntanned, didn't see a single line and not a single phone call. Previously the hunting was good but now everything is destroyed. Everywhere I heard your surname. "In their time, there was order" etc.

'If you don't want to go to a sanatorium [presumably near Moscow] why not go south to Sergo in the Caucasus? Sergo will arrange a good holiday – the sun, good work. . .There, he is the authority. Think about it. I firmly shake your hand. Your Lenin.'[26]

This was a strange suggestion, especially since Kislovodsk was the resort selected. The civil war had ended, but fighting by small units still persisted – especially in the Kuban area where the conflict was to rumble on in the mountains for quite a long time. Kislovodsk was only fifty miles or so from the Kuban River though this was further than it sounded, being rugged mountain country. Lenin clearly believed that Sergo Ordzhonikidze had a proper control over the territory though there had to be an element of danger.

However, Inessa knew Sergo quite well. He had been at the Longjumeau school in 1911 and had also attended the Prague conference in 1912, which Lenin had rigged with Inessa's help. Sergo had actually opposed Lenin on some issues, which had given the conference a tiny shred of authority.

The idea of a holiday had a great appeal for her, especially since Andre was not well and would benefit from the mountain air, So she accepted Lenin's offer. It was to be a momentous decision.

FOURTEEN

The Caucasus 1920

The Caucasus, which divides Europe from Asia, is one of the greatest mountain chains in the world, with six peaks rising above 16,000 feet, twenty that top Mont Blanc, the highest in the European Alps, and 125 square miles of glaciers. Stretching some 650 miles from Novorossisk on the Black Sea to Baku on the Caspian, the grassed and wooded plateau of the north rises to the mountains in a series of terraces, divided by plains cut up by deep fissures.

It is a wild area – this high craggy terrain, alternating with fast flowing rivers and primeval forests – and enabled the Caucasians to hold off the Great Russians for 160 years of continuous fighting. The mythology is rich. This is where Prometheus was said to have been chained to a rock for stealing fire from the gods; where the Argonauts came in search of the Golden Fleece; where the 'fearless' Amazon virgins reputedly once lived.

As promised, Lenin issued his orders to Ordzhonikidze. 'Comrade Sergo, Inessa Armand is leaving today. I am asking you not to forget your promise. Send a telegram to Kislovodsk giving the order to make arrangements for her and her son as appropriate and follow up the execution of this order. If you don't, nothing will be done. Answer me please by letter or, if possible, by telegram [confirming]: I have received the letter. I will do everything. I will check it correctly.'

Clearly, Lenin was starting to worry whether he had chosen the best place for her holiday. 'In view of the dangerous situation in the Kuban,' he continued, 'I ask you to establish contact with Inessa Armand so that you can evacuate her and her son if necesssary to Petrovsk and Astrakhan without delay … and in general to take all [necessary] measures.'[1]

He had already given Inessa a signed letter to the district Administrator of Resorts and Sanatoria requesting that everything possible should be done 'to provide the best accommodation and treatment for the bearer, Comrade Inessa Fedorovna Armand and her sick son.'[2]

Still, Lenin wasn't happy. Two days after she had left, on 20 August he wired Ordzhonikidze again 'Don't forget you promised to arrange for treatment for Inessa Armand and her sick son who left here on 18 August.'[3]

She arrived with Andre and Polina Vinogradskaya on 22 August after a journey that had taken four days. Kislovodsk was a pretty spa town that, together with three others in the area, had been financed by the Tsar. In those heady times, it had been popular with officers on leave and there had been a lively social scene. The local springs gushed a sparkling mineral water called Narzan that was prized in Russia, and bathing in it was supposed to cure venereal disease. It was a place of green hills, with juniper and buckthorn bushes, skylarks and tall poplar trees.

It should have been just what Inessa needed – except, as it soon became apparent, for the sound of gunfire at night. The civil war was supposed to have ended in April, but White 'bandits' were active, especially a group under General Fostikov which had remained in the hills not far from the spa town.

Inessa's long-time friend Lyudmila Stal, who had worked with her in Paris on the early plans for *Rabotnitsa* in 1914, was already there with her husband G.N.Kotov, but Inessa was in no mood for socialising. 'She looked tired, worn out and emaciated when she arrived,' recorded Stal.

The 'sanatorium' was an exaggeration, being a large dacha the local authorities had taken over on the edge of the town. There were no health facilities and food was short. In spite of Lenin's intercession, she had no vouchers, which were needed for accommodation in the principal building, which anyway was overcrowded. However, a voucher was produced for her and a room was found, although it had no electric light nor even proper bedding.

Local party workers, who knew Vinogradskaya had arrived with

Inessa, approached her in a very agitated state with a telegram, presumably from Sergo. '"Could you tell us what to do?" they asked. "We will do everything if Lenin himself is worried." So we all went to see Inessa, who said she didn't need anything except a pillow ... Three pillows arrived.'[4]

The situation with the White 'bandits' was disturbing. The guests, and those patients who were well enough, were issued with rifles and divided into detachments to fight off the enemy, reported Polina. 'The Whites were not very strong in this region and did not mount serious attacks – but created diversions by sudden sorties.'

During alerts, the Revolutionary Committee would summon the defenders by siren to the party HQ, including the armed sanatorium guests. Oddly, in her writings, Inessa makes no reference to this drama or to carrying guns, but she was much occupied by dark thoughts during what must have been some kind of psychological breakdown.

Kotov reported that White 'bandit' attacks were fairly distant at first but the night alerts were alarming. 'People were very frightened. Even party members behaved like cowards.'

Inessa was in no state to fight anyone. 'At first I slept night and day,' she wrote to Inna. 'Now on the contrary I sleep badly. Andre and I have been here three weeks and I can say he is brighter, but he has not yet put on weight ... He has made a lot of acquaintances and likes playing croquet.

'I sunbathe and have showers but the sun here is not very hot – nothing like the Crimean sun – and the weather is not good. There are often storms and yesterday was quite cold. I can't say I'm particularly taken with Kislovodsk.' No mention, it will be noted, of night alerts.[5]

However, three weeks was a long time to wait before writing to her beloved Inna and it was an indication of her state of mind. 'She was not the same,' wrote Kotov, Lyudmila's husband. 'She was exhausted from overwork. She wanted to stay by herself. She used to go for walks in the forest and the mountains. I tried many times to persuade her to play croquet and to enjoy the company of the other people there, but she always answered: "Later. We still have time. Just for now I'll go and rest in the sun."'

He played croquet with 'Andrushka who was a merry companion' and amused Polina. 'I remember with a smile my arguments with Andre,' she recorded, 'because he broke the rules of the game. Inessa, of course, always took his part in the arguments.'

Kotov was watching Inessa anxiously. 'She was drunk on loneliness,' he wrote colourfully. 'If we didn't have to eat, or there hadn't been a bell, she would have stayed on her own [instead of venturing to the dining room in the main building]. This went on for about two weeks. Then she started to become herself again. She was looking better and gaining weight.'

Vinogradskaya was also worried about her. 'I remember her tall, svelte figure in a black cape and white hat, with a book in her hand, slowly climbing higher and higher into the mountains.'

It was nine days after their arrival, on 1 September that Inessa began to write a diary.[6] 'Now I have time, I'm going to write every day, although my head is heavy and I feel as if I've turned into a stomach that craves food the whole time. [Up here] you don't know anything and don't hear about anything.

'I also feel a wild desire to be alone. I am tired even when other people are talking around me, let alone having to speak myself. I wonder if this feeling of inner death will ever pass.

'I have reached a point where I find it strange when other people laugh and have such pleasure in talking. Now, I hardly ever laugh or smile because I feel joy, but just because I have to smile sometimes [to be polite].

'I am also surprised by my indifference to nature [the spectacular scenery, presumably]. I used to be so moved by it. Now I don't like people so much. Previously I approached everyone with a warm feeling. Now I'm indifferent to everyone and bored by them all.

'The only warm feelings I have left are for the children and V.I. In all other respects it's as if my heart has died; as if, having given up all my strength, all my passion to V.I. and the work, I have exhausted all sources of love and compassion towards people to whom previously I was so richly open. I have no one apart from V.I. and my children. I have no relations with other people, except in my work. And people feel this deadness in me and they pay me back with the same indifference and antipathy. And now even my attitude towards my work is fading.

'I remember the biblical Lazarus who rose from the dead. He knew the sign of death in him remained and it scared people, made them need to get away from him ... I, too, am a living corpse and this is terrible – especially when life around me is so active.'[7]

The phraseology is strange, hinting at a presentiment of death.

After a few days, Kotov reported, 'real battles had started near Kislovodsk. All day long we could hear the noise of artillery and feared that Kislovodsk could be cut off by White Guards. The panic started. Inessa was one of the few people who stayed calm. She tried to stop others leaving, wanting the weak and ill and family people to leave first.'

Dr I.S.Ruzheinikov, another guest, wrote that a new threat was 'a guerrilla, Colonel Azarov,' who was commander, it seems, of a kind of commando unit. 'Everything was mobilised [for defence] against attack by the Azarov detachments.'

Then one night, two members of the committee were killed, which concentrated Inessa's mind when she continued her diary on 3 September. 'Some patients [here] are very worried. They are afraid of attacks. I'm worried only for Andrushka, my little son. In this respect I am weak – not like a Roman matron who could easily sacrifice her children in the interest of the republic. I could not. I am terribly worried about my children.

'I was never a coward for myself, but I'm a big coward when it concerns my children, especially Andrushka. I can't even begin to think about what I could live through if one day he has to go to the front, as I'm afraid one day he will have to. The war [presumably the international revolutionary war] will last a long time when our foreign friends will rise.

'We are still very far from the time when the personal interest and that of society will coincide. Now there is no personal life because all our time and effort is devoted to the common cause. Or maybe other people can find a bit of time and a little corner of happiness. I don't know how to do it for myself.'

On 2 September, Lenin had signalled Sergo again: 'Please add fullest details about the progress of the fight against banditry and about arrangements you have made in Kislovodsk for Soviet functionaries about whom I spoke to you here personally.'[8]

When this had filtered through, two men – the district Red Army Commander Davydov, and Stepanov-Nazarov from the local party committee – called to see Inessa. They decided she should be evacuated. She refused, saying she wanted no special treatment. She would leave when everyone left.

According to Kotov, Nazarov was under pressure from the Regional Command, following Lenin's repeated signals. He warned her that if she would not leave with him he would use the Red Army to move her – which was not the way to handle Inessa. It is apparent that Nazarov did not carry out his threat. At least not then, and not in that way.

Vinogradskaya had decided to return and urged Inessa to come with her, but Inessa declined. She was there for a holiday and was going to finish it. She even teased her 'in a light hearted way' – which hardly matches Inessa's diary gloom – for leaving before the end of her vacation, almost ranking her with the *shkurniks*. This was what she called the healthy people who wanted to 'save their skins' at the expense of those who were ill. However, it is strange that she did not consider leaving for Andre's sake, in view of her private comments about not being a Roman matron.

After another day, the military situation had improved. The White Guards had been driven off, but they were still there in the more distant hills. Nazarov decided that since there was still danger of further attacks, he would evacuate the town, though this would take some days to organise. Already some people had left – the very ill, who had been sent off in 'ambulance' carriages or trains; and others, who had their own horse-drawn transport.

On the eve of Polina's departure, Inessa played the piano for the guests in the sanatorium after dinner. Presumably Lyudmila knew she was a pianist, perhaps remembering their Paris days in 1914 when Inessa took much trouble to get a piano in the aftermath of her emotional crisis with Lenin; her talent as a musician was a surprise to Vinogradskaya.

Oddly, she was reluctant to play, since usually she found the piano so settling, but at last she consented.

'At first,' wrote Polina, 'she was not at ease. Then she got involved with the playing. Her face became warm. Her scarf slipped from her shoulders. She played a sonata by Beethoven, a Schumann concerto, a Lizst rhapsody. I can still see her at the piano and hear her playing. It was her swan song.' She continued at the piano, as she was well able to, for the rest of the evening – a dramatic scene against the sound of distant gunfire.

Inessa remained untouched by the danger around her and oddly distanced from it. By 9 September, she had been resting for the best part of three weeks, yet the gloom still enveloped her. It is hard to see why, though logic, of course, cannot necessarily produce contentment or repair a chronic condition. She had been severely overworked and badly needed a holiday but her situation was one which many women would have greatly envied.

As the head of the Women's Section of the Central Committee, and with easy access to Lenin, she was arguably the most powerful woman in Moscow. Her job was to make conditions better for millions of women but, by contrast to Emmeline Pankhurst and other women in several other democratic countries still fighting for equality in the vote, she could to some extent enforce it. (By 1920, five US states had granted female suffrage and in that year an amendmnent to the Constitution became law.)

Her relations with Lenin, now the unquestioned ruler of Russia, were clearly extremely close, as demonstrated by the concern behind all his signals. She even had a warm friendship with his wife who, despite her behaviour after the assassination attempt, still regarded herself as a favourite aunt to Inessa's children.

Finally, as seen in her earlier diary entry, Inessa's faith that their revolution, to which she had devoted so much of her life, would spread throughout the world was still untarnished by doubt.

What more could she want? Why did the future seem so dark? 'It seems to me,' she wrote in her diary at this time, 'that I walk among people, trying to hide my secret from them – that I am a dead person among the living. Like an actor who a hundred times has to repeat the same scene which no longer inspires him, I repeat by memory the gestures, smiles, even the words that previously I used when I felt emotional.

'But now my heart is dead, my soul is silent and I cannot manage to hide from people my sad mystery. There is a cold breeze which people can feel from me. They move away. Now I am no longer tired, but this inner deadness remains within me. And because I have no warmth, as I no longer radiate warmth, I am unable to give happiness to anyone.'

Her last diary entry, two days later, on 11 September, gives a glimmer of a clue. She has devoted herself to a man she loves – and who, judging by his behaviour, loves her – but he has convinced her that the cause has priority over personal feelings, over the individual. It is a stark denial of human emotion, of human nature in a woman for whom love, as she has shown both in her life and in her writings, is an eternal theme.

'For romantic people,' she confided to her diary, 'love takes first place in the life of a person. Love is higher than anything else. And until recently I was nearer to this idea than I am now. It is true that, for me, love was never the only thing. Together with love, there was always the cause and in the past there were many times when I sacrificed my happiness and my love for it.

'Previously, it seemed that love was as important as the cause. Now this is not the case ... It is true that in my life even now love has a big place and makes me suffer much and takes up many of my thoughts. But not for a moment do I cease to recognise that, however painful for me, love and personal relationships are nothing compared to the needs of the struggle ... '

What is she saying? What has changed? That she now realises that the cause is more important than love. That she has given up much for it, though one wonders what she means by this. The children? Exile and prison had, of course, parted her from them fairly often and, in the war, for the best part of three years. Volodya's death? Would he have died, but for those hard, freezing months in Mezen? Yes, probably, but maybe he would have lived longer.

Perhaps she included Lenin, though their parting in Cracow was

218

his decision rather than hers. Lenin and the cause were inextricably linked. Without the cause, it is doubtful if he would have appealed to her.

Her musings were soon to stop. Five days later she consented, under pressure until the last minute, to leave Kislovodsk and, with Andre, boarded a rail coach linked to an armoured military train that would take them to Vladikavaz. Lyudmila and Kotov were with her, as well as Dr Ruzheinikov and his pregnant wife. There was one other woman, who was also pregnant.

Vladikavaz was some 130 miles to the south and the plan was to move on from there by branch line to Nalchik, to the north west, which was deemed to be safer. The journey took them across the Kabarda plain, through country that had mountains to the west and plains to the east.

Repeatedly, they came under both machine gun and artillery fire. 'Inessa was very calm,' reported Dr Ruzheinikov, 'but she was worried for Andrushka and our two pregnant women.'[9]

At last, they passed through Beslan and approached Vladikavaz, once a Russian fortress since it lies in the foothills of Mount Kasbek, a crucial position on the Georgian Military Highway and one of the two main passes through the mountains from the south. The station was very dirty which was not encouraging since there had been a few cases of cholera earlier in the year. Inessa went into the town to find accommodation but it was crowded with Cossacks and refugees from Georgia and she concluded that their best option was to continue sleeping on the train.

The next day Sergo Ordzhonikidze arrived at the station and offered her a car so she could explore the Georgian Highway. Inessa thought she was being offered special treatment again since the car was too small to take everyone. However, she was pressed and reluctantly accepted. There was more on her mind than sightseeing.

'After two days,' wrote Dr Ruzheinikov, 'it became clear that it would be better for us to go on [as planned] to Nalchik,' where they could relax.

The next day, the train set off for Nalchik, but was forced to stop at Belsan for a day and a half because of bandit activity further up the line. Belsan was 'terribly filthy', so the doctor reported, even worse than Vladikavaz 'with no accommodation, inadequate and disgusting toilets, and nowhere to buy food. We ate what we could find – a lot of raw fruit and melons.'

Inessa was worried because Kotov, who had second degree TB, needed milk and eggs. She went to the village, asking people, and she evidently had some success for the doctor reported she 'came back radiant and immediately started cooking and preparing something for Comrade Kotov,' though he omits to say what. It was at Belsan, in the doctor's view, that she contracted cholera.

However, there was no sign she was unwell the next day when the train moved off. And at last they reached Nalchik, less sophisticated than Kislovodsk with old men in tall astrakhan hats called *papakhas* and Caucasian women, with shawls over their heads.

The local party had arranged a dacha for them and, with the doctor, she visited this though, after the experience of the journey, almost anything would have satisfied them. Then in the evening they attended a meeting of the local party. Inessa discussed Lenin's brochure, *The Childish Illness Of Left Wing Communism* although her friends in the Baugy Group, and indeed herself, were presumably its target, but she could not speak of Lenin without enthusiasm. Not even then, in the gloom described in her diary.

That night she fell ill, though she did not want to disturb anyone, so it was not until the next morning that the doctor found her suffering from convulsions, vomiting and diarrhoea. During the convulsions, the doctor and his wife, Rogova, started massaging her feet, but Inessa protested that the pregnant Rogova was putting herself and her child at risk.

The doctor arranged a bed for her in the local hospital. By then, she was so weak she could hardly walk. In the hospital cholera was diagnosed. She was put in a separate ward, with a special medical staff. Dr Ruzheinikov and Andre stayed with her.

By the evening her condition was much worse. The convulsions were increasing. Again the doctor, the medical sister and Andre took turns to massage her feet, which must have been very distressing for the boy. Later, when Andre left the ward for a moment, Inessa asked the doctor to send him away in case he contracted the disease – and Ruzheinikov did as she asked.

The Nalchik doctors feared a heart attack – and gave her an intravenous injection of saline solution, using common salt. After about half an hour, she appeared to improve. The colour returned to her face. The vomiting and convulsions stopped. Her voice became clear and she calmed down, apologising that she was spoiling Dr Ruzheinikov's holiday. She persuaded him to return to the dacha and get some rest. Then she fell asleep.

The next morning when Andre arrived, she spoke to him through the window. She told him to eat something. By noon she was declining again and the cholera symptoms returned. They repeated the saline solution injections and, as before, she became a little calmer. Later, she asked Ruzheinikov to call Andrushka and she talked to him for few minutes and told him not to worry. Even though it was daytime, she suggested he should go and catch up on his sleep because she was feeling better. Again she insisted that the doctor should do the same and to please her he went into the next room. She instructed the staff that no telegrams were to be sent to Moscow about her condition.

That evening, 23 September, she was worse and this time the saline solution had no effect. At midnight she became unconscious. The medical staff stayed by her bed all night, doing everything they could for her. But her system was exhausted and her heart was weak. She failed to respond to treatment.

'In the morning,' the doctor concluded briefly, 'she left us.' It was 24 September, 1920.[10]

Just over two weeks later, early in the darkness of the morning of 11 October, Lenin stood on the platform of Moscow's Kazan station. With him were Nadya, Alexander and Inessa's four older children, and Polina Vinogradskaya whom Lenin had awoken by phone at 3 a.m. to suggest she join them. Also present was the new Kremlin Commandant, Abram Belenky, and several women from Zhenotdel. A catafalque was waiting with two white horses, in traditional decorative bridles, harness and ornamental head-dresses that covered their ears.

Seventeen days had passed since Inessa had died. For eight of these she had lain in the Nalchik mortuary waiting for a zinc-lined coffin and a suitable rail car to take her to Moscow.

Suddenly, on 9 October, forty-eight hours before their bleak, early morning vigil on the platform, it had dawned on a distraught Lenin, or more probably Nadya, that no one had thought about Andre who, at sixteen, would have had little more than pocket money. Telegrams were sent at once to the Revolutionary Committee at Vladikavaz, the Executive Committee of Nalchik and the local Chekas, ordering a search to be made for the boy, reports to be made to Comrade Klishin at the Hotel Russia in Stavropol who had been ordered to accompany him to Moscow.[11]

Since the train bearing Inessa would already have left, Andre might not be on it and it is strange that Dr Ruzheinikov did not mention him in his report of those sad events since they were in daily contact. 'Together with the local organisation,' he wrote, 'we organised a farewell to Comrade Inessa at the railway station as appropriate to a revolutionary figure.' There was no mention of Andre or of any of the guests from the sanatorium who surely would have taken care of a boy who must have been overwhelmingly shocked by his mother's sudden death. Georges Bardawil reports that he was on the train with his mother's body. Certainly this is what would be expected and there is no doubt that he did, in fact, arrive safely at some stage. According to his son, Vladimir, he continued to live in the apartment by the Kremlin in Manege Street.

At last, in the morning darkness, the train from the Caucasus drew into the station. The coffin, with a black drape and red overlay, was moved from the rail car to the waiting catafalque.

Dawn was breaking as the procession moved off from the station. 'We tried to persuade Lenin to sit in the car,' wrote Vinogradskaya, 'since it was a long way, but he refused. "I will walk behind the coffin," he said.' 'The long walk through the deserted streets behind her horse-drawn hearse,' wrote R.C.Elwood, 'was a form of penance for the Bolshevik leader.'

'He walked with his head down,' Polina wrote, 'absorbed by his thoughts. From time to time he slightly raised his hand, his eyes narrowed [in grief].' He had much to disturb him. If he had not urged Inessa to go to the Caucasus and not made all those elaborate arrangements she would still be alive. It was a desolate irony that, had it not been for his continued signals, which had scared the local party into action, she would have stayed in Kislovodsk and finished her holiday in good health, physical if not mental.

The cortège progressed by Kalanchevskaya Square and Myasnitskaya, where the buildings were dilapidated, as Polina commented, being 'unrepaired since the start of the war.' Workers were on their way to their factories and offices – more of them than usual because the trains were not running and, seeing the procession, some of them stopped and joined it. Others asked: 'Is it Lenin?'

At last they reached the House of Unions where Inessa was to rest in state until the next day, with an overnight guard of honour provided by women she had worked with at Zhenotdel. There was a wreath of white hyacinths on the coffin with the words 'To Comrade Inessa from Lenin,' as well as wreaths from other friends.

She lay in a high-ceilinged room next to the big hall where Alexander, and Inessa herself for a short while, once sat as a member of the Moscow Duma; where Inessa, together with Alexandra Kollontai, had addressed an audience of more than a thousand women the previous year.

The next day, in bright autumn sunshine, she was borne from the House of Unions by catafalque to Red Square in procession, this time a big one, with women from all the organisations in different regions with which Inessa had been involved.

There were banners inscribed with such slogans as 'The leaders die but their deeds live' – and, according to *Izvestia*, a military band.

The Bolshoi Theatre Orchestra also played Chopin, Beethoven and Mozart. There were speeches – one rather surprisingly by Inessa's rival, Alexandra Kollontai, who spoke of the collaboration Inessa had inspired 'among the working women in Russia and in the international arena.' But, again surprisingly, no one from the left-wing Baugy Group which she had supported, nor from among her companions in exile, gave an address.

'It was not until the end of the speeches that Lenin appeared, with

223

Nadya, to say goodbye to his friend,' reported Polina. 'He stood with bare head in his autumn coat, buttoned to the neck, at the side of the newly-dug grave.'

He shocked the women who were present. 'He was unrecognisable,' reported Alexandra. 'He was plunged in despair. At any moment we thought he would collapse.'

Angelica Balabanov was equally overwhelmed. 'Not only his face but his whole body expressed so much sorrow that I dared not greet him, not even with the slightest gesture ... He seemed to have shrunk ... his eyes seemed drowned in tears held back with effort.'

Inessa's body was slowly lowered into the grave beside the high red brick walls of the Kremlin as the crowd of mourners sang the *Internationale*. 'So Comrades come rally, and the last fight let us face ... '

Polina's description was vivid: 'NK was crying, but Lenin stood straight, intense, immobile, his face contorted with anger.' Then Nadya embraced Inessa's children. And the massed voices echoed across Red Square with the stirring final verse of the anthem, written to celebrate the Paris Commune of 1871 ...

'No saviour from on high delivers; no faith have we in prince or peer; our own right hand the chains must shiver, chains of hatred greed and fear ... '

As many in that great square would have noted, with the sound of the singing fading, it was the ideal to which Inessa had devoted most of her adult life.

AND AFTERWARDS ...

By the time of Inessa's funeral in October, 1920, the dangers to the Bolshevik Communist regime had declined. The White armies had been fought off. The socialist opposition had been sharply curbed, with 5,000 Mensheviks being sent to prison camps in 1919 and the leading Social Revolutionaries being put through show trials in 1920.

At last Lenin could concentrate on his new order – limited within Russia for the time being. But he did not have long to live himself.

At the time of Inessa's death, Inna was twenty-two, Varya was nineteen and Andre was sixteen. According to Inna, Lenin and Nadya 'became the guardians of my sister, my youngest brother and me.' The girls and, presumably, Andre already had passes into the Kremlin, but they now spent much time in the apartment and at the mansion in Gorki, though Inna and Andre moved for several weeks after their mother's death to the Chaika rest home on the Moscow outskirts.

For Andre, the sudden loss of his mother must have been traumatic and Inna, perhaps the closest to Inessa of all her children – and politically in tune with her – must have found it almost as hard. Lenin understood this, may even have found some consolation in sharing the mourning with her children, and took to visiting them there.

He set Andre some chess problems. He also urged them to take up skiing, as he had urged their mother. The next year, according to Boris Souverine, who worked with Inna, 'she used to live in the Kremlin in Lenin's home where she was the object of great affection.'

In 1922 Lenin learned that Inna had fallen ill during a holiday in the Crimea. He wrote to the doctor in charge of her, asking for details of her diet and condition, ordering him to keep him informed, an almost eerie reflection of her mother's last weeks. And a scared doctor kept her in bed for a week longer than was needed.

He sent Varvara with Sasha to Teheran, under the protection of the

Soviet Ambassador, hoping the change of scene would appeal to them. Sasha was appointed secretary to the Russian Trade Commission there but Varvara was not very happy, so he recalled her. Later, Sasha worked in the Commission for Heavy Industry, finishing up as its head of research.

Inna married Hugo Eberlein, a prominent German Communist, and joined him in Berlin, where she worked in the Soviet Embassy, and had a daughter named Inessa. When Hitler took power, Eberlein fled to Russia, only to be arrested in the purges and to die in prison. Inna became an editor of Lenin's collected works.

Varvara became a decorative artist and married Yakov Blomas, an artist and academician of note. She had a daughter, Blona. After the Second World War a retrospective exhibition of Varvara's work was held in Moscow.

Fedor, the only one of Inessa's children who never joined the party, remained in the air force, becoming an instructor.

Andre trained to be an engineer and worked in the automobile works in Moscow and Gorki. He only joined the party in 1944, before being killed in World War II.

Lenin's health had been poor since early 1921 – coming so close to Inessa's death, this was one reason why Alexandra Kollontai, romantic as ever, suggested it was a cause of his decline – but he became steadily worse through the next two years, with several strokes, and had to accept that, as he said, 'My song is sung.'

Maria and Nadya were constantly at war over his care, his sister believing that visits from young people were damaging to him, while Nadya was convinced he enjoyed them. On one occasion the arrival of Inna and Sasha at Gorki was the cause of so heated a quarrel between the two women that his personal bodyguard quietly suggested that the Armands should leave.

Nadya could not accept a situation in which they could not visit. In the summer, she wrote to Inna in Germany, starting 'Dear sweet girl,' and asking: 'Why can't you stay with us? On the contrary, this year we're going to live in a more "family-like fashion" … since it is impossible to occupy V.I. more than eight hours a day … he'll be delighted to have guests.'

Lenin died in January, 1924 and the next day Nadya wrote to Inna. 'My very own dearest Inochka, we buried Vladimir Ilyich yesterday ... Lenin's death was the best outcome. Death had already been suffered by him so many times [in strokes] in the previous year.' Several months before, she had written that 'I wanted so much to have a child' and saying how alone she felt.

Inna replied to the news about his death. 'Don't think you are completely alone. You still have us, your little girls as you call us. We love you very much and are grieving with you about Vladimir Ilyich. He was so dear, so loved. I did not believe it. Here everyone cried.'

Nadya was disgusted by the plan to preserve the body and place it on public display in the marble mausoleum. 'What they should have done,' she wrote Inna, 'was to bury him with his comrades so that they could be together beneath the red wall.' This was remarkable. The meaning is clear.

'Nadya had a generous spirit,' wrote Robert Service. 'Something made her want to keep the two families together even in death; she was willing for her husband to lie by his former lover Inessa in the cold Moscow ground.'

In April, 1921 Lenin had written to Kamenev, as chair of the Moscow Soviet, about placing a permanent memorial to Inessa in Red Square but it hadn't happened in the form he planned. In time, Inessa shared a granite memorial stone with John Reed, author of *Ten Days That Shook The World*, and two other comrades of lesser fame.

Nadya did more still for Inessa, writing articles in her memory and, in 1926, editing a collection of essays, *Pamyati Inessy Armand* with contributions by former colleagues.

After the death of Lenin, Nadya developed a working relationship with Stalin who approved of her help in building the Lenin cult, but it was not always easy. In 1925, when she was supporting Kamenev and Zinoviev against him, he advised her to take care. 'Otherwise,' he is reported to have said, 'I will tell the world who was really Lenin's wife.'

Andre married a feisty young wife named Hienna who bore him two sons and is reported, in Armand lore, to have made such a scene with 'visitors' from the NKVD (which had replaced the Cheka), threatening to call Stalin's secretary, that the 'heavies' retired in disorder.

This is not as strange as it sounds since the Armands survived relatively untouched, with no arrests, throughout the entire period of Communist rule – unlike most of the more notable early Bolsheviks or even those who travelled on the Sealed Train. As has been seen, the Armands were allowed to keep their estate Alyoshino, and the family still has it, though with a smaller house. Inessa's six-room flat on the fourth floor of 9, Manege Street, procured for her on Lenin's order, stayed in the possession of her descendants for fifty years until 1970, both Blona, Varvara's daughter, and Vladimir, Andre's son, spending their childhood there.

Alexander, Inessa's husband, married again in 1927 – not his prewar companion Anna Arbels but Stepanida Karasyova. There was a state farm, as well as a family home, at Alyoshino and Alexander applied in 1930, after collectivisation, to be a member. His former peasants were surprised and embarrassed, but voted for his admission. He worked there as a blacksmith, not with horses, but with ironwork generally and was also expert with engines. When he died in 1943, according to Alexei Davidovich Armand, he was mourned by the community. 'We've never had such a good blacksmith as our old boss,' is a reported remark.

He did not entirely escape class censure, though. A meadow near Alyoshino was showing muddy signs of overgrazing. When Alexander suggested the cattle should be grazed elsewhere, he was sharply reminded: 'You're not in charge here now!'

It was the old people who suffered most. Alexander's father Evgeny and his uncle Emil died in 1919, as did Inessa's mother, Natalie. Varvara Karlovna, Alexander's mother, lingered on until 1923 – reportedly in a makeshift old people's home under a watchtower next to the church where Inessa was married. By then the big Armand complex at Pushkino had been taken over by the state.

In Moscow, Kollontai stepped into Inessa's post as head of the Women's Section of the Central Committee, only to be dismissed in 1922. Soon after this Zhenotdel was disbanded.

After 1926 Inessa's memory faded from public view. This was

partly because of her suspect relationship with Lenin, now repesented as a god-like image, but also because of her background as a rich young wife, which did not fit the picture of a proletarian revolution.

The feminist advances that Inessa had worked so hard to promote soon died under the reaction of what was still a patriarchal society. 'She was,' wrote R.C.Elwood, 'one of those "herrings with ideas" – an intellectual Communist woman for whom Stalin had no use whatever.'

By 1930, the crèches and communal dining rooms and laundries had gone. Despite the liberal divorce laws, many women were forced back to what was once derided as the dying concept of the bourgeois marriage. 'The withering away of the family,' as Beatrice Farnsworth, Kollontai's biographer, has commented, 'became just another socialist myth.'

So what was there to remember Inessa for? She had devoted her life from 1909 to helping Lenin give flesh to his dream of a new world, being a sounding board, doing his dirty work, feeding his courage, celebrating his successes with him. Once, he told Maxim Gorky that the children of that day would 'have happier lives than we had. They will not experience much that we lived through. There will not be so much cruelty in their lives.'

There *was* as much, of course, and indeed far more, for Stalin institutionalised what Lenin had started. It is arguable that, without the bloody years of revolution, social democracy, in its modern milder form, would not have become accepted so widely. But the price was high.

This book records a tragedy. For the millions of people who died or were tortured or suffered in the gulags. For Lenin because he was proved to be so wrong. For Inessa because, if revolution was for her a religion, the god she worshipped turned out to be false.

She was a woman of great courage, of loyalty, of vision, of enormous effort directed at the improvement of the state of women and, indeed, also of mankind. She deserves to be remembered.

NOTES

CHAPTER ONE – Pushkino 1893

Main sources: RTsVKhIDNI(Central Party Archives), members of the Armand family; R.C. Elwood *Inessa Armand – Revolutionary and Feminist*, Georges Bardawil *Ines Armand* and notably the pre-marital letters of Inessa gained from Armand family sources; Pavel Podliashuk *Tovarishch Inessa*, a Russian biography written under Communist control. Lev Krasnopecvtsev, Curator of the Museum of the Patrons (including Armands), Nikolai Lepeshkin, keeper of the Pushkino Museum, Robert Service *Lenin – A Biography*.

1. I call her Nadya, as close associates did. Others addressed her formally as Nadezdha Konstantinovna, or NK or Krupskaya, her codename and also her maiden name.
2. Bardawil, p. 37, *Le Figaro* obituary 29 December 1885, supported by certificates and Theodore Stephane's reviews. Also Podliashuk.
3. Inna Armand in E.D. Stasova (ed.) *Slavnye Bol'shevichki*; Podliashuk.
4. This and subsequent pre-marital letters: Bardawil and Armand family sources, p.95.
5. Bardawil and Armand family sources, p.124.
6. Podliashuk, p.16.
7. A photograph of the cast list is in the possession of V.M. Fedoseyev-Yegorov (see acknowledgements).
8. Bardawil, p.108. Elwood, p.27.
9. Bardawil, and Armand family sources, p.116.
10. ibid. The ward, Vladimir, later married the younger sister of Stephannida Karassiova, Alexander's second wife.
11. ibid., p.120.
12. ibid.
13. The events of Lenin's life up to his meeting with Inessa have been described in many biographies, but I have leaned on Robert Service's *Lenin – A Biography* in this and subsequent chapters.
14. Elwood, p.40.
15. Bardawil, Elwood, p.39.
16. Vinogradskaya, *Sobytiia i pamyatnye vstrechi*, 209.
17. To Inna, autumn 1916. *Stat'i, Rechi, Pis'ma*, 247.

18. To V.E. Armand (Vladimir), 20 Dec 1908. 'Pis'ma Inessy Armand' *Novyi Mir*, 218.

19. For Minna Gorbunova-Kablukova and the societies Inessa was involved with, see Elwood pp.26–62; Bardawil pp.109–13; Podliashuk pp.19–20.

20. Elwood, p.32.

21. Podliashuk, p.22.

22. To A.E. Armand (Alexander), late April 1899. 'Pis'ma Inessy Armand', *Novyi Mir*, 1989, 197–8.

23. Elwood, p.33.

CHAPTER TWO – Moscow 1902

Main sources: Unpublished autobiography of David Levovich Armand; Elwood; Bardawil; Podliashuk and Armand family, especially Alexei Davidovich Armand. Also Inessa's letters to Alexander, 'Pis'ma Inessy Armand' in *Novyi Mir*, 1970, No 6, p.196–218; E.D. Stasova (ed) *Slavnye Bol'shevichki*.

1. By this date the title 'Cossacks' was used broadly. Historically, most Cossacks came from the Dnieper and Don Rivers. They were independent, brave fighters, but changeable, usually working for the Tsarist state, but often being involved in the revolutions. By the turn of the twentieth century, the word was used to cover almost anyone on a horse used for quelling civil revolt, though the real Cossack regiments remained in existence and were prominent in the civil war of 1918-1920.

2. Elwood, pp.34–5.

3. Unpublished autobiography of David Levovich Armand.

4. ibid.

5. ibid.

6. Bardawil, p.145.

7. Elwood citing Podliashuk: *Zhenshchiny Russkoi Revolutsii* (1968), p.28.

8. Bardawil, citing police records, p.157.

9. To A.E. Armand in the Far East for the Russo-Japanese War, Oct 1904, *Novyi Mir*, 199–200.

10. ibid.

11. 7 Jan 1905, ibid.

12. 14 Jan 1905, ibid. In fact, the Japanese did fund propaganda.

13. Inessa refers to this in a letter to Inna in E.D. Stasova (ed) *Slavnye Bol'shevichki*.

14. Elwood, p.46.

15. Inessa to Inna in September, 1914. RTsVKHIDNI, 1910-1917, 127, 1, 35, p.18.

CHAPTER THREE – Moscow Basmannaya Jail 1905

Main sources: Bardawil, I. Ehrenberg *People From Life*, *Novyi Mir*, Elwood.

1. Bardawil, citing police records, p.173.
2. p.174, ibid.
3. p.175, ibid.
4. Elwood, p.46.
5. To Alexander, beginning of summer 1905. 'Pis'ma Inessy Armand', *Novyi Mir*, p.203.
6. To Alexander, beginning of summer 1905 (Letter no 2), ibid.

CHAPTER FOUR – Nice 1905

Main sources: S.K. Morrisey *Heralds of Revolution*; Abram Ascher *The Revolution of 1905*; Ehrenberg; RTsVKhIDNI; *Novyi Mir*; Service; S.T. Possony *Lenin: The Compulsive Revolutionary*; V. Sanov *Sever*; Elwood; Bardawil.

1. To A.E. Armand, 9 Nov 1905, from Nice. *Novyi Mir*, p.205.
2. Elwood, p.49.
3. E. Vlasova in Krupskaya (ed) *Pamyati*.
4. Bardawil, citing police records, p.189.
5. To A.E. Armand from Finland, end of July 1906. *Novyi Mir*, p.207.
6. Elwood, p.51.
7. E. Vlasova in Krupskaya (ed) *Pamyati Inessy Armand*.
8. Elwood, p.50.
9. Inessa to V.E. Armand, May 1907. *Novyi Mir*, p.206.
10. E. Vlasova, op.cit.
11. Bardawil, p.198.
12. Podliashuk, p.56; Elwood, p.53.
13. Bardawil, p.199.
14. Inessa to V.E. Armand from prison, July 1907. *Novyi Mir*, p.206.
15. Bardawil, p.199.
16. The negotiations, police activity and journey to exile are in V. Sanov 'Mezenskaia Ballada' *Sever* 12 (1971) 82-96.
17. Both Elwood and Bardawil have described her departure and she refers later to her bouquet, writing to Alexander from Mezen.
18. Service, whom I have followed for the Finnish material in this chapter; and also Krupskaya, *Memories of Lenin*.

CHAPTER FIVE – Mezen 1907

Main sources: Sanov; RTsVKhIDNI; 'Pis'ma Inessy Armand' *Novyi Mir* (all quoted letters from Inessa); Krupskaya (ed) *Pamyati Inessy Armand*; Bardawil; Elwood; Service.

1. Inessa to Alexander from Mezen mid-Dec 1907. 'Pisma Inessy Armand', *Novyi Mir*, p.207.
2. ibid.
3. Inessa to her children at Pushkino mid-Dec 1907, ibid p.208.
4. ibid. It appears to be her last mention of Volodya (ward) who presumably left the family after sixth form.
5. Sanov (including Zubrovich account). It is doubtful if Inessa was the author. *Rech* was the newspaper of the Kadet Party with a readership that was bourgeois.
6. ibid.
7. Inessa to A.E. Armand in prison, 16 Feb 1908, ibid p.211.
8. Inessa to A.E. Armand in Switzerland (on holiday with their two sons) prior to exile based in Rubaix in France) from Mezen, 13 Aug 1908. RTsVKhIDNI Fond 127, op 1.36.
9. Inessa to Inna, before July 1908, from Mezen. RTsKVhIDTN Fond 127, op 1.34.
10. Inessa to V.E. Armand from Mezen, 8 May 1908. 'Pisma Innessy Armand'. 212.
11. Inessa to A.E. Armand, May 1908. RTsVKhIDNI Fond 127 Op 1.36
12. Sanov.
13. Sanov, p.91.
14. Service, p.190.
15. Inessa to Inna, 25 July 1908 from Mezen. 'Pisma Inessy Armand' 212.
16. Inessa to Anna Askenazy Aug 1908. 'Pisma Inessy Armand' ibid.
17. Inna has challenged Zubrovich's account, saying someone else (unnamed) had arranged this, though Zubrovich had helped.
18. To V.E. Armand at Beaulieu (near Nice), 1 Nov 1908. 'Pisma Inessy Armand' 214.
19. To V.E. Armand, 2 Nov 1908. ibid. 215.
20. To V.E. Armand, end Nov 1908. ibid. 216.
21. To A.E. Armand at Rubaix, 14 Dec 1908. ibid. 217.
22. To A.E. Armand at Rubaix, 26-27 Dec 1908. ibid. 218.
23. To V.E. Armand at Beaulieu, 20 Dec 1908. ibid. 217.
24. Several writers have written that Vladimir died in Switzerland but Elwood says that he died in Nice, confirmed by Inessa's daughter and the fact that Inessa's correspondence was sent to Beaulieu. Elena Vlasova quotes

Inessa, when she meets her in Paris, as saying that he died in Switzerland, but I have followed Elwood's argument.

25. Bardawil p.226. A degree of speculation, but it seems likely, as Elwood agrees. Alexander was always 'base' for her; her sons were with him; although she would have made no plans yet, France was an obvious place for her immediate future, since she could not return to Russia without risk of arrest. Evidence of her movements during this period is either non-existing or in conflict.

26. Vinogradskaya *Sobytiia*, 212.

27. Inessa to Inna, late 1916. I.F. Armand *Sta'ti rechi pis'ma* 251.

28. Vlasova in Krupskaya (ed) *Pamyati*. Her quote that Vladimir died in Switzerland has been shown to be wrong, as discussed earlier. So possibly is the reference to TB, septicaemia being suspected, but she was writing some fifteen years after the event.

CHAPTER SIX – Paris 1909

Main sources: Service; Krupskaya *Memories of Lenin*; Possony; Bardawil; Elwood; L. Fischer *The Life of Lenin*; RTsVKhIDNI – in particular Fond 127,0p 1.d.61 (a letter to Lenin, also in *Svobodnaye Mysel'* 3 (1992) p.80-88) catalogued as December 1913 (though later research by Elwood indicates January 1914).

1. Elwood, p.73.
2. Bardawil, p.243.
3. Inessa's letter to Lenin – see above.
4. ibid.
5. ibid.
6. M. Body *Alexandra Kollontai. Preuves* Paris (2) 14, 17.
7. Lydia Fotieva *Iz zhizni Lenina*, (1967) 10.
8. Service, p.199.
9. Service, p.206.
10. RTsVKhIDNI Fond 127, op.1.36,77; Elwood, p.91. Speculation.
11. Bardawil, citing police records, p.270.

CHAPTER SEVEN – St Petersburg 1912

Main sources: Safarov and Malakhovskii in Krupskaya (ed) *Pamyati*; RTsKhIDNI; R.B. McKean *St Petersburg between the Revolutions*; Podliashuk; Inna in Stasova (ed) *Slavnye Bol'shevichki*; Possony; Krupskaya *Memories of Lenin*; Elwood; Bardawil; Pipes *The Unknown Lenin*; I.F. Armand *Stati Rechi Pis'ma*.

1. Bardawil, citing police records, p.270.
2. Safarov in Krupskaya (ed) *Pamyati*.
3. McKean, *St Petersburg between the Revolutions*, p.92.
4. Elwood, citing Leninskaya *Pravda, 1912-14* (1972) 64.
5. Bardawil, citing Okhrana dossier, September 1912, p.271.
6. Safarov in Krupskaya (ed) *Pamyati*.
7. Bardawil, p.272.
8. Elwood, citing Stasova in *Pravda* (8 May 1964) 4.
9. Podliashuk, p.124.
10. To Inna, summer 1915. I.F. Armand *Stat'i Rechi Pisma*, 231. Stavropol is not actually on the Volga so presumably they went on to Stavropol by land or possibly some kind of tributary.
11. To A.E. Armand, 4 Aug 1913. RTsKhIDNI Fond 127,1,36,54.
12. ibid. 127,1,36,59.
13. ibid. 61.
14. ibid. 65.
15. ibid. 66.
16. ibid.69.
17 ibid. 71.
18. ibid. 74.
19. To V.I. Lenin. Fond 127,0p 1.d.61 (also I.F. Armand *Svobodnaye Mysel'* (1992) 3 80-88
20. R.C. Elwood 'New evidence on an old affair', *Canadian Slavonic Papers*, Vol XLIII, No. 1, March 2001.
21. Prior to 23 June 1914. Pipes *The Unknown Lenin*.
22. There have been conflicting arguments about how long Lenin stayed in Paris on this visit. There is no doubt that he was in Brussels by 25 January (Vol 43 Lenin *Collected Works*) and Elwood, quoting three sources, insists that the stay only lasted a week. It is relevant only because the letters between Lenin and Inessa following this visit were exceptionally warm, especially, as will be seen, from him.

CHAPTER EIGHT – Paris 1914

Main sources: V.I. Lenin, *Collected Works*, 4th ed. (English) Vols 35 and 43 (including letters first published in Russian 5th ed.); Krupskaya, *Memories of Lenin*; Pipes, *The Unknown Lenin*; the Ros Archiv (letters previously censored); Inessa in RTsKhIDNI; Elwood.

1. 18 Dec 1913, Lenin *Coll. Wks* (35) p.130.
2. End Dec 1913, ibid.(35) p.131.
3. Before 22 Jan 1914, ibid. (43) p.377.

4. Before 26 Jan 1914, ibid. (43) p.378.

5. 25 Jan 1914,ibid.(43) p.377.

6. 26 Jan 1914, ibid.(43) p.379.

7. The missing pages. There are a lot. Censors would not tear them out – as is shown by those previously censored but now released. I believe that, as discussed later, Lenin tore them out himself when he recovered them from Inessa. He left in the politics because he believed these would be part of his testament.

8. 23 Feb 1914. Ros Archiv.

9. Inessa to Inna, spring 1914. RTsKhIDNI, 127,1,35 (1910-1917).

10. Inessa to Inna, spring 1914. RTsKhIDNI 127,1 35.

11. After Mar 15 1914. Lenin *Coll. Wks* (43) p.394.

12. 1 Apr 1914. ibid.(35) p.136.

13. 7 June 1914. Pipes, p.26.

14. Before 23 June, 1914. ibid. p.27.

15. 25 May 1914. ibid. p.26.

16. 25 May 1914. Lenin *Coll. Wks* (43) p.402.

17. Inessa to Nadya, 16 March to 1 Apr 1914. *Stat'i, Rechi, Pis'ma* 219.

18. Inessa to Nadya, July 1914. RTsKhIDNI, 127,1.

19. Elwood, p.132.

20. Before 4 July 1914. Lenin *Coll. Wks* (43) p.406.

21. Before 6 July 1914. ibid.(43) p.408.

22. ibid. p.410

23. 3 July 1914. Pipes, p.27.

24. 10-16 July 1914.Lenin. *Coll. Wks* (35) p.146.

25. Before 23 June. ibid.(35) p.27.

26. Before 13 July. ibid. (43) p.417.

27. Elwood, p.139 (including other aspects of the conference).

28. 19 July 1914. ibid. (43) pp.423–5.

29. Elwood, p.141.

30. Before 12 July.1914. Pipes, p.27

CHAPTER NINE – Berne 1914

Main sources: V.I. Lenin *Collected Works* 4th ed. (35) and (43); RTsKhIDNI; I.F. Armand *Stat'i, Rechi, Pis'ma*; Krupskaya *Memories of Lenin*; Elwood; Bardawil.

1. To Inna from Genoa, Aug 1914. RTsKhIDNI 127, 1, 35.

2. To Inessa from Inna, Cardiff, 3 Sept 1914. Armand family sources.

3. To the children in Russia, late 1914. RTsKhIDNI, 127,1,35 18/20.

4. To Inna from Berne 1915. *Stat'i, Rechi, Pis'ma* 239.

5. 17 Jan 1915. Lenin *Coll. Wks* (35) p.180.

6. To Inna, *Stat'i, Rechi, Pis'ma* p.246.

7. To Inna, 1915. RTsKhIDNI 127,1,35,37.

8. To Inna, after June, summer 1915, from Sorenburg. RTsKhIDNI,127,1,35.

9. To Inna, after June 1915, from Sorenberg. RTsKhIDNI, 127,1,35.

10. To Inna, autumn 1915, from Berne. RTsKhIDNI, 127,1,35.

11. Elwood, p.167. Also other aspects of the Paris venture.

12. Bardawil, citing records from the Okhrana Paris bureau.

13. 15 Jan 1916. Lenin *Coll. Wks* (43) p.505.

14. 19 Jan 1916. ibid.

15. Krupskaya (ed) *Pamyati Inessy Armand*.

16. Lenin *Coll. Wks* (43) p.507.

17. *Leninskii Sbornik* XXXVII, 38

18. Jan 1917 Lenin *Coll. Wks* (43) p.603.

19. 20 Nov 1916. ibid. (35) p.246.

20. 13 Nov 1916. Pipes, p.33.

21. 17 Dec 1916. Lenin *Coll. Wks* (43), p.588

22. 30 Dec 1916. Pipes, p.33.

23. 6 Jan 1917. ibid. p.34.

24. 14 Jan 1917. Lenin *Coll. Wks* (43) p.599

25. Pearson *The Sealed Train*, p.39.

26. ibid.

27. 19 Jan 1917. Pipes, p.34.

28. 13 Mar 1917. Lenin *Coll. Wks* (43) p.615.

29. Elwood, p.194. Also guidance on arguments.

30. 22 Jan 1917. Lenin *Coll. Wks* (43) p.606.

31. ibid.

32. ibid. (35) p.247.

33. 30 Nov 1916. ibid. p.250.

34. 23 Dec 1916. ibid. p.264.

35. Between 25 and 31 March 1917. ibid. p.306.

36. Elwood, p.199. Also other background aspects.

CHAPTER TEN – Zurich 1917

Main sources: this chapter, and the one that follows, cover a wide stretch of history in detail, from the departure of Lenin's group from Switzerland (including Inessa, of course) to his seizure of power in the October revolution. The sources for this, apart from personal aspects of Inessa's life, are similar to those for Pearson: *The Sealed Train*, which ends with that second revolution.

These include: Lenin's *Collected Works*, Vols 35 and 43; Krupskaya's *Memories* and a long article by her in Pravda, 1924, No 87, 16 April; R.H. McNeal *Bride of the Revolution: Revolution in Russia*; W. Hahlweg *Lenin's journey to Russia 1917*; G. Zinoviev *V.I. Lenin*; E. Wilson *To the Finland Station*; Z.A.B. Zeman and W.B. Scharlau *Merchant of Revolution* (Helphand); the German and British Foreign Office files; F. Platten *Lenin's journey through Germany in the sealed car*; N.F. Platten *From the Spiegelgasse to the Kremlin*; Grani.

1. 15 March 1917. Lenin *Coll. Wks* (35) p.294.
2. After the outbreak of war, the name St Petersburg was deemed to appear too German, so it was changed to Petrograd. Later it became Leningrad for some decades before being allowed to revert to its original name. I stay with St Petersburg, except in quotes. Our characters normally called it 'Peter'.
3. In 1915 Lenin had considered moving to Scandinavia to have easier access to Russia than he had in Switzerland, surrounded as it was by warring nations. This probably followed a talk with a one-time comrade from whom he had long been estranged (see note 9).
4. 18 March 1917. Lenin *Coll. Wks* (43) p.616.
5. 19 March 1917. ibid. p.616.
6. ibid.
7. 23 March 1917. ibid. (43) p.620.
8. 25 March 1917. ibid. (35) p.306.
9. In 1915 Helphand, after contact with the Germans, had gone to Berne to seek a meeting with Lenin. He approached Lenin in a café when he was dining with Nadya and Inessa. Lenin would have received him coldly, since he despised him, but the two men did go off for a private meeting. It is presumed that Helphand wanted Bolshevik help to organise a strike in Russian factories in order to demonstrate to the Germans what he could do for them.

Almost certainly, he also sought Lenin's co-operation with the 'revolutionising' plan and almost certainly Lenin rejected him because he was 'tainted'. It is not known if anything was agreed, but it is probable that Helphand's organisation was used after the February revolution to help the Bolsheviks.
10. 31 March 1917. Lenin *Coll. Wks* (43) p.623.
11. This was the date in Switzerland, but Russia was still using the Julian Calendar, which was thirteen days behind the Gregorian calendar of the West. So what to the West was the March revolution was the February revolution to the Russians. Almost a year later, on 1 February 1918, the Russian calendar was changed to conform with the Gregorian. For the events in Russia until that date, I use the local calendar, quoting both when it is not obvious.

12. There is a degree of mystery about the number of travellers. On arrival in Russia, Lenin stated that the party consisted of thirty-two. This would conform with the statement signed by twenty-nine travellers on the day of departure in Zurich, which excluded two children and Fritz Platten, the Swiss. But two people left the party in Stockholm, reducing the number actually reaching Russia to thirty. So Lenin was either speaking loosely or two others whose identity is unknown replaced those who left.

13. Accounts of the journey were written by ten of the travellers, either in book form or in articles. See particularly Olga Ravich 'Journey across Germany', *Pravda* (1927) 88 and Karl Radek 'In the Sealed Carriage', *Pravda* (1924) 91, Krupskaya *Memories of Lenin*, p.209, and Lilina (Zinovieva) Leningradskaya *Pravda* (1924) 87.

14. Telegrams of September and December from the German Secretary of State to the Kaiser. For this and further evidence, see Katkov *Russia 1917*, International Affairs, April 1956: German Foreign Office documents on financial support of the Bolsheviks, or *Sealed Train* p.290.

15. Card from Inessa to her children from Stockholm, 1917. RTsKhIDNI, 127,1,35

16. Service citing G.E. Zinoviev *Vospominanaya*, p.260

17. Accounts differ as to whether Kollontai was waiting with her bunch of flowers at the Finland Station or at Belo-ostrov the border town, where Lenin was joined by Kamenev and senior colleagues. The former, reported by Shlyapnykov, seems most likely.

CHAPTER ELEVEN – St Petersburg 1917

Main sources: N.N.Sukhanov *The Russian Revolution 1917*; Leon Trotsky *The History of the Russian Revolution*; Pearson *The Sealed Train*; V.D. Bonch-Bruevich *Battle Positions in the February and October Revolutions*; N.I. Podvoisky *The Year 1917*; John Reed *Ten Days That Shook The World*; Elwood; Bardawil.

1. Sukhanov, p.286.
2. Vinogradskaya, Polina *Semenovna Pamiatnye Vstrechi* 219.
3. Later than 12 May 1917. *Leninskii Sbornik* XXXVII 58.
4. Before 12 May 1917. ibid. 57.
5. 20 April 1917. ibid. 56.
6. An unknown witness, supported by Sukhanov, pp.415-18; Pearson, p.188.
7. Elwood, p.210.

CHAPTER TWELVE – Moscow 1917

Main sources: Y. Got'e (Gautier) *Time of Troubles*; on what happened to the

Armand family, Armand family sources; Service; Inessa's letters to her daughters; Orlando Figes *A People's Tragedy*, especially on the Terror, the Cheka etc and what was happening to ordinary people; Elwood; Bardawil.

1. Got'e, p.72.
2. This Andrei is not, of course, Inessa's son Andre, who was only thirteen at this time, but another member of the family.
3. Got'e, p.213.
4. Elwood, p.214.
5. Elwood, p.214.
6. Wolfe, *The Bridge and the abyss*, p.71.
7. Figes, p. 527.
8. Service, p.365.
9. Service, p.334.
10. To Inna, in Astrakhan, after 16 Sept 1918. RTsKhIDNI, 127,1,35.
11. Service, p.343.
12. Elwood, p.214.
13. Armand family sources.
14. ibid.
15. ibid.
16. To Inna in Astrakhan around 16 Sept 1918. RTsKhIDNI, 127,1,35.
17. Got'e, p.300.
18. To Inna, around 16 Dec 1918. RTsKhIDNI 127,1,35.
19. To Inna, after 16 Sept 1918. RTsKhIDNI 127,1,35.
20. To Inna, between 3 Oct and 6 Nov 1918. *Stat'i, Rechi, Pis'ma*, 254.
21. ibid.
22. ibid.
23. Around 16 Dec 1918 RTsKhIDNI, 127,1,35.

CHAPTER THIRTEEN – Moscow 1918

Main sources: Figes; Cathy Porter *Alexandra Kollontai*; Service; Elwood; Volkogonov *Lenin: Life and Legacy*; Got'e (Gautier); Bardawil; *Leninskii Sbornik* XXXVII; Letters to Inna *Stat'i, Rechi, Pis'ma* and RTsKhIDNI; Vinogradskaya; Armand family.

1. There have been descriptions by many historians of this attempted assassination. I have leaned most heavily on Volkogonov.
2. Volkogonov, p.227.
3. V. Armand *Novyi Mir* 4 (1967) p.198.
4. To Inna, after 16 Sept 1918. RTsKhIDNI, 127,1,35.
5. *Biog. Khron* (VI) p.317.

6. Service, p.380.

7. Got'e, p.207.

8. Figes, p.646.

9. Figes, citing Bochkareva, p.208.

10. Porter, p.325.

11. To Inna, around 16 Dec 1918. RTsKhIDNI, 127,1,35.

12. Elwood, p.222.

13. R.K. Debo 'The Manuilskii Mission' *International History Review* 8, (1986) p.214.

14. To Inna. Feb 1920. Previously unpublished letter. Bardawil, p.361.

15. Bardawil, citing *Aviation & Astronautique* 12 (1968).

16. Got'e, p.282.

17. Inessa to Ivan Popov. RTsKhIDNI 127,45.

18. Elwood, p.24. And the follow-on from formation of Zhenotdel.

19. Vinogradskaya in Krupskaya (ed.) *Pamyati* pp.61-63.

20. *Leninskii Sbornik* XXXV, 108.

21. ibid.

22. Not later than 16 Feb 1920. Ros Archiv.

23. ibid.

24. ibid.

25. Krupskaya in Krupskaya (ed) *Pamyati*, p.33.

26. Aug 1920. *Leninskii Sbornik* XXXVII 233.

CHAPTER FOURTEEN – The Caucasus 1920

Main sources: P.S. Vinogradskaya *Sobytiia I pamiatnye vstrechi*; Krupskaya (ed) *Pamyati*: L. Stal; G.N. Kotov; I.S. Ruzheinikov; Lenin *Polnoe Sobranie Sochinenii*, 5th ed., (LI); RTsKhIDNI; *Svobodnaye Mysel'* 3 (1992); N. Farson *Caucasian Journey*; M. Pereira *Across the Caucasus*; *Pravda* 12 Oct 1920; *Izvestia* 12/13 Oct 1920; Elwood; Bardawil; A. Balabanov *Impressions of Lenin*.

1. To Sergo Ordzhonikidze 18 Aug 1920. Lenin *Coll. Wks* 5th ed. *Polnoe sobranie sochinenie* (PSS) LI 261

2. To the Administrator of Health Resorts and Sanatoria, 17 Aug 1920. Lenin: PSS LI, 261.

3. To Sergo Ordzhonikidze, 20 Aug 1920. Lenin: PSS Vol LI, 262

4. Vinogradskaya has twice described the events in the Caucasus, as indicated above. For the writing of these scenes in Kislovdsk, I have merged the two sources.

5. Armand *Stat'i, Rechi, Pis'ma*, 257.

6. Inessa's diary *Svobodnaye Mysel'* 3 (1992).

7. This assumes much. St John, in the Gospel (11) says that some of the Jews who witnessed the Lazarus miracle went to the Pharisees and reported what they had seen. The Chief Priests and the Pharisees met in council and saw it as politically dangerous. It is probable that people did feel uncomfortable in Lazarus' presence but St John does not actually say so.

8. PSS, LI, 173.

9. Dr Ruzheinikov's detailed account of the last days of Inessa's life appears in Krupskaya (ed) *Pamyati*.

10. There have been suggestions that, in her state of deep depression, Inessa committed suicide or was even murdered. The detailed evidence of Dr Ruzheinikov and G.N. Kotov makes it quite clear she died of cholera. Also it is hard to believe that she would have committed suicide without making proper arrangements for the care of Andre whom she had always adored – as emphasised in the diary she kept in Kislovodsk.

11. *Biog. Kron.* IX, 346.

BIBLIOGRAPHY AND OTHER SOURCES

Agafanov, V.K. *The Okhrana Abroad* (1918).

Armand, Inessa F. *Stat'i, Rechi, Pis'ma* (Moscow, 1975)

Armand, Inessa F. 'Pis'ma Inessy Armand' 6 *Novyi Mir* (1970) 196.

Armand, Inessa F. *in* E.D.Stasova (ed) *Slavnye Bol'shevichki* (Moscow, 1958).

Armand, Inessa F. *Svobodnaya Mysl'* (1992) [Letter to Lenin December 1913 (later to be shown to be January 1914) and a diary written over the days before her death.(Also includes Krupskaya letters to Inessa's daughters Inna and Varvara.)]

Armand Inna A. *in* E.D. Stasova(ed) *Slavnye Bol'shevichki* (Moscow, 1958).

Armand, Varvara A. 'Zhivaia nit (Iz vosponianii I perepiski s N.K. Krupskoi)' 4 *Novyi mir* 178.

Ascher, A. *The Revolution of 1905* (1988).

Balabanoff, A. *Impressions of Lenin* (1964).

Bardawil, G. *Ines Armand* [French](1993).

Body, M. *Alexandra Kollontai Preuves* (Paris, 1952))

Carr, E.H. *The Bolshevik Revolution* 3v. (1950).

Chernyshevsky, N. *What Is To Be Done?* (Engl. trans. 1983).

Clements, B.E. *The Life of Alexandra Kollontai* (Bloomington, 1979).

Debo, R.K. 'The Manuilskii Mission' *International History Review*, 8 (1986) 214.

Ehrenberg, I. *People and Life, Memoirs of 1891-1917* (1961).

Elwood, R.C. *Inessa Armand–Revolutionary and Feminist* (1992).

Farnsworth, B. *Alexandra Kollontai* (1980)

Farson, N. *Caucasian Journey* (1951).

Fischer, L. *The Life of Lenin* (1965).

Fofanova, M. 'Memories of 1917' *Leningradskaya Pravda* 19 (1928).

Fortnightly Review 108 (July-Dec 1917).

Fraser, E. *The House by the Dvina* (1984).

Freville, J. *Lenine à Paris* (Paris, 1968).

Freville, J. *Une grande figure de la Revolution: Inessa Armand* (Paris, 1957).

Futrell, M. *Northern Underground* (1963).

Gankin, O.H. & Fisher, H.H. *The Bolsheviks and the World War* (1940) .

German Foreign Office Documents on Financial Support to the Bolsheviks. International Affairs (April,1956).

Gorky, M. *Days with Lenin* (1932).

Got'e (Gautier), I.V. *Time of Troubles* (1988).

Hayden, C. E. 'Zhenotdel and the Bolshevik Party' *Russian History*, 3 (2) (1976) 150-73.

Izvestia Reports of Inessa's funeral 12/13 October 1920.

Katkov, G. *Russia 1917* (1967).

Kollontai, A. *A Great Love* (trans. Cathy Porter) (New York, 1981).

Kotov, G. in *Pamyati Inessy Armand* (Krupskaya, N.K. ed) (1926).

Krupskaya, N.K.(ed) *Pamyati Inessy Armand* (Moscow, 1926). (Contributions from. N.K. Krupskaya, L.B. Kamenev, L. Stal, E. Revlina, P. Vinogradskaya, E. Vlasova, G. Kotov, I.S. Ruzheinikov, V.L. Malakhovsky, G. Safarov).

Latyshev, A.G. *Rassekreechennyi Lenin* (1996).

Lenin, V.I. *Collected Works*, 4th edition, 35,43.

Lenin, V.I. *Leninskii Sbornik*.

Lenin, V.I. *Works* 4th Edition in English, 43.

Lenin, V.I. *Collected Works* 5th Edition. *Polnoe sobranie sochinenie*

Lenin, V.I. *Vladimir Ilyich Lenin: Biograficheskaia Khronika* (1970-).

Lilina (Zinaida Zinovieva) 'Comrade Lenin Departs for Russia' *Leningradskaya Pravda*, 87 (1924).

Morrisey, S.K. *Heralds of Revolution* (1998).

Krupskaya, N.K. *Memories of Lenin* (Moscow, 1959).

McKean, R.B. *St Petersburg Between the Revolutions* (1990).

McNeal, R. *Bride of the Revolution* (1972).

Payne, R. *The Fortress* (1967).

Payne, R. *The Life and Death of Lenin* (1964).

Pearson, M. *The Sealed Train* (1975).

Pereira, M. *Across the Caucasus* (1973).

Pipes, R. *The Unknown Lenin* (1996)

Platten, F. *Lenin's Journey through Germany in the sealed car* (1924).

Platten, N.F. 'From the Spiegelgasse to the Kremlin' *Grani*, Nos 77, 79 (1972).

Podliashuk, P. *Tovarishch Inessa* (1964).

Podvoisky, N.I. *The Year 1917* (1958).

Porter, C. *Alexandra Kollontai* (London, 1980).

Possony, S. T. *Lenin: The Compulsive Revolutionary* (1964).

Pravda 12 October 1920 [Inessa's funeral]

Radek, K. 'In the Sealed Carriage' *Pravda* 91 (1924)

Ravich, O. 'The Journey across Germany' *Pravda* 88 (1927)

Reed, J. *Ten Days that Shook the World* (1960).

Ruzheinikov, I.S.(Dr) in *Pamiati Inessy Armand* (Krupskaya, N.K. ed) (1926).

Safarov, G. 'Comrade Lenin' *Leningradskaya Pravda* 877 (1924)

Sanov, V. 'Mezenskaya ballada' *Sever* 12 (1971) 82-96.

Schapiro, L. *The Origin of the Communist autocracy* (1955).

Shukman, H. *Lenin and the Russian Revolution* (1967).

Senn, A.E. *The Russian Revolution in Switzerland 1914-1917* (1971).

Sokolnikov, G. 'The return of Lenin from exile' *Leningradskaya Pravda* 90 (1928).

Smith, E.E. *The Okhrana* (1967).

Stal, L. *in Pamyati Inessy Armand* ((Krupskaya, N.K. ed) (1926).

Stasova, E.D. *Pages of life and fighting* (1957).

Stites, R. 'Kollontai, Inessa and Krupskaya' *Canadian-American Slavic Studies* IX(1) (1975) 84-92.

Stites, R. 'Zhendotdel: Bolshevism and Russian Women' *Russian History* 111(2) (1976) 174-93.

Sukhanov, N.N. *The Russian Revolution 1917* (1955).

Trotsky, L. *The History of the Russian Revolution* 3v (1932).

Trotsky, L. *Lenin* (1925).

Ulam, A.B. *Lenin and the Bolsheviks* (1966).

Ulyanova, M. Reminiscences of V I Lenin, 1960 ®

Valentinov (N.V. Volsky) *Encounters with Lenin* (1968)

Vinogradskaya, P. *Sobytiia I Pamyatnye Vstrechi* (Moscow, 1968).

Vinogradskaya P. *in Pamyati Inessy Armand* (Krupskaya, N.K. ed) (1926).

Volkogonov, D. *Lenin: Life and Legacy* (trans. Harold Shukman) (London, 1994).

Wilson, E. *To the Finland Station* (1960).

Wolfe, B.D. *The Bridge and the Abyss* (1967).

Wolfe, B.D. *Three who made a revolution* (1956).

Wolfe, B.D. 'Lenin and Inessa Armand' *Slavic Review* XXII(1) (1963) 96-114.

INDEX

Abbreviations used throughout, **I** *for* Inessa Armand, **L** *for* Lenin.

INDEX

Soviets 173-174, Zurich station 149-150; temper 140, 172; *What Is To Be Done?* 23, 27; in Zurich (1915) 134, 135, (1917) 149-50
Les Avants 125, 135
letters 28; from Inna to I 125-126, 129; from I to Adrienne Veigele 17; to Alexander 19, 25, 31, 37, 43, 63-64, 95, 102-103, 105; before marriage 1, 5, 6-9; in Roubaix 68-69, 77-78; to Anna Asknazy 66, 73, 80; to children 64-65, 69-70, 125, 201; to Inna (1918) 69, 73, 103, 181, 184, 186, 188, 201; to L 90, 106-112, 210; to Nadya 119, 133; to Volodya Armand 17, 75-76, 78 *see also* Lenin, letters to I
library, secret 30, 48
Liebknecht, Karl 187
Lipinskaya, Alexandrovna `Kurskaya' 30-31
'The Liquidators' 87
literature, forbidden 14-15, 28, 30, 34, 46, 47, 83, 116
London, SDs in (1903) 26
Longjumeau school 88-91,99,210
Lopuklov, Dmitri 25
love, I's views on 77, 128-129, 130
Lovran 120, 124, 125
Lublin 97
Lunacharsky, Anatoly 26, 83
Luxemburg, Rosa 82, 83, 138, 140, 187
Lyons, I's parents in 4

Malakhovsky, V I 100
Malinovsky, Roman 94, 104, 112, 115, 118, 120, 154
Malinovsky Commission 147, 154
malitsa 62, 74
Malkov, Paul 190
Malyantovich 95
Mamontovs 11
Manuilsky, D Z 201-203
marriage, concept of 206, 229; I's 1-2, 10, 23-25; L's 91, 92, 191-192, 226
Martov, Yuli 13, 26, 56, 83, 91, 92, 147, 173
Marxism 15, 17, 22
Marx, Karl 13, 15, 85
Marx, Laura 13, 85
Maryanova, Lidiya 184
Mazanova, Katya 88, 91, 111, 115, 117
Mazanovs 85
Memories of Lenin 89, 126, 130, 191
Mensheviks 44, 48, 56, 87, 97, 205;

Congress of Soviets (1917) 167, 173; newspaper 120; origins 27; post Revolution 176, 225; Prague Conference 93-94; and 'Sealed Train' 149; Zimmerald conference 131
Merrheim, Alphonse 132
Mezen, I's exile in 58-59, 62-71, 73-74; police 66-68
Military Revolutionary Organisation 163; absorbed into Cheka 178
Military Union 47
Milyukov, Paul 147, 149, 161, 165, 171
Ministry of the Interior, Russia 17, 22
Minkin 66-67
Montreux, I in 19; L in 27
Moscow, apartments; Arbat, Denezhnyi Lane 160, 176, 184, 188; Neglinnaya St (Manege St) 190, 207, 222, 228; Bolshoi Afanasievsky Lane 46; Granatny Lane 29; Arbat police HQ (1907) 49; Armand family in, post Revolution 183, pre Revolution 11, 19, flat raided 21, 22; Basmannaya Jail 35-39; Chaika rest home, children at 225; Chuka HQ 189; Duma 19, 29, 61, 166, 199, 223, I elected to (1917) 166; Economic Council, I chairs 192; exile from 10; House of Unions 199, 223; I in, (1907) Yaroslavsky Station 54; (1917) 159-160, 166, 170; (1918) National Hotel 183, 186; Armand house 19, 21-25; arrives from exile 74-76; funeral 221-224; Ostozhenka Street 29-30; I in prison in, (1905) Basmannaya Jail 35-39; (1907) Arbat police HQ 49; Prechistenska Jail 51-53, 76; Kazan station, coffin arrives at 221-222; Kremlin (1917) 175, (1918) 189, (1920) I's funeral 224; L in 163, 183, 221-224; Moscow Forest Protection Committee 19; National Hotel 183, 186; Ostozhenka Street house 29-31, 33-34; post Revolution, government in 183; prostitution in 18; Red Sq. 223, 224, 227; Regional Party Committee 183; Revolution 175-176; Rumyantsev Museum 209; SDs regional conference (1917) 160; social conditions 12; Society for the Improvement of the Lot of Women 17-18; Sokolniki Park 192; Soviet (1917) 166, I delegate to Congress of Peasants 177; I elected to 166; strikes 33, 41; Trubnikovsky Lane 183;

253

BOOKS BY MICHAEL PEARSON

The Secret Invaders
(with Bill Strutton)

The Millionaire Mentality

The £5 Virgins

The Million Dollar Bugs

Those Damned Rebels: The American Revolution as seen
through British eyes.

The Sealed Train

Tears of Glory

NOVELS

The Store

The Keys of the City

The Shadow of Elisabeth